KNOW YOUR
VIKING

KNOW YOUR VIKING

JACKIE DODSON
with JAN SAUNDERS

CHILTON COMPANY

RADNOR, PENNSYLVANIA

Published in Radnor, Pennsylvania 19089, by Chilton Company
No part of this book may be reproduced, transmitted or stored
in any form or by any means, electronic or mechanical,
without prior written permission from the publisher

Designed by William E. Lickfield
Cover and insert photos by Larry Brazil
Manufactured in the United States of America

Library of Congress Cataloging in Publication Data
Dodson, Jackie.
    Know your Viking.
    (Creative machine arts series)
    Bibliography: p. 190
    Includes index.
    1. Machine sewing.   2. Sewing machines.
I. Saunders, Janice S.   II. Title.   III. Series.
TT713.D648   1988   646.2'044   87-48010
ISBN 0-8019-7870-X (pbk.)

1 2 3 4 5 6 7 8 9 0   7 6 5 4 3 2 1 0 9 8

The following are trademarks or registered trademarks of the Viking
White Company (Viking Sewing Machines, a division of VWS, Inc.):
    Pictogram™
    Satin Elements™
    Sewing Advisor™
    Trimotion™
Other protected trademarks used in this book are:
    Fray-Check™
    Lycra®
    Pellon™
    Spandex™
    Teflon®
    Ultrasuede®
    Wonder-Under® Transfer Fusing Web

Contents

Foreword x   Preface xii   Acknowledgments xiii

Chapter 1 Getting Started   1
    Love your Viking 2
    Presser feet 3
    Accessories 6
        Bias binder 6
        Circular sewing attachment 6
        Eyelet plates 6
        Dual feed foot (walking foot) 7
        Ruffler 7
        Glide plates 7
        Roller foot 7
        Narrow hemmers 7
    Supplies 8
        Threads 8
        Needles 9
        Batting, fleece, and fiberfil 11
        Fusibles 11
        Stabilizers 11
    Helpful hints for sewing 12

Chapter 2 Adding Stitches to Your Fabric   13
    Lesson 1. Using utility and decorative stitches 13
    Lesson 2. Using free machining: darning, whipping, feather stitching 15
        Project: Buttons and Pendants 21

Chapter 3 Adding Texture to Your Fabric   25
    Lesson 3. Building up sewing stitches 25
    Lesson 4. Applying thick threads from the top and bobbin 29
    Applying thick thread through the needle 30
    Couching thread down on top of fabric 30
        Project: Greeting Card 31
    Attaching cord pulled through the raised seam guide 35
    Using thick thread from the bobbin 35
        Project: Tote Bag Square (Cabling) 38
    Lesson 5. Fringing yarn and fabric 40
        Project: Fringed Denim Rug 41

Lesson 6. Adding buttons, beads, shisha 43
    Attaching buttons 43
    Attaching beads and baubles 43
    Attaching shisha mirrors 46
        Project: Bird Collage 47
Lesson 7. Smocking and gathering 51
    Smocking 51
        Simple gathered smocking 52
        Smocking with cordonnet 53
        Embroidering with thick thread in the bobbin 53
        Smocking with elastic 53
    Gathering 55
        Using cord 55
        Using elastic 55
        Using a gathering foot 55
Lesson 8. Pulling threads together 55

Chapter 4 Adding Fabric to Fabric: Appliqué   **57**
Lesson 9. Methods of applying appliqués 57
Lesson 10. Appliquéing with feed dogs up 60
    Satin stitches three ways 60
        Standard method 60
        Stained-glass method 60
        Reverse appliqué 60
        Project: Tote Bag Square (Modified Reverse Appliqué) 61
    Blindstitching 63
    Edge stitching 63
        Project: Tote Bag Square (Edge-Stitch Appliqué) 63
        Project: Tote Bag Square (Straight Stitch) 65
    Cording edges 67
Lesson 11. Appliquéing with feed dogs lowered 67
    Blurring 68
        Project: Flower of Sheers and Overlays 68
    Scribbling 70
    Stitching Carrickmacross 72
        Project: Carrickmacross Doily 72
    Layering transparent fabrics 74
        Project: Shadow Work Picture 74
        Project: Stitching Three-Dimensional Appliqués 77
    Helpful hints for appliqué 79

Chapter 5 Stitching Across Open Spaces   **80**
Lesson 12. Cutwork and eyelets 80
    Cutwork 80
        Project: Cutwork Needlecase 81
    Eyelets 83

Lesson 13. Free-machined needlelace 83
Lesson 14. Battenberg lace 85
        Project: Buttterfly-shaped Lace 85
Lesson 15. Hemstitching 89
        Project: Infant's Bonnet 90
Lesson 16. Stitching in rings 94
        Project: Christmas Ornaments 94
Lesson 17. Making Alençon lace 96
        Project: Alençon Pincushion 96

Chapter 6 Drawing Threads Out of Your Fabric **99**
Lesson 18. Needleweaving 99
        Project: Openwork on Sleeves 99

Chapter 7 Layering Fabrics: Quilting **103**
Lesson 19. Quilting with feed dogs up 103
        Project: Tote Bag Square (Appliqué and Quilting) 104
Lesson 20. Quilting with feed dogs lowered 106
Lesson 21. Trapunto 107
Lesson 22. Italian cording 107
        Project: Tote Bag Square (Italian Cording) 107

Chapter 8 Adding Interesting Seams to Your Fabric **110**
Lesson 23. French handsewing by machine 110
    Making entredeaux 112
    Sewing French seams 112
    Stitching rolled and whipped edges 112
    Gathering rolled and whipped edges 114
    Applying insertion 115
    Joining scalloped lace 115
    Using entredeaux 115
    Gathering lace edging 117
    Attaching straight-edged lace to rolled and whipped edges 117
    Attaching entredeaux to lace insertion 117
    Sewing lace to lace 118
    Fagoting 118
    Special marking foot techniques 118
        Project: Wedding Handkerchief 119
Lesson 24. Seaming with feed dogs up and lowered 123
    Using a narrow hemmer 123
    Sewing a fake lapped hem 123
    Seaming with a side cutter 124
    Stitching over yarn on knits 124
    Imitating hand-piecing on quilts 125
    Joining veiling with a scallop stitch 125
    Using utility and decorative stitches 125
    Creating seams with feed dogs lowered 126

Chapter 9   Adding Hems and Edges   **127**

> Lesson 25. Turning hems once   127
>> Using double needles on knits   127
>> Hemming with a double needle on sheers   128
>> Hemming with utility or decorative stitches on front   128
>> Quilting a hem   129
> Lesson 26. Blind hemming   129
> Lesson 27. Sewing narrow hems   130
>> Straight stitching   130
>> Sewing on lace   130
>> Attaching scalloped lace   131
>> Stitching shell edging   132
>> Roll and shell hemming   132
> Lesson 28. Using bias tape   133
> Lesson 29. Zigzagging a narrow edge   134
> Lesson 30. Covering wire for shaped edges   134
> Lesson 31. Cording edges   135
>> Covering cords   135
>> Creating crocheted edges   136
>> Reshaping knits with elastic   137
> Lesson 32. Making thread fringe   137
> Lesson 33. Piping edges   139
> Lesson 34. Topstitching   139

Chapter 10   Machine Tricks: Adding Threads to Threads   **140**

> Lesson 35. Making cord   140
>> Twisting monk's cord   140
>> Stitching belt and button loops   142
> Lesson 36. Making tassels   142
>> *Project:* Tassel Collar   143
>> *Project:* Covered Wire Tassel   144
>> *Project:* Doll Tassel   145
>> *Project:* Making Two Tassel Tops by Machine   145

Chapter 11   Decorative Stitches   **148**

> Lesson 37. Stitches   149
>> Using rows of decorative stitches   149
>> Cablestitching with a double needle   149
>> Creating plaids and stripes   151
>>> *Project:* Decorative Messages   152
>> Sewing, pleating and folding paper   153
>>> *Project:* Heirloom Christmas Stocking   154
> Lesson 38. Decorative Motifs and Pictograms   157
>>> *Project:* Pictogram Motif Buttons and Earrings   158
>> Satin Element design lines   159
>>> *Project:* Tote Bag Square (Landscape Pictogram)   161
>>> *Project:* Tote Bag Square (Viking Crest)   164

Lesson 39: Machine accessories used with decorative stitches   167
 Seven-hole foot   167
  Project: Vest with Corded Design   168
 Friendship bracelets   169
 Hemstitching   170
  Project: Hemstitched, Fagoted and Embroidered Detachable
 Collar   171

Chapter 12   Making the Tote Bag   **173**
 Finishing the squares   173
 Tote bag construction   174

A Brief History of the Viking   180

Viking Presser Feet and Attachments   182

Sources of Supply   186   **Bibliography   190**   **Index   191**

Foreword

In 1987 we published a book by Jackie Dodson called Know Your Bernina. *Jackie and I had met more than ten years ago by accident on a tour bus in Chicago. Since then she has showered me with wacky, inspiring letters. This is a woman who is brimming with laughter and ideas, sharing both freely. Most of the letters arrived with swatches of machine-embroidered fabric pinned to them. "Have you tried this?" she'd ask, again and again.*

When it came time to revise my machine-embroidery book, I knew who to ask for help as a designer and critic: Jackie. Next I asked her to write a book about her teaching methods; the result was the Bernina book.

The editors at Chilton and I knew Know Your Bernina *was a good book, but even we were surprised at the enthusiastic response: we had to reprint it four times in the first six months. We also received letters and calls from storeowners and home sewers saying, "I bought the book, even though I don't have a Bernina—but I wish you'd publish one for my brand."*

So we did. In Spring 1988, we published a generic version called Know Your Sewing Machine. *Having taught on all major brands, Jackie adapted her techniques to include all of them. She kept the same lesson format, but changed all the tote-bag squares and some of the projects, added a chapter on using decorative stitches, and showed some of the projects on color pages, along with inspiring artists' work.*

But as the second book developed, Jackie and I realized we could barely touch on the unique features of each brand. Like cars or computers, sewing machines are not all alike. They each have special features, stitches, feet, capabilities: that's why Jackie and I own so many machines. (We've been known to buy a brand-new computer sewing-machine that does everything but your income taxes . . . and to hold on to four old machines "because I love the feather stitch on this one and the buttonhole on this one and I'm keeping this one in case my daughter wants it and this one in case all the others fail.")

So Know Your Viking *was born. I contacted Jan Saunders, whose work I had admired for years. From Columbus, Ohio, Jan is the author of* Speed Sewing: 103 Sewing Machine Shortcuts. *She is Swiss-trained and has worked extensively with consumers and fabric stores to upgrade and update sewing skills.*

Jan stitched her way through the entire manuscript, making changes appropriate to Viking machines. Again, Jackie changed all the tote design squares and many of the project designs. Then Jan wrote two special chapters—"Why I Love my Viking" and Chapter 11 on using Viking's unique decorative stitches. Meanwhile, we canvassed the country, looking for creative work done on the Viking, which we've shown on the color pages (and it is only the tip of the iceberg—we wish we could have included much more).

We are also publishing versions for other brands—Elna, New Home, Pfaff, Singer, and a revised Bernina book, so far—in which knowledgeable co-authors have adapted the book to their brand and have contributed a unique chapter on decorative stitches. All of the decorative stitch chapters are completely different, as are all of the tote-bag squares, so even if you don't own that brand, be sure to read the book. Your head will be filled with enough ideas to make clever gifts, garments, and accessories for many years to come.

And best of all, after stitching your way through the book(s), you will truly know your sewing machine.

Robbie Fanning

Series Editor, *Creative Machine Arts,* and co-author
The Complete Book of Machine Embroidery

Are you interested in a quarterly magazine about creative uses of the sewing machine? Robbie Fanning and Jackie Dodson are planning to start one. For more information, write:
The Creative Machine
PO Box 2634, Ste. 2
Menlo Park, CA 94026

Preface

When our children were small, we took long car trips. I remember one that took longer than planned. We all grumbled about being lost, but one of our boys said, "It's just one of Dad's long-cuts."

We loved that new word, so we came up with dictionary meanings.

Long-cut (noun): When it takes longer, but Dad convinces everyone he wanted it that way. A "little something extra." An adventure. An educational side-trip. You are happier when you finally reach your destination. And so on.

What does this have to do with the Viking? This book contains long-cuts, those adventurous techniques that help you and your sewing machine create something special, something out of the ordinary.

Most of us learned basic techniques of sewing when we bought our machines—how to thread it, wind a bobbin, make a buttonhole, sew a straight seam. We were shown each presser foot and how to use it. . . and, I'll bet, except for the zipper and buttonhole feet, you haven't looked at those other feet again.

But there's so much more to learn. Join me on an educational side-trip. By the time you're done with this book, you'll truly know your Viking.

Let's begin by exploring how we can change a piece of fabric: we can add texture to it, appliqué it, quilt it, stitch across holes in it, draw thread out of it, gather it up and decorate it. We can stitch in space with our sewing machines, make cording–but, more importantly, once we understand the machine, it makes all our stitching easier.

As we explore all these effects, which are presented in 39 lessons, we'll make small samples for a notebook; make finished 6'' squares to fit on a totebag, displaying what we've learned; and make 33 other projects. In the process of stitching the samples and projects in the book, you'll take an educational side-trip as well. You'll learn to adjust and manipulate your Viking until you can use it to its full potential.

This workbook of ideas does not take the place of your Operating Manual or *Viking Owner's Handbook*. Instead, it is to be used as a reinforcement and supplement to what you already know. By working through the lessons, you will come to know your machine better.

Yes, there is much more to sewing than straight stitching. And wouldn't you rather go that long-cut route–to make your stitching more interesting and original?

In my classes I often hear this progression: "I can't do that" to "Can I really do that?" to "I can do that!" I hope this book is the next best thing to having me prompting, prodding, patting you on the back in person.

Jackie Dodson
LaGrange Park, Illinois

Acknowledgments

Thank you:

To Viking White Sewing Machine Company for time, assistance, and commitment to sewing education.

To Sue Hausmann, who answered my questions no matter how busy she was.

To Robbie Fanning, for her wonderful books that "introduced" us.

To Jackie Dodson, for answering endless questions and offering her support and sense of humor in the face of almost impossible deadlines.

And most of all, to my husband John Moser, who has offered me the encouragement, support and understanding needed to complete this project.

J.S.

Thank You:

To Viking White Sewing Machine Company, for answers and willing help, with a special thanks to Sue Hausmann.

A special thank you to Ed and Flo Perk, who let me work out these lessons with students at their shop.

To Caryl Rae Hancock, Nora Lou Kampe, Gail Kibiger, Pat Pasquini and Marcia Strickland for sharing ideas; Ladi Tisol who helped me before I had to ask; and Marilyn Tisol, critic, sounding-board, and special friend.

To Chuck, who took the photos, and to the rest of my family, who accept chaos as normal and never complain.

To Robbie Fanning, for her optimism, encouragement, and endless support.

Especially to Jan Saunders for beating deadlines, for working tirelessly to make our book exceptional, and for becoming a good friend.

J.D.

CHAPTER **1**

Getting Started

by JAN SAUNDERS

This book is organized by the changes you can make to a piece of fabric—add stitches, add texture, subtract threads, and so on. Following this introductory chapter, each chapter consists of several lessons, and some projects. Each lesson asks you to stitch up practice samples for a notebook or for finished projects. The largest project in the book is the tote bag (directions for making it are in Chapter 12). It was designed to show off interchangeable decorative squares, which you'll make as you proceed through the lessons.

For the practice samples, you will want to set up a three-ring notebook—the kind with the largest rings—to keep track of your stitching (Fig. 1.1). Buy plastic pockets and blank notebook paper (both available at office supply stores). Write the settings you've used directly on the stitched samples and slip them into the plastic pockets for future reference.

Clip pictures from magazines that trigger ideas. Ask yourself: Could I get that effect if I loosened the bobbin? Which presser foot would I use for that? Which thread

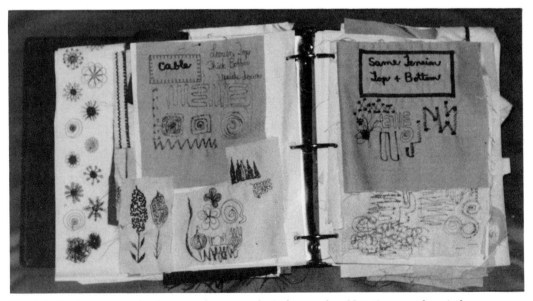

Fig. 1.1 A reference notebook, open to a page of stitch samples. Notations on the stitchery will help you reset the machine.

would produce loops like that? Write notes to yourself with ideas to try and add these to the notebook along with the magazine pictures.

Love your Viking

When I turned ten years old, my best present was to have use of Mom's sewing machine. On my eighteenth birthday, Mom and Dad gave me a White to take to college. I made all those tailoring and draping projects home economics majors make, as well as formals, bridesmaids' dresses, and the funky clothes of the 70s. All this I stitched with a straight stitch and zigzag, even though my machine had 20 built-in stitches.

After graduation, I finally learned how to use those stitches. Soon I was off to the races, finding new ways to use them to simplify clothing construction and ways to imitate hand stitchery by machine. By then, I was in the market to update my equipment. I wanted a machine that was easy to operate without sacrificing decorative potential. I found both in my Viking 990.

For the first time, I didn't have to test for the best stitch or appropriate setting for the fabric I was using. Oh, I could make an educated guess, but now I let my Viking computerized *Sewing Advisor* select the stitch, the width and length. If we disagree on the recommended settings, I can override it. But honestly, the Sewing Advisor is right 99% of the time and is so much faster. It even knows when to make tension adjustments and what presser foot to use so seams won't pucker on fine fabrics, yet I still have all the power needed for mending my husband's jeans. My Viking 990 makes five different types of buttonholes that can be programmed to come out the same length every time. If I could only get it to cook, clean and do the laundry, I'd have it made.

As far as decorative potential, I have recently discovered what the *Pictogram* feature is all about. Essentially, all the *Satin Elements* necessary to make anything from flower petals to intricate edge stitches are programmed in a cassette. Simply decide what shape or design you want, program it in, and the same tapered line of satin stitching is sewn perfectly time after time. The finishing button is also a great help. When you come to the end of a motif, the finishing button stops at the end of the program. The next motif starts at the beginning, great when creating flower petals or a decorative treatment where each element needs to be the same every time it's stitched. The finishing button automatically knots off thread ends, eliminating the need to tie them off by hand. Those clever Swedes have also included a special pair of embroidery scissors to cut the threads off, right at the fabric.

Another feature I love is the 6mm stitch width. The decorative stitches look big, bold and—since my Viking automatically adjust the tension for each stitch—the decorative effects are beautiful.

If you have a youngster at home, the sewing machine is usually off-limits. However, Viking has thought of that, too. The on/off switch turns the machine off even when it is plugged into the outlet. If I'm afraid of little hands turning it on, however, I simply put a bobbin on the bobbin winder which automatically disengages the needle even though the machine is on.

Bobbin winding can be done from the needle; or you can leave your work under the presser foot and wind a bobbin at the same time without disturbing the program. Bobbins are specially marked so you don't wind or thread them incorrectly, and are transparent so you can easily check thread supply.

Another reason I chose the Viking over other brands was because of the control and precision you get only with a Viking. The foot pedal can be used in three different positions to control the maximum sewing speed. It works similar to "cruise control" on your car, so you are able to zip up a seam, or slow down for precise topstitching or intricate decorative work.

Other machines stop sewing with the needle up, even if you want to leave the needle in the fabric to turn a corner. I can stop the needle wherever I want with the touch of the foot pedal. Viking calls it "stop right" control because you stop right where you want—no more need to turn the flywheel by hand.

After sewing on other brands, I realize I sometimes take these special Viking features for granted: two lights, one over the needle, one over the bed of the machine; 13 needle positions; a big accessory tray that works as a sewing table around the slim free arm; measuring guide in inches and centimeters; snap-on and -off feet; and easy maintenance (no oiling is necessary). The no-jamming feature and open threading is great for beginning sewers and children.

I have enjoyed getting to know my Viking and love to use it for machine stitchery. Notice that I did not say "machine embroidery." Embroidery is only one part of machine stitchery, which also includes making lace, needle weaving, and appliquéing in creative ways, to name a few we'll touch on in this book.

How can you find the right Viking for you? A good starting place is to ask friends about their Vikings. Then check out the models they recommend by asking for demonstrations at the dealer's. Bring along fabric of every description and try them all yourself. When you finally purchase your machine, be sure you've bought only as much machine as you need.

So let's begin. Get out the dusty box of accessories and presser feet that came with your machine, as well as the Operating Manual. If you can't find it, contact the dealer and arrange to purchase another.

What type of Viking do you have? Not the model number, but what are its capabilities? Can it zigzag and blind stitch?

Then you can stitch up the projects and complete the lessons in this book. If your machine includes other built-in stitches, you'll find they're not neglected here either.

Presser feet

But built-in stitches are only part of this book. Presser feet are also a part of it—an important part. When you purchased your machine, you probably asked what built-in stitches were included, but didn't think of asking about the presser feet. Most sewers don't look beyond the standard A and zipper feet, even though presser feet expand the capabilities of your Viking.

Do you know how each presser foot is used? Turn each over and look at the bottom; it's the most important part. Foot C, the buttonhole foot, will have two deep grooves to keep the fabric moving freely and in line as the beads of satin stitches are stitched in. The utility B foot or transparent appliqué foot will have a wide groove cut out in the back and is open in front to allow the fabric not only to feed freely as the decorative stitches are sewn in place, but also let corners be turned easily. There are presser feet that create pintucks, sew down braids accurately, make blindstitching a breeze, keep edges from tunneling when overcasting them, help you edge stitch or topstitch accurately and quickly—the list goes on. Find out about the ones you own and do a sample for each, write on the fabric which foot you've used, and file it in your notebook. Though I'll include some of the basics in this book, you'll learn new ways to use them as well. You can't use your machine to its full potential until you understand what the presser feet can do and then take advantage of that knowledge.

Each Viking model comes with standard accessories and presser feet. What is included varies from model to model, and many more presser feet are available, as well as such accessories as the bias binder,

Chart 1.1
Presser Feet and Accessories Included with Viking Machines

Lettered Feet	Manufacturer's Number	100/600 Series	900 Series	6000 Series
"A" Standard	411 73 86 45	•	•	•
"B" Utility	411 73 88 45	•	•	•
"C" Buttonhole	411 73 89 45	•	•	•
"D" Blind Hem	411 73 91 45		•	•
"D" Blind Hem	411 73 91 45		•	
"D" Blind Hem	411 53 31 45	•		
"E" Zipper	411 73 93 45	•	•	•
"E" Zipper	411 29 89 01			•
"F" Raised Seam	411 73 99 01	•	•	•
"H" Teflon	411 85 30 45	•	•	•
"J" Overcast	411 85 27 45	•	•	•
"J" Overcast	411 42 47 01			•
Transparent Appliqué foot	412 00 16 45	•	•	•
Standard Machine Accessories				
Edge Guide	401 54 20 01			•
Edge Guide	411 73 95 01	•	•	
Attachment Screw	411 13 99 01			•
Glide Plate	411 77 93 01	•	•	•
Glide Plate	411 77 91 01	•	•	•
Glide Plate	411 42 43 01			•
Button Reed	411 17 32 01	•	•	•
Bobbins, Transparent	411 44 01 01	•	•	•
Raised Seam Guide	411 39 25 01	•	•	•

circular sewing attachment, eyelet plate, and dual feed (walking) foot. Remember to mention the model number to your dealer when purchasing these accessories so you get the correct one to fit your machine.

All new snap-on feet will fit any Viking with snap-on feet. However, any old feet from a 6000 series Viking will not feed correctly on a 100, 600 or 900 series because the feed dogs on newer models are de-signed for a 6mm stitch width. Therefore, the grooves under older feet are not in correct alignment to mesh with today's feed system.

Chart 1.1 lists presser feet supplied with each model. Chart 1.2 lists presser feet and accessories I find important in my work and recommend throughout the book. I've indicated which ones are available for each model. If you have an older Viking, the feet

Chart 1.2
**Presser Feet and Accessories Available for Viking Models
as Separate Purchase**

	Manufacturer's Number	100/600 Series	900 Series	6000 Series
Braiding Foot	411 85 00 45	●	●	●
Braiding Foot	409 30 05 01			●
Braiding Foot, Narrow	411 85 09 45	●	●	●
Braiding Guide	411 85 01 45	●	●	
Bias Binder	411 85 04 45	●	●	●
Circular Sewing Attachment	411 85 26 45		●	
Circular Sewing Attachment	411 58 13 01			●
Cording Foot—5 Hole	411 45 38 01			●
Cording Foot—7 Hole	411 85 11 01	●	●	
Darning Foot	411 28 98 61			●
Darning Foot	411 73 90 45	●	●	
Eyelets Plates—4mm	412 00 69 01		●	
Eyelets Plates—6mm	412 00 69 02		●	
Eyelets Plates—4mm	411 58 55 01			●
Eyelets Plates—6mm	411 58 55 02			●
Eyelets Plates—4mm	412 00 71 01	●		
Eyelets Plates—6mm	412 00 71 02	●		
Dual Feeder	411 85 84 45		●	
Dual Feeder	411 42 94 01			●
Gathering Foot	411 85 02 45	●	●	
Gathering Foot	411 43 81 01			●
Hemmers—2mm	411 85 22 45	●	●	●
Hemmers—5mm	411 85 17 45	●	●	●
Hemmers—3mm	411 85 20 45	●	●	●
Hemmers—2mm	411 85 24 45	●	●	●
Piping	411 85 10 45	●	●	●
Roller Presser Foot	411 85 29 45	●	●	●
Roller Presser Foot	411 39 01 01			●
Ruffler	409 30 20 01			●
Ruffler	411 85 88 45		●	
Special Marking Foot	411 85 03 45	●	●	●
Special Marking Foot	411 39 31 01			●
Hemstitcher	401 53 67 45	●	●	●
Rug Foot	411 29 64 01	●	●	●
Weavers Reed—30mm	411 34 58 01	●	●	●
Weavers Reed—45mm	411 34 58 02	●	●	●
Straight Stitch Foot	411 85 35 45	●	●	●

Chart 1.2, *continued*

	Manufacturer's Number	100/600 Series	900 Series	6000 Series
Buttonholer	491 30 00			•
Darning Plate	412 00 68 01		•	
Darning Plate	412 00 68 01	•	•	
Glide Plate Zipper and Buttonhole	412 01 41 45	•	•	•
Raised Seam Foot and Guide	412 01 42 45	•	•	•
7 Hole Foot and Threader	412 01 43 45	•	•	

are not lettered, but they are the same feet as for the 6000 models.

New presser feet are introduced often. Use Chart 1.2 to keep a record of the ones you have. When you come to know your Viking well, you will quickly realize that a blind hem D foot is not only for blindstitching, a braiding foot is not only for soutache, and many feet can do the same job.

I love my Viking! One of the reasons my enthusiasm never wanes is because I have a group of friends who also love their Vikings. We exchange sewing advice, pass on our creative discoveries, recommend books to each other, and sometimes meet to try new ideas. If you don't have such friends already, you'll find them in classes at your dealer, where new ideas are taught regularly.

While at the store, check out the books and magazines. There are also educational leaflets and project ideas published by the Education Department of Viking.

What else can you use to make your sewing easier? Following is a list and description of some accessories I find useful.

Accessories

Bias binder

The Viking bias binder is used for binding edges in one operation, and can be used on quilted or non-quilted fabrics. Use 1″ (2.5cm) unfolded bias tape or cut the bias binding yourself. What's nice about this binder is that the funnel is adjustable, depending on where you want the line of stitching to fall. It can also be used with a straight stitch, zigzag or decorative stitch, so you can bind and decorate an edge at the same time.

Circular sewing attachment

This attachment fits onto your presser bar like the edge guide and enables you to sew a circle that returns to the exact starting point. Use it for making patches, buttons, coasters, and circular decorations. Try utility and decorative built-in stitches with it, as well as straight and satin stitches.

If you don't have the attachment, you can easily make perfect circles as described in Fig. 1.2.

Eyelet plates

The eyelet plate snaps over your feed dogs and can be used to make Battenberg rings, as well as English eyelets. I've used this to make flower centers or eyelets for belts and bags. It is available in a 4mm or 6mm size.

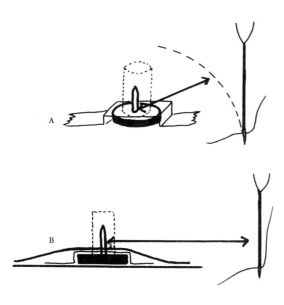

Fig. 1.2 A. Make your own circle maker by taping a thumbtack upside-down on the bed of the machine a radius away from the needle. Tape it in place. B. Place material in a hoop and stick the fabric onto the thumbtack wherever you want the center of the circle to be. Secure the fabric with a cork. Keep the fabric taut between the thumbtack and the needle as you sew a circular design.

Dual feed foot (walking foot)

The dual feed foot—also referred to as a walking foot—is great for stitching stripes and plaids together perfectly, sewing plastics, leathers, vinyls, knits, napped fabrics, slippery fabrics, and layers of fabrics such as quilts. It can be used with the straight stitch, zigzag or any Trimotion stitch. It has a top set of feed dogs that help pull the fabric through the machine without causing the fabric to shift, slip, slide or come up short.

Ruffler

This attachment ruffles fabric and also pleats it. The ruffler adjusts to the proper fullness for your ruffle or pleats. Always do a sample first, using the fabric you plan to use on your finished project, so you can determine how much fabric you will need. The ruffles or pleats are not adjustable once they are sewn in.

The Viking ruffler has two fabric guides so you can also gather or pleat while sewing a ruffle between two layers of fabric; you can also trim the pleated edge with a narrow tape or bias binding while pleating.

Glide plates

One of the best presser feet that comes as a standard accessory with all Vikings is the Teflon H foot. It's great on synthetic suedes, leathers and very fine fabrics. Like the dual feed foot, it helps keep top and bottom fabric layers even when sewing long seams. Teflon glide plates are available for the zipper and buttonhole feet and function similarly to the Teflon presser foot.

Roller foot

The roller foot works like a bulldozer. It rides up and over varying thicknesses, like jeans seams, and is great for sewing sticky, heavy leather or vinyl. The rollers allow the fabric to move freely between the foot and feed dogs.

Narrow hemmers

Viking makes 2mm, 3mm, and 5mm narrow hemmers. Use the narrow ones for fine rolled shirt-tail hems. Use the wider ones for deeper rolled hems or to simplify the second step of a flat-felled seam. Use a straight stitch on wovens, a zigzag on knits. For a shell tuck, use a longer zigzag stitch or blindstitch.

Supplies

In addition to your Viking and a good supply of threads, here's a shopping list of what you'll need for the lessons. (Each lesson will give you a detailed materials list). You probably have many of the supplies in your sewing room.

1. Scissors and shears: sharp embroidery scissors, plus shears for cutting fabric and paper-cutting scissors.
2. Water-erasable markers for light fabrics; white opaque permanent marker for water-soluble stabilizer; slivers of soap or light-colored chalk pencils for dark fabrics.
3. Vanishing markers are great when you need an accurate but temporary mark. The ink is air-soluble and disappears within 24 to 48 hours (sometimes sooner if you live in a humid climate). I have also found that the amount of time the mark takes to disappear depends on the type and amount of synthetic fiber used in a fabric. When in doubt, test.
4. T square or 6" × 24" (15.0cm × 61.0cm) plastic ruler; 6" (15.0cm) and 12" (30.5cm) see-through rulers are also helpful.
5. Wood and spring-type hoops in varied sizes, maximum 7" (17.8cm) for ease.
6. Rotary cutting wheel and board.
7. Extra bobbin case.

Have fabric ready for stitching samples. A handy size is a 9" (22.9cm) square. It will fit in the 7" (17.8cm) hoop and can be trimmed slightly for your notebook. Cut up a variety of fabrics from extra-light-weight types like organdy, lightweights like calicos, medium-weight poplins, and heavy-weight denim. Extra-heavy-weight canvas scraps will be left over from your tote bag and can be used for experiments.

In the projects, you'll also use felt, transparent fabrics, bridal veil, 1/8" (3.2mm) and 1/2" (12.7mm) satin double-faced ribbon, lace insertion, scalloped lace, lace beading, Battenberg tape, fleece, batting, stabilizers and fusibles. Now let's discuss your choices of threads needles, and other supplies.

Threads

One of the most useful charts I have in my notebook is a piece of doubled fabric with line after line of satin stitches on it. Each row is stitched using a different type of thread. I recommend that you make one, too. More important than telling you which thread to use, your chart will graphically convince you that what is called machine-embroidery cotton is usually more lustrous and covers an area more quickly and more beautifully than regular sewing thread. It's easy to compare differences among threads.

Generally, sewing threads are not used for machine embroidery. Ordinary sewing threads are usually thicker, stretch more (if polyester), and do not cover as well as machine embroidery threads. However, for durability or when you need a certain color, try using a 100% cotton Zwicky sewing thread. I never use thread from the sale bin—the ones that are three spools for 88 cents. This thread does not hold up to heavy use; it breaks, shrinks, knots, and, after all the time spent stitching with it, looks sloppy. If I am going to take the time to sew or embroider anything, then it deserves quality thread.

Machine embroidery rayons and cottons are more lustrous and have a softer twist than ordinary sewing thread. Rayon embroidery threads are silky and loosely twisted, but if you use a #90 stretch needle and sew evenly and at a moderate speed, they are easy to use. The Viking Satin Elements used for Pictograms are programmed to rayon "Sulky" thread, available through your Viking dealer (see Sources of Supply). However, don't use rayons or any other machine embroidery threads for clothing construction because they aren't strong enough.

Besides regular sewing threads and those used for machine embroidery, there are others to become acquainted with. The fine nylon used for lingerie and woolly overlock used for serging are just a couple of them. Another is Zwicky darning thread: It's often used on the bobbin for machine embroidery because it's lightweight and you can get so much more of it wound on. It comes in only a few colors, so it cannot always be used should you want the bobbin thread to be seen on the surface.

Monofilament, another popular thread, comes in two shades. One blends into light-colored fabrics, the other darks. It is not the wild, fish-line type anymore, so don't be afraid of making it work. I use it on the top and bobbin constantly.

If you use silk and silk buttonhole twists as well as fine pearl cottons, crochet and cordonnet, the needle must be large enough to keep the threads from fraying against the fabric and the eye large enough to enable the thread to go through smoothly. Sometimes top-stitching needles are called for. Or you may have to use a needle larger than you normally would embroider with.

Waxed or glacé finished quilting thread should never be used on your machine, as the finish wears off and does your machine no good.

Chart 1.3 is a handy guide, showing which needles and threads to use with which fabrics. More about where to purchase threads can be found in Sources of Supplies at the end of the book.

Needles

It is important to choose the right needle for the job. Match fabric weight, thread, and needle size, as well as type of material. The lighter the material, the smaller the needle and finer the thread should be. The heavier the fabric, the larger the needle should be.

Like presser feet, needles come in different sizes and shapes and produce different effects. I once had a student in quilting class who struggled to get a needle out of her machine—it was rusted in. "I don't do much sewing," she said. (Why didn't that surprise me?) No matter how mind-bog-

Chart 1.3
Needle and Thread Chart

Fabric	Thread	Needles
Very heavy (upholstery, canvas, denim)	Heavy-duty cotton; polyester; buttonhole twist; cordonnet	18 (110)
Heavy (sailcloth, heavy coating)	Heavy-duty cotton; polyester	16 (100)
Medium weight (wool, poplin, velvet)	Ordinary sewing cotton and polyester; machine-embroidery cotton and rayon	11/12, 14 (80, 90)
Lightweight (shirt cotton, dress fabrics, silk)	Extra-fine to ordinary sewing cotton and polyester	9, 11/12 (70, 80)
Very lightweight (lace, net, organdy, batiste)	Extra-fine sewing cotton and polyester	8, 9 (60, 70)

gling this sounds, I know that few sewers change needles unless they break, even though a new needle keeps thread from fraying, fabric from being damaged, and your stitches from skipping. The correct size and shape enables you to stitch through the heaviest or the flimsiest materials with ease. Also, wing needles for hemstitching and double needles allow you to create unique, decorative work.

But all needles do not fit all machines. Viking uses a 130–705 system which is equivalent to the American 15 × 1 system.

Needles are available in sharp point, used for heavy woven fabrics and are sometimes referred to as denim or jeans needles. Ballpoint needles are sometimes used for knits to minimize cutting threads and causing runs in the fabric. The universal-point needle is all-purpose and can be used for knits, as well as woven fabrics. Instead of cutting through the fabric, the slightly rounded point deflects off the threads and slips between them. Because of its versatility, it is the needle in greatest use today.

Following is a list of needles and their uses:

Universal Needles: All-purpose sewing.
Fine Ballpoint Needles: Fine fabrics, including knits and wovens.
Medium Ballpoint Needles: Heavier knitted fabrics.
Medium Ballpoint Stretch Needles: Available in sizes #75/11 or #90/14, the stretch needle is designed to prevent skipped stitches when sewing interlock knits, elastic, Lycra swimwear and Spandex. I also use the size #75/11 for sewing Ultrasuede and the #90/14 for free-hand embroidery and free-machining.
Extra-Fine Point Needles: Used to pierce closely woven fabrics such as canvas or denim; often called jeans needles.
Topstitching Needles: Equipped with an eye and thread groove larger than a regular needle of the same size. Use buttonhole twist or double thread when topstitching. Use them for embroidery, too.
Double and Triple Needles: Used for sewing with more than one thread on top. Double needles come in five sizes (1.6mm, 2.0mm, 2.5mm, 3.0mm, 4.0mm).
Wing Needles: Double and single types for hemstitching.
Leather Needles: Often called wedge needles because of their cutting points. Use them on real suede and leather. Or use a regular #110 needle in place of a leather needle.

To keep your machine running trouble-free, change the needle often. Be sure the needle is straight and has no burr on the point. Damaged needles damage fabric and machines.

If your machine is noisy and is skipping stitches, change the needle (assuming the machine is clean). Be sure you've used the correct needle for the job and be certain you've placed the needle in the machine correctly. Most of the time a damaged needle is the only problem—and an easy one to rectify.

To make it easier for you to prepare appropriate supplies before beginning the

	Very Fine	Fine	Medium	Strong	Large	Very Large	Hemstitching
U.S.	8	9	11/12	14	16	18	—
Europe	60	70	80	90	100	110	120

lessons, let's discuss items often called for and the terms I'll use.

Batting, fleece, and fiberfill

Batting, both cotton and polyester, is used between fabric layers for quilting. Different weights and sizes are available, as well as different qualities. For our use, most of the projects can be quilted with bonded batting, which holds together firmly, or with fleece, which is a filler that's thinner than bonded batting and about as thick as a heavy wool blanket. Alternative fillers can be flannel, when only a light garment is desired, or a wool blanket. Fiberfill is the shredded batting used to fill toys. Or stuff toys with batting.

Fusibles

Fusibles are used to hold appliqués to background fabrics so edges are held firmly for the final step of stitching them in place. Plastic sandwich bags or cleaner's garment bags can be used. Stitch Witchery, Fine Fuse, Magic Polyweb and Jiffy Fuse are commercial fusible webbings. To use, place them between two pieces of fabric and press with a hot iron until the webbing melts and holds the two fabrics together. Use a Teflon pressing sheet to protect your iron and also to allow you to press the fusible to one fabric at a time. The Applique Pressing Sheet or Teflon sheet has eliminated any problem with the fusible melting on your iron: it looks like opaque wax paper, is reusable, and comes in handy sizes.

A fusible webbing already backed by paper, which saves one step in application, is called Wonder-Under Transfer Fusing Web. Press rough side of Wonder-Under against wrong side of fabric. Press for 3 seconds with a hot, dry iron. Let fabric cool. Draw your design directly onto paper before cutting. Cut this new fusible fabric into desired shape. When you're ready to fuse, gently peel off paper backing. Position fusible fabric, coated side down, on background fabric. Cover with damp press cloth. Set iron to "wool" setting and press for 10 seconds.

Appliqué papers are paper-backed products that look very much like freezer wrap, but act like the transfer web. One side of the paper has a glue finish.

See Chapter 4 for more about fusibles.

Stabilizers

Stabilizers are used behind fabric to keep it from puckering when you embroider. At one time, we used typing paper, but today we have more choices of stabilizers, available at fabric and quilt shops and through mail-order (see Sources of Supplies).

The old standby, typing paper, still does the job. Or, use shelf paper when stitching large pictures and adding-machine tape for long strips of embroidery. A problem with paper is that it dulls machine needles faster than tear-away stabilizers do. It's also harder to remove from the back of the embroidery, although dampening the paper will help.

Another stabilizer you probably have in the cupboard is plastic-coated freezer wrap. I find I'm using it more and more. If I'm embroidering a fabric that could be damaged by the hoop, I back it instead with freezer wrap, which I iron to the back of the fabric. The freezer paper adheres to the fabric and stiffens it. When I finish my embroidery, I peel off the freezer paper. I like using it if I have a small piece of fabric to embroider. I iron the small piece to a larger, easier-to-manipulate piece of freezer paper.

Tear-away stabilizers come in crisp or soft finishes and some are iron-ons. When embroidering, place them between the fabric and machine. When the embroidery is completed, they tear away from the fabric easily.

Don't confuse stabilizers with interfacings. Interfacings are permanent and don't tear away. They can be used, of

11

course, and so can fabrics like organdy, but they are usually used when you plan to leave the stabilizer on the back of the embroidery after it's completed.

One of the newest stabilizers is a thin film of plastic, available by the sheet or the yard, that will dissolve when wet. Clamp it into the hoop along with the fabric. It is transparent, and can be used on top of the embroidery, too. It can be marked on, but choose a water-erasable marker or permanent white opaque marker (available in art supply stores) that will not leave ink on your embroidery when the plastic is dissolved. When your embroidery is completed, rinse out the stabilizer. It will become gooey, then disappear. I'll refer to it as water-soluble stabilizer.

Helpful hints for sewing

Before beginning to sew, check out the following general helpful hints:

1. Every machine has its own idiosyncracies, so the settings I recommend for each lesson are only suggestions; your machine may prefer different ones.

2. Take your Viking in for regular checkups whether you think it needs it or not. Between checkups, keep it clean. No matter what model Viking you have, you must keep the inside free of lint and threads. Clean the bobbin area first by removing the bobbin, then wiping out all the lint. The lint brush that comes with your Viking works well and so does canned air. It's used for cameras to blow out lint from hard-to-reach areas. I sometimes vacuum out lint from inside the machine. Remember to clean the feed dogs whenever you finish sewing or during a long period of stitching nappy fabrics such as corduroy, fur, or velvets.

3. Do you know what stitch length really means? Here are the conversions:

Setting	Number of Stitches per 1" (2.5cm)
0.5	60
1	24
2	13
3	9
4	6
5	5
7	4

Now gather your supplies together and begin the adventure—to know your Viking.

CHAPTER 2

Adding Stitches to Your Fabric

- ■ **Lesson 1. Using utility and decorative stitches**
- ■ **Lesson 2. Using free machining**

In this chapter you'll become acquainted with the range of stitches your machine can produce. By the end of it, you'll easily switch back and forth from stitching with the feed dogs up to stitching with feed dogs down. To demonstrate your new facility, you'll make beautiful small buttons and pendants.

Lesson 1. Using utility and decorative stitches

The first thing I did when I bought my machine was to try all the built-in stitches. I wanted a reference, so I sewed stitches in rows at different widths and lengths and put them in a notebook, along with notations from the Operating Manual. I was determined to know my sewing machine, and this has been so helpful to me that I've made it your first lesson too.

To save you time, practical and decorative stitches have been built into your machine and more are available on cassettes for your Viking 990 or other Viking model. I classify stitches as "closed" and "open." "Closed" refers to those where the beauty is in stitching it close together (wide stitch width, stitch length 0.3–0.5), like the satin stitch or scallop stitch. On the Viking 990, Satin Elements can be used alone or combined to make "closed" Pictograms. "Open" utility stitches, like the three-step zigzag stitch, blindstitch, overlock and overcast stitches, are usually sewn at a stitch length longer than 0.5.

To practice the utility stitches and make a record of them, first set up your machine as indicated at the beginning of the lesson.

Note that, throughout this book, stitches on cassette 2 for the 990 are referred to as "decorative stitches" or Satin Elements. They will also be referred to by the number of the cassette and the number of the stitch. For example, Tulips, 2-10; Train Engine, 2-21; etc. I keep Fig. 2.1 in front of me while sewing, for easy reference, and number the rows of stitches as shown.

Stitch width: widest
Stitch length: varies
Needle position: center
Needle: #90/14 stretch needle
Feed dogs: up
Pressure: normal
Presser foot: utility B or transparent appliqué
Utility or decorative stitch: varies
Tension: *top*, normal; *bobbin*, normal
Fabric suggestion: medium-weight striped cotton
Thread: Sulky machine-embroidery to contrast with fabric, different colors in top and bobbin
Accessories: fine-point marker
Stabilizer: tear-away or iron-on freezer paper

13

Stitch lines of the utility and decorative stitches found on your machine (Fig. 2.2). The striped fabric will help you keep them straight. Start by using the settings suggested in the manual. Vary the settings as you stitch, making the stitches wider and narrower, longer and shorter. If there is a setting you find particularly useful, mark it right on the fabric with a marker to show where that setting begins.

On a separate piece of fabric, stitch one of the open decorative stitches in varying lengths, widths, elongated, matched,

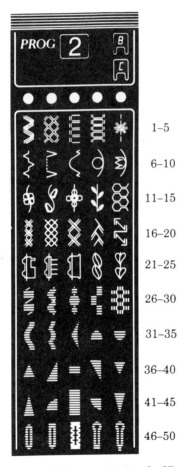

Fig. 2.1 Cassette #2 for the Viking 990, with rows numbered for easy reference.

combined with other stitches, mirror imaged, stitched with double needles or stitched as a single motif. Sew in a straight line, a circle, or curve and keep this sampler for future reference (Fig. 2.3). When you have time, make a sampler for each open decorative stitch for your notebook. You'll be amazed what you'll discover about your Viking.

This is a good time to determine the precise width and length settings for the best-looking closed, decorative stitches.

Using different colors of thread on top and bobbin will help you adjust the machine to find the perfect stitch. Adjust tension by loosening the top tension slightly and leaving the bobbin tension normal. The top thread should be pulled down and show underneath the fabric and should mound slightly on top when making satin stitches. Note that the 990, 980, and 950 automatically loosen top tension for closed embroidery stitches.

Start by stitching the zigzag, with the widest stitch width, stitch length 2. Adjust the length as you stitch until the satin stitch is perfect. This will be somewhere between 0.3 and 0.5 length. Write the setting on the sample.

When you finish your record of the utility stitches, practice mirror images. This is as simple as pushing a button on your 990, 980 and 950. If you have an older Viking, now is the time to practice and learn to make them manually. Check your Operating Manual.

There are a number of variables with mirror images or matching a pattern back-to-back. Are you feeding the fabric through exactly? Don't pull on one side when the other has been fed through freely. Did you start the second row at exactly the right spot? Just one stitch off will make a difference. Do you have the same thickness of fabric under both sides of the design? If you're stitching on top of a seam allowance, the needle may go off the two layers.

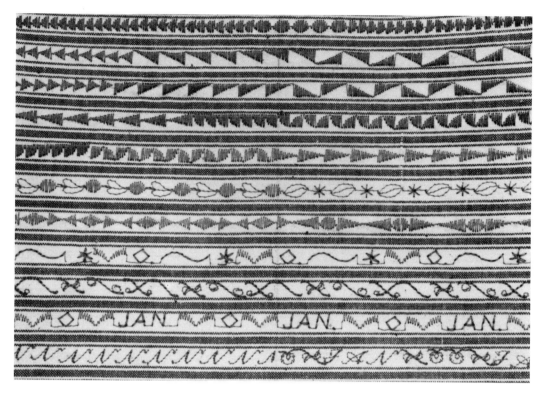

Fig. 2.2 Striped fabric is used to make a record of utility and decorative stitches on my Viking 990.

Not only can you make a mirror image by pushing a button, but you can also program the machine to stop after the last stitch of the design with the finishing button. Also, the design can be elongated by lengthening the stitch or the stitch can be narrowed. Make a record of each possibility.

As you sew line after line of practical and decorative stitches, imagine how they can be used. For example, the blindstitch is used for blind hems and for a shell tucked hem.But it can also be an invisible way of stitching on a patch pocket or an appliqué, or the stitch to use when couching down heavy cords.

Lesson 2. Using free-machining: darning, whipping, feather stitching

In free machining, you — not the presser foot — control the movement of the fabric, which in turn determines the length of the stitch. With fabric stretched tightly in a

hoop, it is easy to move your work forward, backward, in circles, whatever way you wish.

I suggest working with a wooden hoop

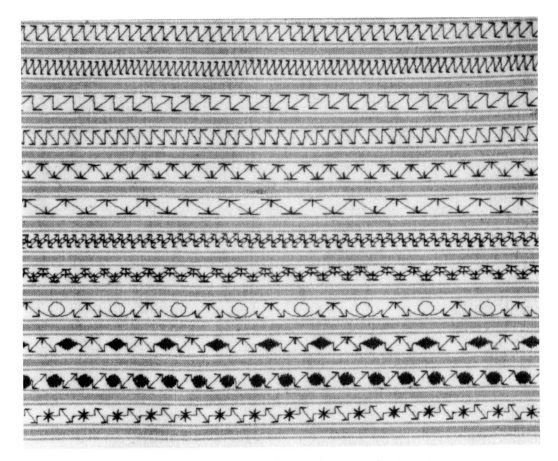

Fig. 2.3 One stitch pattern variation: regular, shortened, elongated, mirror image, with double needles, and combined with other motifs.

when first learning machine stitchery. Choose one that has a smooth finish, and slips easily under the darning foot. But whatever wooden hoop you use, be sure it is the screw type, as that will hold the fabric tightly. To be sure that it does, the inside ring of the wooden hoop should be wound with narrow twill tape. This keeps the fabric from slipping. Take a few hand stitches at the end of the tape to hold it firmly.

If your needle will not clear the hoop you've chosen, turn the hoop on its side and slip it under the darning foot or put the hoop together and carve out a small wedge to make it easier. Then wrap the inside part with tape.

Fabric is placed in the hoop upside-down from the way you would put it in a hoop for hand embroidery (Fig. 2.5). Pull the cloth as tightly as you can. Tighten the screw; pull again; tighten. Tap on the fabric. If it sounds like a drum, it is tight enough. You may or may not want to use a stabilizer under a hoop, depending upon the effect you want and the weight of the fabric.

16

Fig. 2.4 Free-machine darning stitches were used to make a picture.

You can stitch with a darning foot on or without a presser foot (but keep your fingers a safe distance from the needle!).

It is possible to stitch freely without a hoop if you use your fingers to hold the fabric taut while stitching. If you don't use a hoop — or if you use a spring-type hoop — use a darning foot to prevent skipped stitches. On most Viking models, it is not necessary to use a darning foot for free-machine stitching. By removing the foot and releasing the pressure between # and 1, the foot shank acts like a darning foot. However, in certain instances you may be more comfortable using a darning foot available for your machine. The foot shank or darning foot will hold the fabric down each time the machine makes a stitch so the threads interlock correctly under-neath. Also, use a stabilizer under the fabric to keep the stitches from puckering.

Stitch width: 0–5
Stitch length: 0–2.5
Needle position: center
Needle: #90/14 stretch needle
Feed dogs: lowered
Pressure: between # and 1
Presser foot: darning foot or none
Utility stitch: zigzag
Tension: *top*, 4½–7½; *bobbin*, normal to loose
Fabric: light-colored, medium-weight fabric, such as poplin — scrap for practice; 18" x 18" (45.7cm x 45.7cm) square for your notebook
Thread: one color for top, another for bobbin; both should contrast with fabric

17

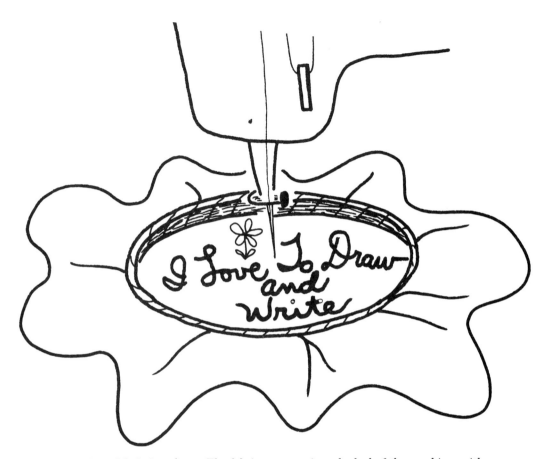

Fig. 2.5 Tighten fabric in a hoop. The fabric rests against the bed of the machine, with the material topside up for machine embroidery.

Accessories: wrapped wooden or spring hoop, no larger than 7″ (17.8cm), fine-point marker
Stabilizer: tear-away or iron-on freezer paper

The two samples in this lesson will give you practice in control and coordination. One sample will be for practice; the other, for your notebook. Keep a record of the new-found stitches you create with your machine and your imagination.

Free machining—darning, whipping and feather stitching—takes practice, but it is worth every minute. It opens up a new world of stitchery to you.

First, you are going to learn to draw, write, and sketch with your machine. It's called the darning stitch.

Place practice square in embroidery hoop with tear-away stabilizer under fabric. Set up your Viking for darning. Always begin by dipping the needle into the fabric and bringing the bobbin thread to the top. Hold both threads to the side while stitching in one place several stitches to anchor the thread. Clip off the ends. When you begin your stitchery, start slowly. Practice moving the hoop slowly, as well. You must coordinate the speed at which you move your hoop and your sewing speed. It is not

18

necessary to stitch at top speed—moderate speed is fine. You'll soon learn how fast is right for you and for the particular stitching you are creating.

Move the hoop back and forth, then in circles—remember the old Palmer Method exercises for handwriting? Stitch faster; move your hoop faster. Then write your name, draw a picture of a tree, your dog, an old flame. It doesn't matter how well you draw; you are really practicing control.

Change to zigzag and try it all over again. Yes, it will take awhile to gain absolute control, but don't give up. Stitch tiny fill-in spirals, figure eights and jigsaw patterns.

Now stitch, hesitate, stitch. The bobbin color may come to the top. Good! That's what we want. To make sure it does, tighten the top tension slowly. When you see the bobbin thread, note where the tension dial is set and write this on the sample. This type of stitchery is called whipping. If the hoop is moved slowly and the machine run very fast, a nubby, thickened line of bobbin thread will appear on the surface. It can be used in place of the darning stitch when embroidering—or used with it for

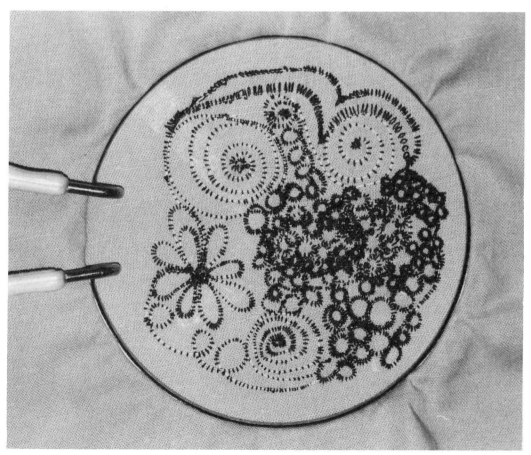

Fig. 2.6 Whipping and feather stitching.

variety. Whipping can be seen in the tiny circles of dark bobbin thread in Fig. 2.6.

For a more pronounced effect, buy another bobbin case and mark it with nail polish. This will be used for tension experimentation and the other bobbin case will be used for normal sewing.

With the top tension very tight and the experimental bobbin case tension loosened, stitch straight lines, circles and spirals. Move the hoop quickly. The top thread is visible as a straight line on top of the fabric. Covering it are looping, feathery bobbin stitches. This is an exaggera-

Fig. 2.7 Draw 36 squares on a piece of fabric, then fill them in with the new stitches and techniques you've learned and will learn. Be sure to record machine settings.

tion of whipping, which is called feather stitching. This can be seen in the hoop in some of the small circles as I went from tight to tighter top tension, and in the larger, spiky spirals (Fig. 2.6) that occurred when I loosened the bobbin tension until there was no resistance on the thread.

Practice is the only way to learn control. When you feel you have accomplished coordination between moving the hoop and the speed of the machine, make the following record of what you've learned: Iron freezer paper on wrong side of the 18″ x 18″ (45.7cm x 45.7cm) square of fabric This way you don't have to put your fabric in a hoop for the next sample. Draw a grid of 3″ (7.6cm) squares, six across, six down (Fig. 2.7). Then fill in your squares with examples of free machining — darning, whipping and feather stitching. Use both straight stitches and zigzag stitches in your squares. Try utility stitches, too. You can stitch your own designs or use mine. But as you practice, write the machine settings on the fabric. Slip this into your notebook. Add new stitches as you discover them and refer to your notebook regularly for stitches you want to use on a project.

For variety, thread your needle with two colors, or try metallics.

Project
Buttons and Pendants

The following one-of-a-kind projects include free machining and stitching with feed dogs up. Get to know your sewing machine by stitching up these small embroideries.

You have a choice of stitches on the designs and they can be finished as large buttons or pendants. Buy button forms at fabric or needlecraft shops. I used a size 75,

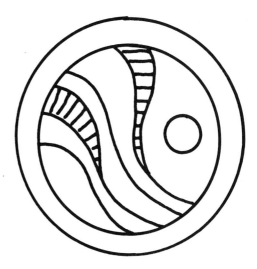

Fig. 2.8 Pattern for embroidered button or pendant, shown in the color section.

which is about 2″ (5.1cm) in diameter. And I was inspired by Mary Ann Spawn of Tacoma, Washington, to finish some of them by attaching cords and tassels to make pendants (see color section for finished embroideries of designs in Figs. 2.8–2.10).

If you use the round design in Fig. 2.8, draw two circles with the same center

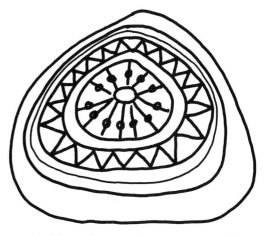

Fig. 2.9 Use whip stitches to make a pendant using this pattern (shown in color section).

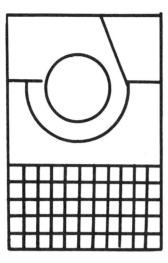

Fig. 2.10 Pattern for a rectangular machine-embroi-
dered pendant, shown in the
color section.

Tension: *top*, loosen, tighten; *bobbin*, normal,
    loosen
Fabric suggestion: medium-weight, tightly
    woven linen
Thread: Sulky rayon or machine embroidery
    in many colors
Accessories: wood or spring hoop, button
    forms or cardboard, batting, craft glue,
    cord, water-erasable or vanishing mark-
    er, small beads (optional), colored mark-
    ers, tracing paper, dressmaker's car-
    bon, empty ballpoint pen
Stabilizer: tear-away or iron-on freezer paper

On small embroidered pendants, I find it
much easier to imitate the decorative or
utility stitches than to actually use them.
This way I can fudge a little on the designs,
either shortening or elongating them, or
making them wider or narrower to fit the
space. Of course you can use utility or decorative stitches if you prefer.

Before I begin any pendant, I plan my
colors by drawing the design on a piece of
paper and coloring it. Once I begin stitching, not only do I sometimes change my
mind about the placement of some colors,
but I may add others and combine some by
sewing next to or on top of the first threads
I've used.

First, find the colored threads you'll
need and then wind bobbins for all the
spools of colors you'll use. If you want to
add small beads to any of the pendants,
keep them well within the outline.

General directions for making the three
pendants follow: For the round pendant,
stretch your fabric (I used a natural linen)
in a hoop and, using a water-erasable or
vanishing marker, draw in your design. Of
course you can trace it from the book, but
it is quite easily done free-hand—as are the
others. Then place the hoop under the needle and slip stabilizer under the hoop.

Begin by satin stitching the two wide,
flat rows. Use normal top and bobbin tension, transparent appliqué foot, feed dogs
up, parrot blue thread in top and bobbin.

point on your fabric. One is the area to be
embroidered; the other circle, ½"
(12.7mm) outside the first, is the cutting
line. It's important to keep the area between the lines free from stitching. Use a
piece of fabric large enough to go into a
spring hoop and place a piece of tear-away
stabilizer underneath.

Embroider, using free machining such
as whipping and darning, as well as satin
stitches. Leave a ½" (12.7mm) margin on
the asymmetric and rectangular designs in
Figs. 2.9 and 2.10, as well. For each, trace
the designs on linen fabric. The threads
are rayon because I liked the contrast between the linen and the shiny threads.

Stitch width: 0–6
Stitch length: 0–0.5
Needle position: center
Needle: #90/14 stretch needle
Feed dogs: up or lowered
Pressure: between # and 1
Presser foot: utility B or transparent appliqué
    foot; darning foot (optional)
Utility or decorative stitch: varies

Taper the line of stitching, using the following Satin Elements:

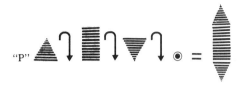

Next, change the top thread to hunter green, and the bobbin thread to parrot blue, using the other bobbin case with loosened bobbin tension. Set your machine for whipping, using the straight stitch, top tension set to 7–7½, and begin stitching by freely drawing the ladder rungs with the whip stitch.

Change top thread to royal blue, bobbin to fuchsia, leaving top and bobbin tension as you did for whip stitching. Use a zigzag stitch and fill in wide spaces.

Change top thread again to purple. Set machine on a straight stitch, with the same tension settings. Start at the center of the circle and stitch around and around to the outside. Put feed dogs up, transparent appliqué foot on, and leave thread and tension set as you did to make the circle. Select the following Satin Elements for a tapered satin stitch and sew a row of stitching over part of the larger areas that have been filled in with the royal blue and fuchsia:

Accent undulating lines with a tapered satin stitch in silver metallic thread:

Add beads to dress up the piece (Fig. 2.7). I also made sure I didn't cover the entire surface with stitches. Why cover a beautiful fabric completely? And also, I think that when fabric is completely hidden by machine embroidery, it looks too much like the appliqués you can pick up at the dime store.

All rows of stitching on the triangular pendant are tapered satin stitches, except the zigzagged line of stitching and the spider lines in the center. I used the same colors as for the first pendant, starting with the darkest colors on the outside rings, lighter colors toward the middle. I let a little of the background fabric peek through between the metallic and fuchsia rows and in the center. The tiny outlines are done with squiggly whip stitches (lowered feed dogs, straight stitch, loosened bobbin tension, upper tension set to 7–7½). The center is created with zigzag blobs. Use the transparent appliqué foot, feed dogs up, a zigzag stitch on a 4 width, stitch length 0, normal tension top and bobbin. Make 8 to 9 stitches, stop with the needle in the middle, then pivot fabric 90 degrees to make another blob, and so on, always stopping and pivoting in the center (Fig. 2.9).

I've included one other small, rectangular pendant that combines darning, whipping, appliqué, and uses a Pictogram to create the checkerboard effect on the bottom half of the design (Fig. 2.10).

First I fused a bright fuchsia fabric to the bottom half of the design with Wonder-Under. Then I programmd the following Satin Elements and stitched the squares in emerald green, picking up and moving the fabric for each motif:

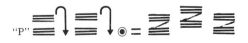

23

I stitched the appliqué down with a tiny satin stitch (length 0.4, width 1), transparent appliqué foot, feed dogs up.

Next, free-machine whip-stitch the circle, starting from the center and working out. Use fuchsia thread on top with top tension set at 7–7½. Red-orange thread is used on the bobbin with a loosened bobbin tension. These colors create an iridescent effect, giving the circle a three-dimensional look. The squiggles in the upper right corner and under the circle are darned with purple thread using normal tension on top and bobbin.

Finish pendant with the feed dogs up. Use parrot blue thread to satin stitch around the circle, using the zigzag stitch, transparent appliqué foot, stitch width 5, stitch length 0.4. Stitch over curve again with a 5 width satin stitch to give some height and density to the stitch. Finally, stitch the two lines on either side of the circle with a 2 width satin stitch in emerald green thread. *Hint:* After stitching this design in a couple of different color schemes, I found that the design looks best if you use the same color family for the appliqué fabric as you use to stitch the circle.

Pendants and buttons are small enough to do quickly and, if you make a mistake, they're easily disposable. There are no two alike. What a delightful way to spend an afternoon—stitching and getting to know your sewing machine.

When you've finished embroidering, cut out the shapes. Use large button forms for the round ones, or cut cardboard shapes to fit your embroidery. Place a piece of batting between your embroidery and the cardboard. Then make an identical circle, triangle or rectangle of plain fabric, batting and cardboard the same way. Use a thick craft glue to glue the fabric edges over the cardboard pieces. Then join back-to-back by dabbing glue between and whipping around the edge by hand. Add tassels if you wish.

By hand, stitch monk's cord (see Chapter 10) around the join of the pendant for a beautiful finish. That same cord can be extended to tie around your neck. Or measure a length of monk's cord, and tie an overhand knot at each end. Stitch the knots to the top or sides of the pendants by hand.

CHAPTER 3

Adding Texture to Your Fabric

- **Lesson 3. Building up sewing stitches**
- **Lesson 4. Applying thick threads from top and bobbin**
- **Lesson 5. Fringing yarn and fabric**
- **Lesson 6. Adding buttons, beads, shisha**
- **Lesson 7. Smocking and gathering**
- **Lesson 8. Pulling threads together**

Add to or create texture on fabrics by building up sewing stitches, using thick threads, attaching fringe or objects like buttons and beads, gathering fabric for smocking or for utilitarian purposes—to stitch elastic on sleeves or bodices, or to make ruffles for curtains.

You'll make samples for your notebook; stitch up a fabric greeting card; cable stitch a tote bag square; make fabric fringe for rugs and doll hair; and make a framed picture. Both projects and samples will suggest numerous other ways to use these stitches.

Lesson 3. Building up sewing stitches

One of the simplest ways to build up texture is to sew in one place many times. Sounds simple and it is. But you can do this in so many ways that even though it is simple, the results aren't. Texture can look studied and exact or free and wild.

I use the following techniques for landscapes, monograms, and flowers. Practice each one for your notebook, recording your machine settings and any notes on how you might use the stitches later.

Begin with my suggested settings, but change them if they are not correct for your machine or not to your liking.

Stitch width: 5
Stitch length: 0–0.5
Needle position: automatically left for 990, left for other models
Needle: #90/14 stretch needle

Feed dogs: up or lowered
Pressure: normal
Presser foot: darning, utility B or transparent appliqué foot
Decorative stitch: Satin Element 2-38 for 990; zigzag for other models
Tension: *top*, preset (990, 980, 950), loosened for other models; *bottom*, normal
Fabric suggestion: experiment with varied weights, types, and colors
Thread: practice with any type, but use machine embroidery thread for good results; include several sizes of pearl cotton, cordonnet, yarns and ⅛″ (3.2mm) ribbon
Accessories: 7″ (17.8cm) spring hoop
Stabilizer: tear-away type or iron-on freezer paper

Note: For samples 3.1 through 3.7, your

Viking 990 really shines. Using the Satin Elements below, the finishing button automatically anchors the threads for you without moving the stitch width or needle position:

"P" ≡ ↰ ≡ ↰ ◉ = ≣

With the feed dogs up, and transparent appliqué foot on, anchor the threads first; then use the widest satin stitch. Sew a block of 6 or 8 satin stitches. Anchor them by using 0 width or touch the finishing button on the 990, 980, or 950, and stitch in place. Move the hoop and do another block of satin stitches. Keep them quite close together, but all at different angles (Fig. 3.1). Use these to fill in areas in other designs.

For the next sample, lower the feed dogs, release the pressure between # and 1, and use the darning foot. Anchor the threads by stitching in one place. Use a 5 width zig-zag, but sew in one place to build up 10 or 12 stitches. Move to another spot close to the first blob of stitches and stitch again. If you wish to achieve the effect in Fig. 3.2, pull the threads into loops as you move from place to place and don't cut them off. You can make flower centers this way. Or finish by clipping between the satin stitches and then, using a different color on top, outlining with straight stitches (Fig. 3.3). Using variegated thread is especially effective.

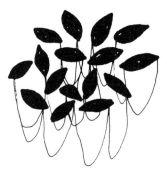

Fig. 3.2 Blobs and loops.

In the next experiment, with feed dogs up, reset pressure to normal, place the utility B or transparent appliqué foot on, and set your machine on the widest satin stitch as before. Anchor the threads and sew a block of satin stitches at the left of the practice fabric. Pull the fabric down about three inches and over to the right slightly. Stitch another block of satin stitches. Pull up and over a bit to the right to stitch another block of satin stitches. Pull down and over for the third block. Continue across the fabric. Change threads and come back with another color. Cross the threads from the first pass as you do (Fig. 3.4). This is a good filler for garden pictures—the stitches become hedges of flowers—or use layers of these to crown trees (Fig. 3.5).

Speaking of flowers, try the ones in Fig. 3.6, with feed dogs lowered, pressure be-

Fig. 3.1 Use satin stitches for flower centers or fill-in background stitches.

Fig. 3.3 Straight-stitching around blobs.

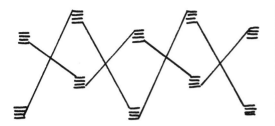

Fig. 3.4 Crossed threads and satin stitches.

tween # and 1, using the same machine settings. Anchor the threads. Stitch one blob of about 10 or 12 satin stitches in one place and, ending on the left side (on the 990, the needle automatically stops on the left side), with the needle still in the fabric, turn the hoop. Do another blob and end on the left side. Turn the hoop and do another and another. Lay in about five or six of these to create a satin-stitch flower. The satin stitches will all have that common center — at needle left.

Make the next satin stitch flower (Fig. 3.7) by first tracing around a drinking glass with a water-erasable marker. With feed dogs lowered, pressure between # and 1, anchor the thread and make a satin stitch blob perpendicular to the edge of the circle. Pull the thread across to the other side of the circle and make another blob. Anchor it. Cut off the thread. Go to another place on, just within, or just outside the circle and stitch another blob. Pull the thread over to the other side, make another satin stitch blob, anchor it, and cut off the thread. Begin again and continue until you have made a flower head.

Now you'll practice filling in shapes, another way to bring texture to your base fabric. Zigzagging is probably the most widely used method to fill in designs. You can use any stitch width, but the wider the setting, the looser the look. I feel I have more control if I use a 2 width — or better yet, I sew with straight stitches to fill in backgrounds. It is more like drawing with a pencil.

Fig. 3.5 This tree was stitched on cotton net. The trunk is encroaching zigzags, the crown of the tree is satin stitches and crossed threads.

Fig. 3.6 Zigzag star flowers.

27

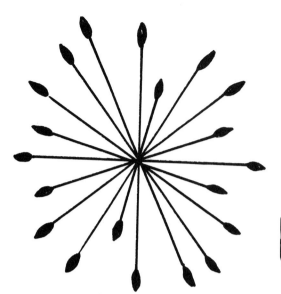

Fig. 3.7 Create flowers using zigzag stitches and crossed threads.

Utility stitch: zigzag
Tension: *top*, preset (990, 980, 950), slightly loosened for other models; *bobbin*, normal
Fabric suggestion: medium-weight cotton
Thread: sewing thread for practice
Accessories: large hoop at least 7″ (17.8cm); water-erasable or vanishing marker

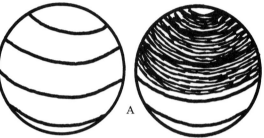

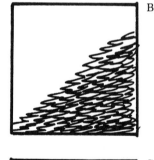

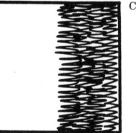

The drawback to straight-stitch filling is that the stitches are very tight to the fabric. Sometimes I want a lighter, loopier look, so I may start with zigzagging to fill in a design and then draw on top of that with straight stitches to emphasize a color, to outline, or to add shading to my embroidery. So I've included three ways to add texture to fabric by filling in designs with zigzag stitches.

Method A

In this method you will follow the contour of your design with zigzag stitches, changing a flat circle into a ball shape.

Stitch width: 5
Stitch length: 0–2.5
Needle position: center
Needle: #90/14 stretch needle
Feed dogs: lowered
Pressure: between ▦ and 1
Presser foot: darning foot or use a wooden hoop with no foot

Fig. 3.8 Filling in designs with zigzag stitches. Method A: Draw guidelines in the circles, then move sideways and back, following the guidelines. Method B: Stair-step method. Method C: Encroaching zigzag.

Using the marker, draw several circles on the fabric in the hoop (I drew around the base of a large spool of thread). Place stabilizer under the hoop. Zigzag the first circle into a ball shape by stitching in curved lines. To make it easier, first draw stitching guidelines inside the circle (Fig. 3.8, method A, *left*).

Start at the top of the circle, stitching and moving your hoop sideways and back while following the curves you've drawn (Fig. 3.8, method A, *right*). Move from top to bottom, creating the ball shape as you stitch. Don't build up stitches too fast in one place. Move the hoop evenly, slowly, and practice coordination.

Try other stitch widths on the other circles you've drawn. Put the samples in your notebook.

Method B

This has been described as the stair-step method. Designs can be filled in by zigzag stitching from lower-left corner to upper-right corner and back again (Fig. 3.8, method B). To practice this, set up your machine as you did in method A. Draw several 1½" (3.8cm) squares on your fabric. Although you will start with a 5 width zigzag stitch, experiment with narrower widths as you did before. Each line of zigzags blends into the one before it. Add your experiments to your notebook.

Method C

Encroaching zigzag is another way to fill in a design (Fig. 3.8, method C). Set up your machine as follows:

Stitch width: 5
Stitch length: 0–2.5
Needle position: center
Needle: #90/14 stretch needle
Feed dogs: lowered
Pressure: between # and 1
Presser foot: darning foot
Utility stitch: zigzag
Tension: *top*, preset (990, 980, 950), slightly loosened for other models; *bobbin*, normal
Fabric: medium-weight cotton
Thread: sewing thread for practice
Accessories: 7" (17.8cm) spring hoop, tear-away stabilizer, water-erasable marker

This time, draw only one 2" (5.1cm) square on the fabric in the hoop, and place stabilizer under it. Keep the hoop in the same position in front of you; don't rotate it. Instead, move it backward and forward as you stitch. Start at the top of the right side of the square you've drawn and stitch down to the bottom, moving the hoop slowly to keep the stitches close together. Move the hoop to the left a bit and stitch back up to the top, overlapping the first stitching slightly. Continue until you have covered the square. Go back and stitch on top of stitches for more texture. Do a sample for your notebook.

Lesson 4. Applying thick threads from top and bobbin

We created texture with regular sewing threads in Lesson 3, but in this lesson we'll change sewing and machine-embroidery threads for thicker threads, such as pearl cotton, cordonnet, and crocheted cotton. We'll explore four different ways to create texture by attaching these thick threads to fabric, including using them on the top spool, couched down on top of fabric, threaded under the raised seam guide, and wound on the bobbin.

Adding texture adds interest to sewing and embroidery. Perhaps it's not essential—a dress is still a dress without textured decoration — but it is a long-cut, that something extra that takes your dress from ordinary to special. Adding cords, fringe, objects, and gathers to the background fabric are all easy techniques once you know your machine.

Applying thick thread through the needle

Thread as large as cordonnet can be sewn with a #110 needle. Topstitching needles also have eyes to accommodate double threads or thick threads like buttonhole twist, and are available in #80– #110 needles.

Whatever you use, the thread must slip through the needle easily and the needle must make a hole in the fabric large enough to keep the thread from fraying.

Couching thread down on top of fabric

If thread is too thick for the needle, try couching it down on top of the fabric using a narrow braiding foot. Pull cord under the clip, from front to back. If you use the narrow braiding foot, as soon as you start stitching the thread will be fed through this clip with no help needed. It will stay exactly in place as you satin stitch over it with a zigzag or other decorative stitch. Cover the cord as closely or sparsely as you wish, using different stitch lengths.

This technique is ideal to preserve children's artwork in stitchery. (Your biggest challenge will be to straighten out the masterpieces after they have been folded or crunched in a book bag or backpack.) Enlarge artwork at the neighborhood copy center. Trace shapes onto tracing paper for the pattern. Generally, I appliqué the piece

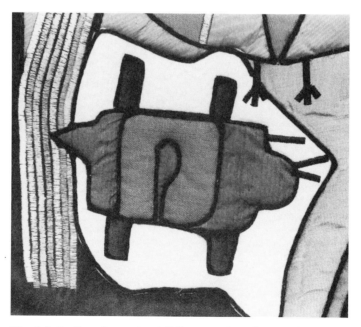

Fig. 3.9 Outline shapes in child's artwork with yarn threaded through narrow braiding foot.

30

or shape (see Chapter 4), then outline shapes with heavy cord, soutache or yarn. You may skip the appliqué and use the appropriate color yarn (rather than finger paints or crayons) to outline shapes (Fig. 3.9).

To outline shapes, thread top and bobbin with nylon monofilament thread. Thread cord or yarn through narrow or standard braiding foot. Use a short stitch length for small areas; use a longer stitch for larger areas. The thread sews into any color cord or yarn without showing and the foot keeps you on track.

You can substitute other feet—raised seam foot F, narrow hemmer, transparent appliqué, invisible zipper foot, narrow or regular braiding foot. You may need to change needle position, depending upon which foot you use. Unlike the regular or narrow braiding foot, which feeds the thread automatically, you may have to guide the cord if you use one of the other feet mentioned.

Because of this, I feel that owning a narrow braiding foot is mandatory. I couldn't sew without it. Covering cord is just one use. I also use it without cord when I want to sew a perfectly straight line of stitches. The center clip is a perfect guide when I line it up with the stitching line on my fabric.

Try multiple cords as well. There is a special 7-hole foot available with holes for the cords. More ideas for the 7-hole foot are in Chapter 11. Use a regular braiding foot with a wide groove underneath like an embroidery foot. Also, try the braiding foot or raised seam foot F for this purpose.

Project
Greeting Card

Practice applying thick threads on top of the fabric by making the greeting card shown in Fig. 3.10.

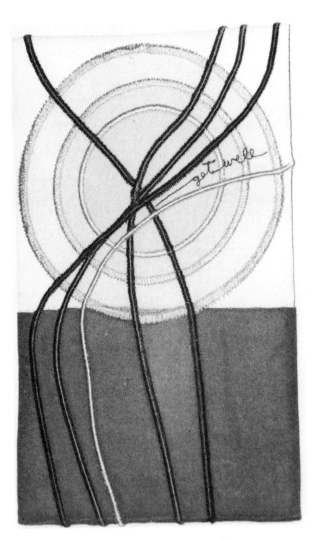

Fig. 3.10 "Even the Rainbow is Upset" greeting card.

Stitch width: 0–4
Stitch length: 0.5–2
Needle position: center
Needle: #90/14 stretch needle
Feed dogs: up or down
Pressure: normal
Presser foot: utility B or transparent appliqué, braiding foot, overcast J, darning foot or narrow hemmer
Utility stitch: zigzag

31

Tension: *top*, preset (990, 980, 950), loosened for other models; *bobbin*, normal

Fabric suggestions: 12" (30.5cm) square of white polished cotton, 6" (15.2cm) square of green polished cotton, 12" (30.5cm) square of yellow organdy

Thread: Sulky rayon in rainbow colors—yellow, red, green, purple, blue; #3 pearl cotton in the same colors; monofilament

Accessories: 7" (17.8cm) spring hoop; circular sewing attachment or thumb tack, transparent tape, cork or eraser; water-erasable or vanishing marker; greeting card folder (available at craft, art, and needlework shops) or picture frame; dressmaker's carbon; empty ballpoint pen

Stabilizer: tear-away

Use the pattern in Fig. 3.11 as a guide, changing measurements to fit the card folder or frame. Trace the pattern from the book, then place the drawing on top of the white background fabric, with dressmaker's carbon between. Transfer it, using the empty ballpoint pen.

Cut a piece from the green fabric large enough for the area at the bottom of the design, plus 1" (2.5cm). Fold under the top edge of the green about ½" (12.7mm) and press it. Hold it in place with pins and apply it using the transparent appliqué foot, with monofilament thread on the top and bobbin, and the machine set on a blindstitch: width 1, length 2.

Next, stretch three layers of yellow organdy over the white and green fabric and put them all in a spring hoop. Back this with tear-away. Set up the circular sewing attachment on your machine. (If you don't have a circular sewing attachment, use the thumb tack method in Fig. 1.2.) Poke the tack through at the center of the three layers of organdy. Place the transparent appliqué foot on the line of the inner circle. Stitch on that line around the circle with a straight stitch. Take the fabric out of the hoop and cut back only the top layer of organdy to the stitching.

Place the greeting card back in the hoop, with the tack back in its original hole. Satin stitch with the machine set on a width of 2, length 0.4.

Then move the tack so the line of the next circle will be centered under your presser foot. Straight stitch around the circle, cut back and satin stitch again as you did with the first. Do the same for the last layer of organdy.

Take the fabric out of the hoop while you stitch over the cords, but place tear-away stabilizer underneath. Each cord is a different color; use the braiding foot to guide the pearl cotton. If you don't have a braiding foot, then use the utility B foot or narrow hemmer. Fit the pearl cotton into the clip or groove and guide it as you stitch. You may have to change stitch width to cover the cord perfectly. Stitch over the cords, using close satin stitches. I prefer to stitch in two passes, attaching the cord first, then stitching in close satin stitches to cover it evenly and smoothly on the second pass.

When the last cord has been covered, and if you have a Viking 990 or 980, program in your message. With all other models, change to the darning foot, feed dogs down, release pressure between # and 1, and use a straight stitch. Use the color you have on your machine—unless it's yellow—to write a message along the top of one of the cords. I wrote "get well," and on the inside I'll write the message: "Even the rainbow is upset."

Finish the edge with a straight stitch. Trim close to stitches and slip into the card folder or finish it for a framed picture.

Also try the braiding foot for sewing down bulky yarn or cords invisibly. Choose the blindstitch (Fig. 3.12). Set up your machine as follows:

Stitch width: 1–1.5
Stitch length: 1–1.5
Needle position: center

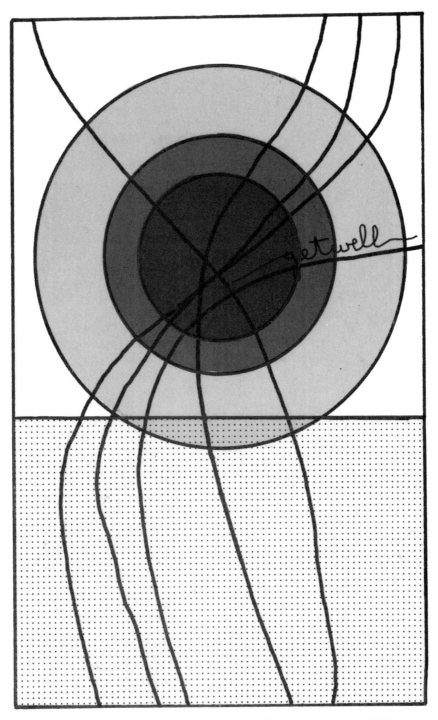

Fig. 3.11 Greeting card pattern. Enlarge or reduce to fit your card folder.

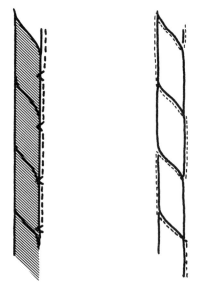

Fig. 3.12 Use the
blindstitch to attach
cord invisibly.

Fig. 3.13 Stitch
alongside, then
across the twist, to
attach cord.

Needle: varies
Feed dogs: up
Presser foot: braiding foot, utility B, transpar-
    ent appliqué foot or narrow hemmer
Utility stitch: reverse blindstitch (2–7)
Tension: *top*, normal; *bobbin*, normal
Pressure: normal
Thread: monofilament on top and bobbin
Stabilizer: tear-away

Stitch alongside the cord. When the needle bites into the cord, it is sewn down with
a tiny, almost unnoticeable stitch. When
the line of stitching is completed, go back
and gently nudge the cord over toward the
stitching line. Now your monofilament will
be completely hidden.

Or, using a braiding foot, utility B,
transparent appliqué, or 7-hole foot, line
up several threads of pearl cotton next to
each other. Use a zigzag, three-step zigzag
or bridging stitch (2-6) to attach them with
monofilament or with a colored thread.
Make colorful shoelaces this way.

Soutache is like a thick cord, and can be
attached perfectly using a braiding foot. It
is not easily done without this special foot,
as there is no way to hold the braid in place
so the needle will enter exactly in the center each time. It's sometimes possible to
feed other narrow braids or rickrack
through the center of this foot. To attach
soutache, trace the design on the topside of
your fabric, using a vanishing marker.
Place stabilizer under the fabric.

Corners are not impossible if you walk
the machine around them. Look at the underside of the braiding foot. You'll see a
groove cut along each side which helps
turn corners. Stop at the corner, needle
down, presser foot raised. Turn the fabric
45 degrees, lower the foot, take one stitch;
then, needle down again, raise the presser
foot, turn the fabric to complete the corner. You'll get a good angle. If you can,
though, choose a design with undulating
curves, which are easier to accomplish.

Use soutache and other braids down
jacket and vest fronts, around sleeves, to
decorate belts and handbags.

If the braid crosses and recrosses itself,
threading in and out like a Celtic interlac-
ing cord, it is still possible to use the braiding foot. The braid will not be threaded
through the foot, but will be hand basted
in place on the fabric, then fit within the
groove as you carefully ride over it and
stitch it down.

For your next sample, use a darning foot
for wool when freely couching down yarn.
To get the feel of the foot, use straight
lines or gentle curves on your first samples. Try a smooth, sport-weight yarn for
your first experiment. Add the result to
your growing notebook.

Here's another invisible way to attach
thick, twisted cord or yarn to fabric (Fig.
3.13). Leave the machine set up for free
machining, but remove the presser foot or
use a darning foot. Drop feed dogs and release pressure between # and 1. Use
monofilament thread on top. Iron a piece

of freezer paper onto the back of the fabric. Begin by drawing the bobbin thread to the top and anchoring the threads. Stitch the end of the cord down. Then move along one side of the cord with a straight stitch. When you reach a twist in the cord, follow it to the other side by stitching in the twist. Once on the other side, follow along that side for a few stitches until you reach the top of the next twist. Cross over again, following the twist. Continue in this manner until the cord is attached.

Attaching cord pulled through raised seam guide

You can also attach thick cords to the surface of fabric by threading them through the raised seam guide. Of course, this method attaches the cord underneath the fabric so you must stitch with the topside of the fabric against the needleplate. To set it up, lay cord across free-arm under the foot. Snap the raised seam guide in place over cord. The guide accommodates one, two or three strands of size #5 pearl cotton cord.

I've used this method of attaching cords using the raised seam guide and the transparent appliqué or utility B foot for collages, when I want to add long lines of thick cords easily and fast. I draw on the stabilizer, which is on top of the wrong side of the fabric, to indicate where I should stitch. The cord is fed evenly through the guide and attached to the fabric with straight or zigzag stitches.

Stitch a record of your experiments with the zigzag stitch. For example, you can use this method to gather by stitching over cord with a 2 width, 2 length zigzag. Also experiment with cord through the guide, using the utility B or transparent appliqué foot and some of the decorative stitches intended for edgings, like the closed scallop stitch. You can also apply round elastic with this method.

In addition to cord, I like to experiment with pearl cotton through the raised seam F foot and guide for pintucking with double needles (see Chapter 5). Try stitching many rows, spacing them according to the spacing on the foot. Mark these and all your samples for your notebook.

Using thick thread from the bobbin

Cable stitching is an embroidery technique using thick thread on the bobbin. The topside of the fabric will be against the bed of the machine. It can be done with feed dogs up, using an embroidery foot for straight or built-in stitches, or it can be done freely with feed dogs down using a darning foot or using no presser foot at all.

Cabling can look like a tightly couched thread or like fluffy fur, depending on the thread you choose. A hard twist thread like crochet cotton will lay flatter, with less beading or looping than a soft, loosely twisted yarn like mohair. The effects you get will depend not only on top and bobbin tension, but on stitch width, stitch length, color and size of cord, color of top thread, feed dogs up or down, color, weight, and type of fabric, how fast you stitch and how fast you move the hoop.

When I say you can use thick threads, I'm not kidding. Did you know that you can use up to a four-ply yarn in the bobbin? Of course, the thicker the yarn, the less you can wind on the bobbin. Usually the bobbin can be put on the machine and wound slowly while you hold the yarn or cord to control it. If you find the yarn must be wound by hand, do so evenly without stretching it.

To use the thicker threads this embroidery requires, you must override that panicky feeling that accompanies loosening and tightening the tension on the bobbin. Most embroiders I know buy extra bobbin cases to use for embroidery only. Buying an extra case is a good idea. It's possible to tighten and loosen the spring screw—or even remove the spring altogether—without the time-consuming adjustments needed to return to normal sewing tension. Mark second bobbin case with nail polish so you don't confuse it with the bobbin case for normal sewing.

Perhaps you've already discovered, as you've changed bobbins, that you can recognize the feel of normal tension. If not, put a bobbin full of sewing thread into the bobbin case and click the thread into the spring. Hold on to the end of the thread and let the bobbin case hang from it like a yoyo. It should drop slowly when jerked. Memorize how this feels with normal tension before you begin to loosen the bobbin tension for cabling. Loosen the tension screw over an empty box, because it has a tendency to pop out and disappear forever. I use a tiny screwdriver that has been attached to my magnetic pin cushion. This magnetizes the screwdriver so if the screw comes out of the bobbin case, it sticks to the screwdriver. Or you can purchase several extra screws just in case.

When adjusting tension for heavy threads, remember that the cord must feed through the bobbin case smoothly. Loosen the bobbin tension by turning the screw counter-clockwise until the tension feels normal to you. You may have to bypass the tension altogether if the cord or yarn is too thick.

Practice cabling on a piece of scrap fabric. Set up your machine with feed dogs up, using an embroidery or Zwicky sewing thread on top. Place your fabric in a hoop and use the utility B or transparent appliqué foot. Stitch and then look under the fabric to be sure the tension is set correctly—do you want tight, stiff stitches or loosely looping ones? Manipulate the bobbin tension for different effects.

I've found tightening the upper tension to 7½–9 keeps the stitches looking neat.

Write on your sample fabric which is the topside, which the back. Also record bobbin tension by using + and − signs. Record top tension using the best number for your fabric and weight of cord.

Don't be afraid of your sewing machine. Change tensions, lengths, speeds, and use it to its full potential. Get to know your machine.

Now prepare a cabling sample for your notebook. Choose a medium-weight cotton or blend. Use a number of the utility and decorative stitches with #3, #5, and then #8 pearl cotton. Try ribbon and yarn as well. Keep the stitch long enough to prevent the cord from bunching up under the fabric. Open decorative stitches work best and simple zigzag is most effective. I like the zigzag opened up to a 2 or 3 length and a 4 stitch width. It gives a rickrack effect.

Stretch a piece of fabric in a hoop, but don't use a stabilizer underneath. Instead, use a stabilizer on top to keep your stitches from pulling. Draw lines or designs on the stabilizer. This is actually the back of your work.

Dip the needle into the fabric, drawing the bobbin thread or cord to the top. Hold the threads to the side as you begin. If you can't bring the cord up through the fabric, then pierce the cloth with an awl or large needle and bring it up. Don't anchor the threads with a lockstitch at the beginning or end. Instead, pull the threads to the back each time you start; when you stop, leave a long enough tail to be able to thread it up in a hand-sewing needle and poke it through to the back. Later you can work these threads into the stitching by hand.

It is also possible to quilt with this technique. Using a white pearl cotton in the bobbin and a top thread to match the fabric, you can get an effect which looks much like Japanese Sashiko (Fig. 3.14).

Apply ⅛" (3.2mm) double-faced satin ribbon as shown in Fig. 3.15. Wind the ribbon onto the bobbin. Thread ribbon through the bobbin tension. Loosen screw until ribbon pulls through bobbin case and

Fig. 3.14 Stitching in the style of Japanese Sashiko.

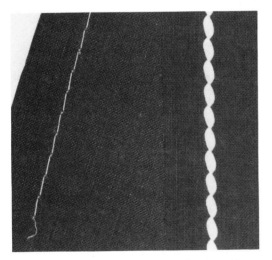

Fig. 3.15 The top and underneath of a ribbon attached by machine stitching.

feels like normal sewing thread. Use the standard A presser foot, right needle position, stitch length about 4, or use the topstitch setting.

When you start and stop in this type of couching, the ribbon is brought to the underside and finished off by hand. This technique is used on the infant's bonnet in Chapter 5.

Next try cabling with free embroidery. Place a medium-weight fabric in a hoop with a stabilizer on top. Lower the feed dogs, release pressure between # and 1, and, using a darning foot or bare needle, freely straight stitch, then zigzag.

Plan the lines of stitching before you begin. If you plan to use a number of different colors, use nylon monofilament thread on the top, through the needle. As you work, sew and peek under your hoop so you can regulate the bobbin and top tensions to your liking. Practice turning, pushing and pulling the hoop, sewing circles and straight lines. When your stitching changes direction, the tension is also changed, so practice how fast you should move your hoop for the effects you want. Often a design can be seen from the back of printed fabric. Take advantage of that to stitch a sample piece for your notebook. Stretch the fabric in a hoop. Water-soluble stabilizer can be used underneath if the fabric is washable. Otherwise, don't use a stabilizer. Instead, be sure your fabric is very taut, and use the darning foot. Embellish these prints by outlining the designs with pearl cotton or thick rayon thread on the bobbin.

Use bridal veiling as your fabric and create original lace. Or, decorate velveteen using velour yarn on the bobbin and monofilament thread on the top.

Project
Tote Bag
Square (Cabling)

Think "spring" with a tote bag square; the pattern is provided in Fig. 3.16. Remember that directions for making the tote and finishing the squares are in Chapter 12.

Stitch width: 0
Stitch length: 0–2.5
Needle position: center
Needle: #90/14 stretch needle
Feed dogs: lowered
Pressure: between # and 1
Presser foot: bare needle or darning foot
Utility stitch: straight stitch
Tension: *top*, 7–9; *bobbin*, loosened for #8 pearl cotton
Fabric suggestions: 9″-square medium-weight white fabric
Thread: green and orange machine embroidery thread (or try variegated threads in these colors); two bobbins each wound with #8 pearl cotton (green and yellow)

Accessories: tracing paper, dressmaker's carbon, empty ballpoint pen, water-erasable or vanishing marker
Stabilizer: iron-on freezer paper

Transfer the design in Fig. 3.16 to tracing paper and then, using dressmaker's carbon and the ballpoint pen, transfer the design to freezer paper. Color in or mark each flower vine and leaf to indicate color. Press this to the underside of your fabric. Always do a sample first, using the same fabric, stabilizer and threads as you will be using on your finished copy. Peek under the sample and adjust the tensions as needed. When cabling, you always work with underside up.

Because you have stabilized the fabric with freezer paper, you will not put the fabric in a hoop. Dip needle into fabric, bringing pearl cotton up through the fabric. Don't anchor the threads at the beginning or the end. Leave ends long enough to poke the thick thread to the back and work into the stitches there later.

Stitch the flowers first. Start at the base of the flower and stitch up the spiral; then come back, stitching as closely as you can to the first row of cording. Stitch the whole flower motif without stopping so you don't have to poke a lot of cording ends to the back. I was able to stitch the flowers with about a bobbin and a half of #8 pearl cotton.

Next, stitch the vine and leaves. Change needle thread to green and bobbin to green pearl cotton, using the same tension and machine settings as before. Again, start at the base of the vine, outline the leaf, then fill it in with three or four rows of cabling.

When you've finished, pull off the freezer paper and work in the pearl cotton beginnings and ends by hiding them in the stitches on the underside. Finish as explained in Chapter 12.

Fig. 3.16 Pattern for tote bag square.

Lesson 5. Fringing yarn and fabric

In this lesson you will learn to make fringe with a weaver's reed, as well as with strips of fabric sewn together and clipped into fringe. Start by using a weaver's reed to make yarn fringe. It can be used for wigs, costumes, rugs, and decorating edges of garments. Weaver's reeds are available in two different sizes, 30mm for narrow fringe, 50mm for wider fringe.

Wrap the reed. Sew down one side, pull the reed toward you, and wrap some more. If making yards and yards of fringe, use Robbie Fanning's method of measuring. Robbie measures the length she wants from a roll of adding-machine tape and stitches her fringe right to the tape. This also keeps the fringe from twisting. When you're finished, tear off the paper and apply the fringe.

Sometimes you may want the fringe sewn in the middle. In that case, make your own weaver's reed by using wire, ranging from the thickness of a coat hanger to as fine as a hair pin. If you make a wire form, it's called a fringe fork. Follow the steps in Fig. 3.17.As you work with the fork, you will understand when to use each method. And don't limit yourself to yarn or string alone. Try fabric. I used it for doll hair for my denim doll.

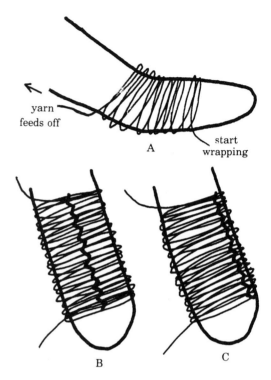

Fig. 3.17 The fringe fork. A. Wrap with yarn or fabric strips. B. Sew down in the middle. C. Or sew at the side of the fork for wider fringe.

Stitch width: 0
Stitch length: 4.5
Needle position: center
Feed dogs: up
Presser foot: rug foot or standard foot A
Presser: normal
Tension: *top*, normal; *bobbin*, normal
Utility stitch: elastic straight stitch
Fabric suggestion: 1"-wide (2.5cm-wide) bias
    strips, several yards
Thread: polyester to match bias
Accessories: 50mm weaver's reed
Stabilizer: adding machine tape

I wrapped the reed with red denim and sewed down the one side over adding-machine tape. When I had enough for hair, I tore the paper off the fringe and pinned the hair to her head in various ways to decide what hairdo I liked best. I sewed it on by hand; I could have left it as it was, but I decided to clip the loops (Fig. 3.18).

But you can achieve almost the same effect with fabric without using the weaver's reed (see Fringed Denim Rug). Work with strips of fabrics, but don't clip them into fringe until after they are sewn to the item you are making.

Fig. 3.18 The doll's hair is fabric fringe, her eyelashes are thread fringe done with the special marking foot.

Project
Fringed Denim Rug

This fabric-fringe project, a little rug, ate up yards of old jeans and denim remnants I picked up at sales; I kept cutting 2½″ (6.4cm) strips on the bias until I had finished the rug.

Stitch width: 0
Stitch length: 2–3
Needle position: right
Needle: jeans needle
Pressure: normal
Presser foot: zipper foot E

Utility stitch: straight stitch
Tension: *top*, normal; *bobbin*, normal
Fabric suggestion: denim, cut into 2½″ (6.4cm) bias strips of blues and red; use remnants and old jeans to cut quantity needed for rug size you want; heavy upholstery fabric for rug backing
Thread: matching polyester thread
Stabilizer: 1″-wide (2.5cm-wide) fusible webbing (measure circumference of rug)

You'll need a piece of heavy fabric the size of the finished rug, plus an inch all around. Measure the perimeter and cut a piece of 1″-wide (2.5cm-wide) fusible webbing. Using a Teflon pressing sheet, press

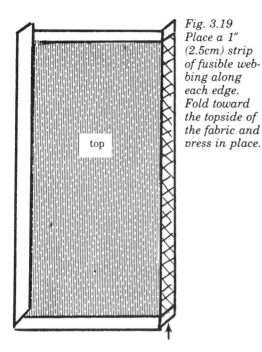

Fig. 3.19 Place a 1" (2.5cm) strip of fusible webbing along each edge. Fold toward the topside of the fabric and press in place.

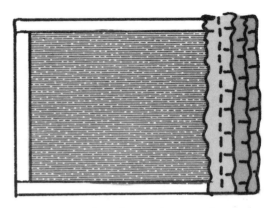

Fig. 3.20 Stitching bias strips onto the rug.

Fold the first bias strip lengthwise to find the center, but open it again and place it ⅛" (3.5mm) from the edge of the upholstery fabric. Stitch down the center crease of each strip from top to bottom (Fig. 3.20). Fold the left side of the strip to the right. Push the next strip as close as you can get it to the first. Sew down the center again; Fig. 3.19 shows the first three fabric strips stitched down. If you run out of fabric for a strip, add another by overlapping the last strip at least 1" (2.5cm).

When you're all done stitching, clip each strip every ½" (12.7mm), staggering the clips for each row. My rug (Fig. 3.21) went into the washer and dryer to soften.

the fusible webbing to the topside of all the edges and fold them back on the topside of the fabric, pressing again (Fig. 3.19). This is the top of the rug, so the edges will be finished when the last strip is stitched down.

Fig. 3.21 The bias strips are clipped into fringe.

Lesson 6. Adding buttons, beads, shisha

Attaching buttons

Once you've attached a button by machine, you won't want to do it any other way, it is so speedy. If you are applying buttons to a garment you've made, be sure the button area is interfaced. Dab glue stick on the underside of the button and position it.

Stitch width: space between holes in the button
Stitch length: 0
Needle position: far left
Needle: #80/11–12 all-purpose
Feed dogs: lowered
Pressure: normal
Presser foot: bare needle or special marking foot
Utility stitch: zigzag
Tension: *top*, normal; *bobbin*, normal
Thread: polyester
Accessories: Viking button reed or toothpick are optional, transparent tape, glue stick, scrap fabrics, buttons, beads and shisha mirrors (see Sources of Supply)

Place the foot shank on top of the button and stitch in the hole to the left 3 or 4 times to anchor the threads (stitch width 0). Raise the needle and move the stitch width so the needle clears the button and falls into the hole at the right. On that setting, stitch back and forth several times. When you have finished, push the finishing button on the 990, 980 or 950; for other models, move the stitch width to 0 and anchor again. That's all there is to it. If the garment fabric is thick, such as coating, you will need to make a button shank; otherwise, the buttonhole will pucker whenever the coat is buttoned. Raise the stitches to create a shank by taping a darning needle or round toothpick between the holes on top of the button before you stitch (Fig. 3.22A). When finished, pull off the tape and remove the darning nee-

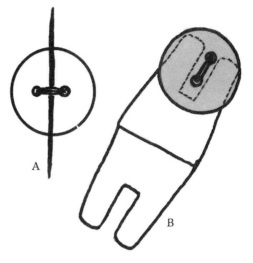

Fig. 3.22 Sew on a button with a shank.
A. Use a toothpick on top of the button.
B. Use the Viking button reed.

dle. Leave a long thread to wrap around the shank and anchor with a hand needle, strengthening the shank.

Or use the Viking button reed (Fig. 3.22B). It is a small gadget made to slip under the button to raise it off the fabric and create either of two shank heights.

The special marking foot can also be used, but it will give you a very high shank, so experiment first.

Attaching beads and baubles

Beads can be attached by machine if the hole in the bead is large enough and your needle fine enough. The thickness of the bead also matters. If in doubt, hand-walk the machine first to see if the needle will clear the bead, and if the sizes of the bead and needle are compatible. Attach the rim of the bead to the fabric by first holding it in place with a dot of glue from a glue stick. Drop the feed dogs, remove the foot, and put foot shank on bead. Anchor the thread

43

Fig. 3.23 If beads are stitched down on only one side, they can be nudged to stand up.

Fig. 3.24 Stitching down both sides to make beads lie flat.

Fig. 3.26 Attach a large bead by threading a cord through it and stitching on either side of the cord.

in the center of the bead by pushing the finishing button (990, 980, 950) and stitching in place three or four times. For other models, straight stitch in place three or four times. Raise the needle. Move the fabric over to anchor the thread on the side of

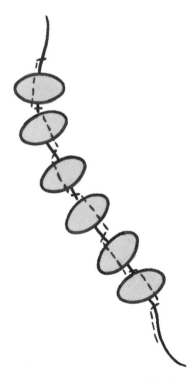

Fig. 3.25 A string of seed beads, attached by machine along dotted line (solid line is thread).

the bead. Go back to the center and anchor again. Repeat until the bead is securely sewn in place and will stand up (Fig. 3.23). If the bead is narrow, you can adjust the width of the zigzag stitch to sew bead to the fabric, rather than moving the fabric under the needle. Nudge the bead to stand on its outside rim when you finish stitching. Wipe off the glue.

If you go back and stitch down the other side as well, your bead will lay flat, hole up (Fig. 3.24).

Attaching seed beads, or other fine or oddly shaped beads can be done in the following way. First string the beads onto a thread. Using monofilament, free-machine stitch one end of the beaded thread down on the fabric. Stitch along the thread the width of one bead. Push the first bead near that end and then stitch over the thread to keep the bead in place. Stitch again the distance of the next bead. Push the bead up to

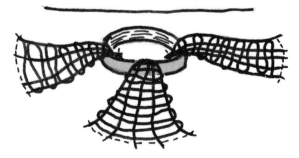

Fig. 3.27 Using needlelace to attach beads.

Fig. 3.28 "The Flop Box," made by Pat Pasquini, has a machine-embellished top by the author. It includes beads held down with needlelace, other beads strung with cord and porcupine quills and couched in place, textures created by stitching cords down, using a double needle to pintuck suede, and stitching blobs and satin stitches in the background. Photo by Robbie Fanning.

the first, stitch over the thread and repeat, as shown in Fig. 3.25.

Or sew beads down by stringing them singly on thick threads and stitching both ends of the threads down (Fig. 3.26).

You can attach beads invisibly, using monofilament thread to couch them down or to string the beads on. Or choose your thread wisely and use the stitching as a part of the decoration.

Another way to hold down beads is to first stitch strips of needlelace on water-

soluble stabilizer. When the lace has been stitched, merely pull off the excess stabilizer and hold your work under a faucet to wash out most of what remains, but leave a bit of the sticky residue. When it is almost dry, shape the needlelace strips and they will dry in that shape. Use two or three of these strips to hold down beads or washers (Fig. 3.27). Thread a strip through the object and stitch down one end. Move the bauble down over your stitching. Arrange the strip, twisting it if you wish. Then stitch down the other end freely and invisibly. Use this method, as I have, on decorative box tops and collages (Fig. 3.28).

Another method of using stones and jewels for wall hangings or pictures is to cover them with net or transparent fabrics, and then stitch down the fabric. Then cut holes in the fabric large enough to let the objects show through and small enough so they don't fall out.

Or make needlelace in the center of wire bent into a circle, rectangle, or other shape. Stretch the lace over an object placed on a background fabric. Attach the lace to the fabric by stitching freely, close to the wire, around the inside of this frame, and cutting off the wire. Embroider the edges if you wish.

Attaching shisha mirrors

Shishas are small pieces of mirrored glass. They are about 1″ (2.5cm) in diameter, but are never exactly circular. It is possible to attach them to fabric if you follow the methods Caryl Rae Hancock of Indianapolis, and Gail Kibiger of Warsaw, Indiana, invented.

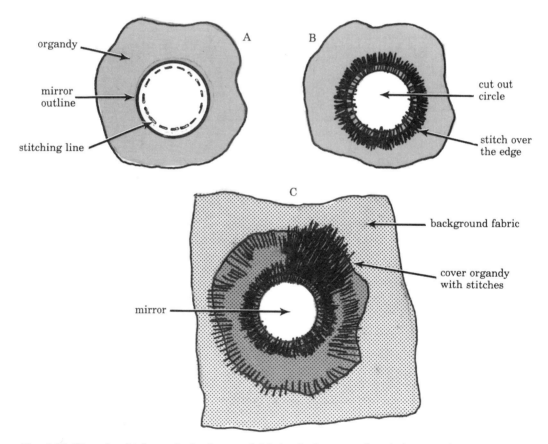

Fig. 3.29 Glue the shisha to the background fabric. A. On organdy, stitch around a circle slightly smaller than the shisha. B. Cut out the center and embroider over the edge. C. Place the organdy over the shisha and stitch it in place on background fabric by straight stitching. Embroider the background to conceal the edge.

46

This is Caryl Rae Hancock's method, illustrated in Fig. 3.29. First, stretch organdy in a hoop. The shisha is placed on top of the organdy and its outline traced. The back of the shisha is dabbed with glue stick and placed on a background fabric, not the organdy.

Sew around—and about ⅛" (3.2mm) inside—the drawn circle. Stitch around two more times. Without taking the fabric out of the hoop, cut out the circle of fabric within the stitching. After anchoring threads, the machine should be set on a medium width zigzag and the circle stitched freely around the cut edge. Turn the hoop as you sew around it, letting the stitches radiate from the edge of the hole to about ½" (12.7mm) beyond. The organdy must be covered with stitches at this time. Anchor threads and take the organdy out of the hoop. Cut very closely around the outside stitching.

With the machine changed back to straight stitch, place the piece of embroidery over the shisha and background fabric and pin organdy in place. Stitch around outside edge of the shisha. Be careful: if you stitch into the glass, the needle and probably the shisha will break.

Leave the machine as set or change to zigzag again and stitch over those straight stitches, following the radiating direction of the original zigzagging. Blend the outside edge of the organdy with the background fabric by radiating stitches onto the background fabric.

Gail Kibiger has a slightly different method. She applies shisha by first placing the mirror on the background fabric, not on organdy, and tracing around it. Removing the shisha, she stitches ⅛" (3.2mm) within this circle three times and cuts out the circle. Gail embroiders on the background fabric as Caryl Rae did the organdy.

The shisha is then glued to a piece of organdy and placed under the finished hole. After pinning it in place, she straight stitches around the mirror to hold it in place.

One of Gail's variations is to work a spiderweb across the hole before the edges are zigzagged.

Silver bangles, the large sequins found in craft and knitting shops, are an excellent substitute for shisha. Not only are they exactly round, unlike the uneven shape of shishas, but they are durable. If you sew into them, your needle doesn't break. Make a record for your notebook of how you have applied buttons, beads and shishas.

Project
Bird Collage

I work with transparent fabrics almost exclusively, so I collect them. Besides fabric stores, garage sales and thrift shops are wonderful sources. I check out the chiffon scarves, colored nylons, lingerie, curtains, as well as glitzy dresses—though it takes courage to buy some of these because of the double-takes at the checkout counter.

This is a beadwork project, which includes appliqué as well. Bird shapes are my favorites. I like them plump like baby chicks, sleek like soaring eagles, even whimsical like African Dahomey appliqués. I've used them on quilts, wall hangings, and in fabric collages.

In this small picture, shown in Fig. 3.30, I added small clay beads by machine to the appliquéd picture.

Stitch width: 0
Stitch length: 0–2.5
Needle position: center
Needle: #90/14 stretch needle
Feed dogs: lowered
Pressure: between # and 1
Presser foot: darning foot
Utility stitch: straight stitch
Tension: *top*, slightly loosened; *bobbin*, normal

Fig. 3.30 Bird collage.

Fabric suggestions: green and gold suede or felt for bird's body and wings; transparent fabrics, such as organdy, chiffon, yellow mesh grapefruit bag, for the wings; moss green bridal veiling to cover the picture; 12″ (30.5cm) square of coarse beige upholstery linen for background; loosely woven taupe-colored fabric for the nest; gold lamé for the eggs; nude-colored nylon stocking; also needed are small clay beads

Thread: several strands of brown and beige coarse thread or string, cut into 1″ (2.5cm) pieces; brown, green and beige shiny rayon; monofilament

Stabilizer: iron-on freezer paper

If this sounds overwhelming, you can substitute any colors you wish, and use only one, instead of a variety, of transparent fabrics. Although I used transparent thread for most of this collage, I added browns, greens and beiges in rayon stitches when my piece was almost complete.

Begin by pulling off a half-dozen threads from the square of background fabric. Cut these threads into small lengths of 1 and 2 inches (2.5–5.0cm) and add them to the other threads you've cut—you will need several dozen. Put them aside.

Iron freezer paper to the back of the linen fabric for stability, as you will not use a hoop for this project. Although not necessary, I always cut the background fabric at least 6"–8" (15.2–20.3cm) bigger than the finished size so I can practice stitching or layering on the edges. Also, I plan my pieces so they look as if they go on beyond the frame. I don't want them to look as if they end inside it.

Fig. 3.31 shows the arrangement, and Fig. 3.32 is the pattern; cut out the fabric pieces as follows: Cut out the oval nest from the taupe fabric and place that slightly below the center on the background. When I cut fabric for collages, I use a cut/tear method. By pulling slightly on the fabric as I cut, I fray the material a bit to keep the edges soft. The bird should be cut from green suede or felt so it will not roll when you cut it out. Be sure to use fabric that has some body, so it will be easy to control. Place the bird on the nest (Fig. 3.30). Cut a gold wing from suede and position that on the bird. Cut out the transparent wings. Place one on top of the gold wing, but shift it a bit so it is not exactly in the same place as the first. Do the same with the other sheers. Your wings will

cross, meet, blend, as if in a watercolor. Over the last wing you will use one cut from a yellow mesh grapefruit bag or a coarse yellow net. Rearrange until the wings look pleasing to you.

Cut the foot and top off a nude-colored nylon stocking and slit the stocking from top to bottom. Stretch it over the picture and pin it down just beyond the image area. As you stretch the stocking, it will lighten in color. It should be almost invisible, but not stretched so tightly it buckles the picture. This holds all the pieces in place, and softens, but does not change, the colors of your picture.

Lower the feed dogs and release the pressure to between # and 1 on your machine. Use a darning foot, as you will have many layers to stitch together. Begin by freely sewing around the bird with transparent thread. Stitch just off the edge of the body and wing pieces. It is not important to be completely accurate; it's fine if you stitch into the body or wings. You might want to stitch in a few feathers on the gold wing as well, giving the bird an at-

Fig. 3.31 Follow this design for assembling the bird picture.

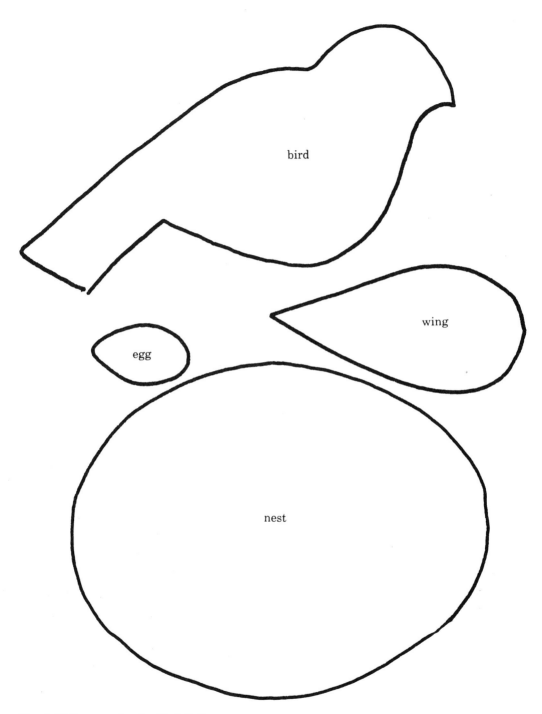

Fig. 3.32 Patterns for the Bird Collage.

50

Tote Bag Squares: (upper left, clockwise) Chapter 4, Lesson 10—Edge-Stitch Applique, Modified Reverse Applique, Straight Stitch Applique; Chapter 4, Lesson 19—Applique and Quilting.

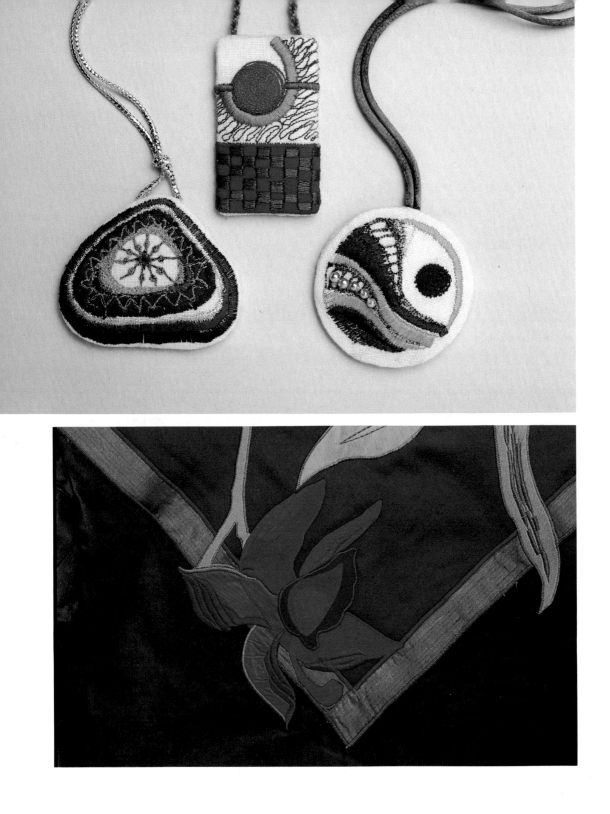

Chapter 2, Lesson 2 (opposite, top)—Pendants are a fast way to practice free machining and satin stitches.

Chapter 11, Lesson 38 (opposite, bottom)—Close-up of jacket with Satin Element design lines.

Schiffli lace collar, left, by Jill Robinson, Corpus Christi, TX—DMC floss on tulle.

Ryan's Art, below (see Chapter 3, Lesson 4)—Interpret children's art fast with applique and corded edges.

*Free-machine embroidery by
Theresa Stafford of Albany, GA—A
photocopy of Thomas Nast's Santa
is sandwiched between organdy and
a foundation fabric, then filled in
with stitches.*

*Pictogram child's quilt by Dawn
Stark, Minneapolis, MN.*

tractive, padded look. Stitch to the outside of the nest and sew that down freely. Then sew all around the outside edge of your picture. Cut off the stocking from the outside edges.

Add three gold lamé eggs under the bird. Over the edge of the nest, scatter half the thread pieces you've cut. Hold all this down by laying a piece of moss green bridal veiling over the picture and pinning it in place.

Again, with transparent thread and a free machine, sew around the eggs, around the outside of the bird and around the nest, managing to catch threads to anchor them. Yes, you will be sewing in a haphazard manner around the nest—and you do not have to sew every thread in place. With a very fine embroidery scissors, cut out the veiling from in front of the bird and the eggs.

String the small clay beads onto some of the remaining "nest" threads. Arrange the threads around the nest on top of those you have already sewn in place. Be very careful as you sew these threads in place;

you don't want to hit beads with the darning foot. With transparent thread, sew above and below the beads to hold them in place (see Fig. 3.26).

An alternative method is to remove the darning foot. Press the fabric firmly against the needle plate as you sew down the threads. Be careful of your fingers. Thread up with a shiny brown Sulky thread. With your machine set up for zigzag stitching, add texture and color to the nest by stitching a blob, lifting the presser foot lever and pulling the picture to stitch again in another spot. Cross and recross threads. I change colors several times (browns, beiges and greens). This also helps anchor the coarse threads.

The bird's eye can be added by sewing on a gold bead by hand, or with your machine, by building up a blob of thread. Your picture is complete. Pull off the freezer paper, or leave it in place. Cut off that extra margin from around your piece. Stretch the picture over a piece of batting and plywood and frame it. These pictures are so much fun to put together, and no two are alike.

Lesson 7. Smocking and gathering

Smocking

In hand smocking, fabric is gathered tightly into channels and embroidery is worked on top of the channels. Stitches chosen are open and stretchy.

Smocking by machine, on the other hand, will not be stretchy like hand smocking. After gathering with thread or cord, machine embroidery stitches usually hold the gathers in place. But if you use elastic, the gathering will stretch—but then, of course, you won't embroider over it.

There are at least a dozen ways to smock on your sewing machine, varying the method of gathering or embroidering, or varying the threads used. Here are several methods you can try. In each one, start

with at least 2½ times the width needed for the finished pattern. For any garment, do the smocking first and then cut out the pattern.

Stitch width: 0-widest
Stitch length: varies
Needle position: center
Needle: #90/14 stretch needle
Feed dogs: up
Pressure: normal
Presser foot: utility B or transparent appliqué foot
Utility or decorative stitch: zigzag or open embroidery type; three-step zigzag, bridging stitch (2–6)
Tension: *top*, normal; *bottom*, varies

Fabric: 2 or more 18" × 45" (45.7 × 114.3cm) pieces of medium-weight cotton; 1 yard (.9m) strip for gathering ruffles; several 12" (30.5cm) or larger pieces of scrap fabrics

Threads: machine embroidery; monofilament

Accessories: water-erasable or vanishing marker

Stabilizer: water-soluble, tear-away type

Simple gathered smocking

First draw at least four lines across the 45"-wide (114.3cm-wide) fabric with a water-erasable or vanishing marker. The lines should be about ½" (12.7mm) apart. Leave the seam allowances free of stitching. Loosen upper tension to 4 and anchor the threads, and then straight stitch along your drawn lines, leaving long ends of thread at the ends of the rows (Fig. 3.33A). Pull on the bobbin threads to gather the fabric to 18" (45.7cm) and knot every two threads together. Pin this to tear-away stabilizer.

Choose a decorative stitch and embroider across the fabric between the gathering lines of stitching (Fig. 3.33A). My favorite on the 990 is the large cross-stitch

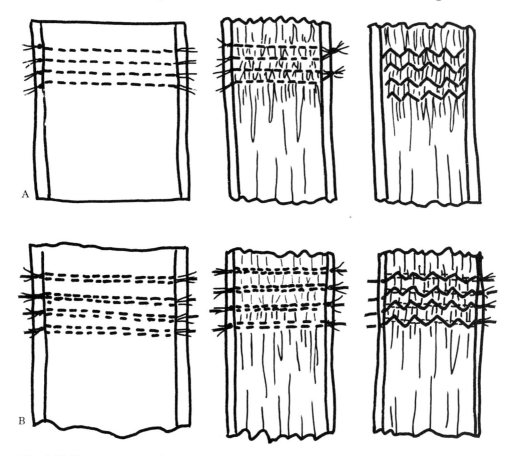

Fig. 3.33 Two ways to machine smock. A. Gather up rows of stitching and embroider between them. B. Gather the fabric, then using a cord and double needle, embroider over the gathers.

(2–18). It anchors gathers better than other stitches, so smocking will be durable. Remove the gathering stitches and tear off the stabilizer.

Smocking with cordonnet

Use another piece of 18″ × 45″ (45.7 × 114.3cm) fabric. Thread the cordonnet under the raised seam guide and snap it on the needleplate. To gather, sew across the fabric, using a double needle threaded with monofilament on top, Zwicky sewing thread on the bobbin. Use the raised seam foot F, width 0, length 2.5 (Fig. 3.33B). Again, leave the seam allowances free of stitching. Use the presser foot as a width guide to sew at least three more rows. Stitch an even number of rows, at least four. Leave tails of cord at the beginning and end of each line.

Tie off pairs of the cords at the start. Pull the cords to gather the material to 18″ (45.7cm). Then tie a knot at the end of each. Remove the cordonnet raised seam foot F and guide.

Place a stabilizer under your work. Embroider over the cords and then remove the stabilizer.

Embroidering with thick thread in the bobbin

This may be used with either of the preceding methods for gathering. First complete the gathering. Turn the fabric over, topside down on the bed of the machine. Place water-soluble stabilizer under the gathers.

Stitch width: widest
Stitch length: varies
Needle position: center
Needle: #90/14 stretch needle
Feed dogs: up
Pressure: normal
Presser foot: utility B or transparent appliqué foot
Utility or decorative stitch: zigzag or open embroidery type (2–6, 2–9, 2–24, 2–25)

Tension: *top*, 7–8; *bobbin*, varies with cord
Fabric: medium-weight cotton
Thread: monofilament or sewing thread for top; #5 or #8 pearl cotton for bobbin
Stabilizer: water-soluble, adding machine tape

When you stitch up the samples, look underneath to see if the pearl cotton is attached evenly and smoothly. Adjust tensions as necessary.

Open utility and decorative stitches look best. My favorites on the 990 are the braid (2–24), stitch length 2.5–3, and the open heart (2–25) on preset length and width. The simple zigzag is also effective. Remove the stabilizer when your stitching is completed.

Smocking with elastic

Use a delicate to lightweight fabric and a fine, round elastic. The best brand of elastic thread is Goldzack. It's made in Switzerland, has a rubber core wrapped in cotton, and has more zip than other types I've tried (see Sources of Supply). Wind bobbin by hand or on the bobbin winder *without stretching it.* Thread bobbin normally. The thread on the top will show, so choose the color carefully. You may also have to tighten the upper tension slightly.

Place a strip of adding machine tape under the fabric and begin sewing with a 2.5–3 length straight stitch. The paper prevents the fabric from gathering before you want it to and the stitches are more uniform. Sew as many rows of elastic thread smocking as desired. Remove adding machine tape so fabric shirrs. You can use this for bodices of sun dresses, nightgowns or swimsuits.

Another way to make fabric stretch, giving a shirred effect, is to use a round elastic through the raised seam guide. Use regular thread on top and bobbin, and a zigzag setting that clears the elastic. Try stitching with a double needle and a straight stitch. Stitch several rows across the fabric using stitch (2–6), width 4, length 1.5–2. Thread the elastic through the opening in the narrow braiding foot or use the groove in the utility B or transparent appliqué foot to guide it.

With the three-step zigzag or bridging stitch (2–6), the gathers can't be changed after they are sewn in, because the needle stitches into the elastic. Stretch the elastic while sewing. The more you stretch it, the more gathers it will create.

The zigzag stitch will sew on either side of the flat elastic and will not pierce it. After stitching, adjust the gathers.

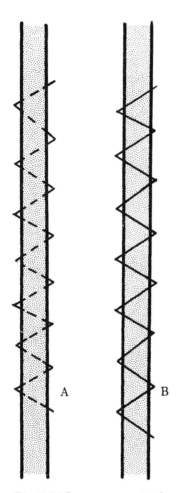

Fig. 3.34 Two ways to attach flat elastic. A. Three-step zigzag stitch. B. Zigzag stitch.

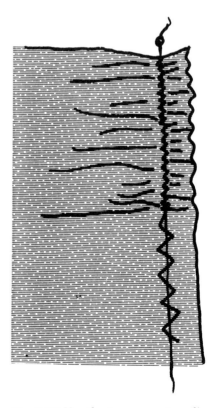

Fig. 3.35 Use the transparent appliqué or utility B foot when zigzagging over cord to gather fabric.

the presser foot as a guide, or draw the rows on the fabric with a water-erasable or vanishing marker before stitching. Don't pull the elastic for gathering until all the stitching is completed. I use this method at the top of children's knit skirts, as well as on waistlines of T-shirt dresses.

With ⅛" (3.2mm) flat elastic, use either the zigzag, three-step zigzag or bridging

54

Gathering

Using cord

To gather light to heavyweight materials, use this, my all-time favorite method.

Stitch width: 2–3
Stitch length: 2
Needle position: center
Feed dogs: up

Zigzag over a cord, such as gimp or cordonnet. To keep the cord in position while stitching over it, use the transparent appliqué or narrow braiding foot. Place the cord under foot or through clip and it will be fed through and covered perfectly (Fig. 3.35). Pull up the cord to gather the fabric. Leave the cord in the fabric.

I use this for everything from skirts to dust ruffles to slipcovers. You won't break the gathering stitch as you often do when pulling on a basting thread. It saves hours.

Using elastic

Using the same settings as you did for cord, thread ⅛" (3.2mm) elastic under appliqué foot or through clip in the narrow braiding foot. Knot the elastic in back. Pull on it from the front while sewing a zigzag over it. I use this for quick sleeve finishes for little girls' dresses. If sewn about 1" (2.5cm) from the finished edge, it creates a ruffle.

Using a gathering foot

Gathering yards of ruffles is easy with a gathering foot. It simultaneously gathers and applies the gathers to another flat piece of fabric. The only drawback is that without seeing your fabric, I can't give you an iron-clad formula for how much fabric is needed to gather into, say, a 15" (38.1cm) ruffle.

The key to your estimates is to stitch a sample. Work with the same material you're going to use for the ruffle. Finer materials need to be gathered more fully than heavy fabrics do. Gathering depends upon fabric weight, tension and stitch length. The tighter the tension, the more gathering. The longer the stitch, the more fullness that can be locked into each stitch and the tighter the gathers — and the more fabric you'll need. I admit I'm a coward and always add inches to be sure.

Even though this foot will gather a ruffle and apply it to fabric at the same time, I prefer gathering and attaching the gathers in two steps because of the difficulty in estimating the yardage I'll need for the ruffles. But, to do both steps at once, place the fabric to be attached to the ruffle in the slot of the gathering foot and the ruffle fabric under the foot. Keep the edges of both pieces of fabric even with the right side of the foot.

This does not exhaust the methods of gathering and smocking on the machine. Check your Operating Manual for others.

Lesson 8. Pulling threads together

Satin stitching on top of loosely woven fabric builds up texture quickly by drawing the threads of the fabric together into ridges. Then you can connect the ridges for even more texture. As you can see in the sample (Fig. 3.36), this technique looks like lace.

If you're hesitant about stitching in open areas, place water-soluble stabilizer behind the fabric before stitching.

Stitch width: 0–6
Stitch length: 0–2.5
Needle position: center

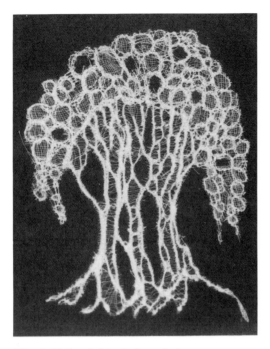

Fig. 3.36 Straight stitch and zigzag over loosely woven fabric produced both lacy and textured embroidery.

Needle: #90/14 stretch needle
Feed dogs: lowered
Pressure: between ⌗ and 1
Presser foot: darning foot
Utility stitches: zigzag, straight stitch
Tension: *top*, slightly loosened; *bobbin*, normal
Fabric: loosely woven cheesecloth type
Thread: machine embroidery, desired color top and bobbin
Accessories: spring hoop, water-soluble stabilizer (optional)

To learn this technique, stitch an imaginary tree of satin stitches and lacy straight stitches. It's not necessary to trace my design as this is done freely.

Put the fabric in a hoop. It must be stretched tightly. Bring the bobbin thread to the top and anchor the threads. Using the widest stitch setting, sew up and down in straight lines. At the down points, move the fabric over a bit and go up and down again. Continue until you have three or four rows of satin stitches. Then go back over them, zigzagging in between. This draws the previous lines together. Cut fabric threads if there is too much pulling and puckering.

Create branches on top and, when you come down to the bottom again, flare the line of stitching to resemble roots. Use the widest zigzags to stitch up and down again. Go back and zigzag over the whole tree again and again until the stitches are built up to your liking.

Change to a straight stitch and begin to stitch small circles at the top to crown the branches. Go from one to another. Cut or poke out the centers of some or all of the circles in the tree top, thus creating a lacy effect.

If you've used water-soluble stabilizer, then wash it out on completion of your work.

In the sample, I trimmed the tree from the background to show you the type of appliqué I add to my collages. It has a lacy look you can see through, which adds depth to the embroidery it's placed over. But sometimes I place the untrimmed appliqué over a background fabric and stitch it in place. After trimming it back to the stitches, I freely embroider over it with more satin stitches, with more ridges, building up more and more texture.

If you do a large enough square of threads pulled together with satin stitches, it can be used as a design for your tote bag. Or leave it untrimmed and still in the hoop for a window hanging.

CHAPTER 4

Adding Fabric to Fabric: Appliqué

- **Lesson 9. Methods of applying appliqués**
- **Lesson 10. Appliquéing with feed dogs up**
- **Lesson 11. Appliquéing with feed dogs lowered**

Once you know your machine as I know mine, you won't be satisfied stitching down all your appliqués with satin stitches. This chapter will show you several ways to place an appliqué onto a background successfully and teach a variety of methods for stitching it in place, including satin stitch, straight stitch, blind hem, and three-dimensional applications.

You'll make tote bag squares, Carrickmacross lace, and shadow work in these lessons. You will also work samples for your notebook to practice other appliqué methods.

Lesson 9. Methods of applying appliqués

Applying fabric to fabric takes two steps. Both are equally important. The first is to place the appliqué on the background in a way that keeps it in place, without puckering the fabric and with edges held down firmly, to enable you to do a perfect final stitching. The second step is the stitching. In Lessons 10 and 11, we'll try blind hems, straight stitching, blurring, scribbling and corded edges.

In appliqué, the best results are achieved when the applied and background fabrics have similar properties. For example, if using a cotton background fabric, it is best to use a similar weight appliqué fabric, and one that can be washed like the cotton. If washable, prepare the fabrics by washing and ironing them. They may be easier to work with if they are starched.

Match the grain lines of the appliqué to those of the background fabric. It's usually necessary to use a stabilizer under the fabric to prevent puckers when stitching. There are several methods for the first step. The first one wastes fabric, but the results are worth it.

Method A

Stretch both fabrics tightly in a hoop. I use a wooden hoop for this step because the fabric can be stretched and held more tightly than in a spring hoop. The fabric for the appliqué should be underneath–on the bed of the machine–with the topsides of both fabrics down. Draw the design on the wrong side of the base fabric, or place a paper pattern in the hoop, either pinning it there or catching it in the hoop with the fabric.

With the machine set up for free machining, single stitch around the design. Take the fabric out of the hoop, turn it over and cut the applied fabric back to the stitching line. Place the fabric back in the hoop with the appliqué on top this time. Use one of the methods for final stitching discussed in Lessons 10 and 11.

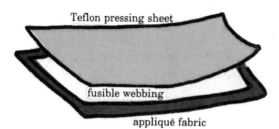

Fig. 4.1 To prepare an appliqué with fusible webbing, first place a piece of the fusible on the back of the appliqué fabric, cover it with the Teflon pressing sheet, and press in place.

down against wrong side of appliqué fabric, and press for 3 seconds. Cut appliqué out, remove the paper, then fuse to background fabric with a damp press cloth.

To use fusible webbing and Teflon sheet, put webbing on top of the appliqué fabric, place the Teflon sheet over it and press until the fusible webbing melts (Fig. 4.2). When it cools, the Teflon can be peeled away. Cut out the appliqué from this piece of fabric and then iron it to the background fabric, using a Teflon sheet on top to protect your iron.

Method B

For the next method, Wonder-Under or fusible webbing and a Teflon pressing sheet are needed. This will produce a slightly stiffer appliqué than the first method, but if done correctly, it will never produce a pucker.

Cut a piece of fabric and a piece of fusible webbing or Wonder-Under slightly larger than the appliqué (Fig. 4.1). For Wonder-Under, place paper side up, rough side

Method C

An alternative to fusible webbing or Wonder-Under is the appliqué paper backed with "glue." To use this paper, cut a piece of it and fabric approximately the size of the appliqué. Draw the design on the non-adhesive side of the paper, then press the paper to the back of the fabric. After it adheres and cools, cut around the design and fabric, then peel the paper off the appliqué. The glue will have been

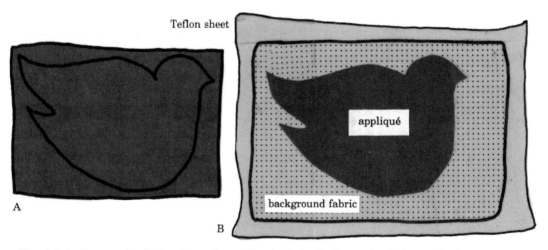

Fig. 4.2 A. Cut out the design from the appliqué fabric. B. Cover the design with the Teflon sheet again to press in place on the background fabric.

transferred from the paper to the fabric. Iron the appliqué to the background.

If doing lettering or an appliqué where direction is important, then remember that this method gives you a flipped or mirror image of the original.

Method D

Plastic sandwich bags can also be used as a fusible–or try cleaners' garment bags. Cut out a piece of plastic the size of the appliqué and place it between the backing fabric and appliqué.

Put brown wrapping paper over and under this "sandwich" so any plastic that is peeking out will be pressed onto the brown paper and not your iron or ironing board. Press it with an iron hot enough to melt the plastic and fuse the fabrics together.

Method E

If you wish to blindstitch around the edge of an appliqué for step two, the appliqué must be prepared in another way (Fig. 4.3).

First, straight stitch around the appliqué on what will be the fold line. Cut the appliqué from the fabric, leaving a ¼" (6.3mm) seam allowance. Clip the edges and turn under on the stitched line. Trim off more seam allowance wherever fabric overlaps or creates bulk. Baste with stitches or a glue-stick. Press the edges flat. Baste in place on the background fabric–I find it more accurate when done by hand. There is a wash-away basting thread on the market. If you use this it eliminates the need to pull out the basting later, and if it gets caught in your final stitching, there's no problem because it simply washes away. Now you can blindstitch the appliqué to the foundation.

If the appliqué is to be embroidered, it is sometimes best to do it first to prevent puckers in the background fabric. Embroidered patches can be appliquéd in many ways, the most common being satin stitching around the edge. But another way is to leave the edge almost devoid of stitching, cut out the appliqué and apply it with the same free stitches as the embroidery, to blend it into the background.

Even if fabric is to be heavily embroidered, embroider first on another piece of fabric, cut it out, and make it an appliqué. Use a glue stick or pin it in place. These appliqués are usually too thick to attach with fusible webbing.

Fig. 4.3 To prepare and apply an appliqué for blindstitching, sew all around it ¼" (6.3mm) from the edge (top). Fold under on the stitching, apply to the background and blindstitch in place (bottom).

Lesson 10. Appliquéing with feed dogs up

Satin stitches three ways

In addition to keeping your machine in excellent condition, the perfect satin stitch is achieved by matching of fabric, needle, and thread. If you have a different model Viking or plan to use different embroidery thread, always sew a sample, using the same fabric and needle that will be used on the finished piece. The Viking 990, 980 and 960 are programmed for a perfect satin stitch using Sulky rayon embroidery thread, and when an embroidery stitch is selected, the computer automatically loosens the upper tension. Don't watch the needle, but keep your eyes on the line you'll be stitching. Check to see if the fabric is being fed through evenly. Open or close the length of the zigzags. Each Viking has its own personality, so you must work this out for yours.

Standard method

Keep a few things in mind when attaching an appliqué with satin stitches: First, the stitch width should not overpower the appliqué. I almost always use a setting no wider than 2, along with utility B or transparent appliqué foot, because the satin stitches fit well inside the groove on the underside of the foot.

Stitch width: 2–3
Stitch length: 0.4–0.6 or adjust for your machine and thread
Needle position: center
Presser foot: utility B or transparent appliqué foot
Utility stitch: zigzag
Feed dogs: up
Tension: *top*, preset (990, 980, 950), slightly loosened for other models; *bobbin*, normal

I prefer to cover the edge of an appliqué in two passes rather than one. Instead of a 0.4 length, start with 0.8. At the same time, set the width for first pass slightly narrower than the final one. Instead of 4 width, set width to 3 for the first pass.

Use a needle appropriate for the thread. The needle must be large enough to let the thread pass through freely and it must punch a large enough hole in the fabric to prevent the thread from fraying. For example, with rayon embroidery thread I use a #90/14 stretch needle; on Zwicky cotton thread, I use a #80/11–12 needle. On woven materials, I use a jeans or denim needle instead of an all-purpose point because I feel it gives me a more perfect edge. (The all-purpose point is slightly rounded, so it deflects off the fibers and slips between them. When satin stitching on closely woven materials, this needle may create an uneven edge.)

Stained-glass method

Stained-glass is a type of satin-stitch appliqué in which your satin stitches are gray to black and extend out from the appliqué to the borders of the design. It is important to remember this, since not every design is appropriate for stained-glass.

Reverse appliqué

Reverse appliqué is the technique of layering from one to many fabrics on top of a background material. A design is straight-stitched through layers, then the fabric is cut away from portions of the design to reveal the fabric beneath. It is finished by satin stitching over the straight stitches. Reverse appliqué can be combined with appliqué from the top as well. To do a perfect reverse appliqué, put both fabrics in a hoop, topsides up, your appliqué fabric underneath. Draw the design on the top fabric or place the pattern on top of the fabrics in the hoop and straight stitch around the design. Remove the paper.

Take the fabrics out of the hoop and cut

out the top fabric inside the design area. Put the fabric back in the hoop, slip stabilizer between hoop and machine, and then satin stitch the edges. When finished, you may want to cut away the extra appliqué fabric on the back to eliminate bulk.

This method often affords better control of the appliqué when applying small pieces to a design.

Project Tote Bag Square (Modified Reverse Appliqué)

This square, shown in Fig. 4.4, could be reverse appliqué. In fact, I began it that way, but found that there were too many layers, so much bulk to sew through that the satin stitches didn't meet my standards. I faked reverse appliqué by using the following layering technique and cut out as much fabric underneath as I could.

Also, I have my reasons for not cutting out each piece and then fitting it all together like a jigsaw puzzle. It takes too much time trying to get them to fit perfectly — they never do — so I'd rather not use that method.

Stitch width: 2–3
Stitch length: 0.4–0.6
Needle position: center
Needle: #90/14 jeans
Feed dogs: up
Presser foot: utility B or transparent appliqué foot
Utility stitch: zigzag
Tension: *top*, preset (990, 980, 950), slightly loosened for other models; *bobbin*, normal
Fabric suggestions: lightweight cotton, 9″ (22.9cm) squares of purple, yellow, red, green

Thread: red, green and purple Sulky or Zwicky cotton thread to match fabrics
Accessories: Wonder-Under, dressmaker's carbon, empty ballpoint pen, tracing paper
Stabilizer: Iron-on freezer paper

Transfer the design in Fig. 4.4 onto tracing paper. Use dressmaker's carbon between the design and the yellow background fabric. Then, with the ballpoint pen, transfer the design to the yellow fabric. This is your guide. Iron on freezer paper to back of yellow square.

Fuse Wonder-Under on green, red and purple squares, following manufacturer's instructions (see Chapter 1). Next, cut apart the design on the tracing paper. Using the pieces of the design, cut out your fabric in this manner: The centers of each triangle will be cut exactly as shown in Fig. 4.4. You will be making three tracings, one for each color. For the green fabric, trace and cut out the top triangle. Then trace and cut the two larger triangle shapes with a ¼″ (6.4mm) seam allowance outside the stitching line. Trace and cut larger red triangles ¼″ (6.4mm) outside the stitching line. Cut centers out of red triangles exactly as shown. Trace and cut triangles out of the purple border.

Before fusing shapes in place, free-hand monogram your initials in purple thread as pictured. Use a 3 width zigzag, lower feed dogs, release pressure to between # and 1. Practice on a scrap first. If you have a 990 or 980, you may want to stitch your name with programmed letters instead.

Place shapes on background so monogram shows through green triangle cutout. Be sure no seam allowances are peeking out where they don't belong.

I prefer lifting off all the layers and then, beginning with the first layer, place and press, go on to the second layer, place and press, and so on. The pieces will adhere better.

Cutting and placing the appliqués in this

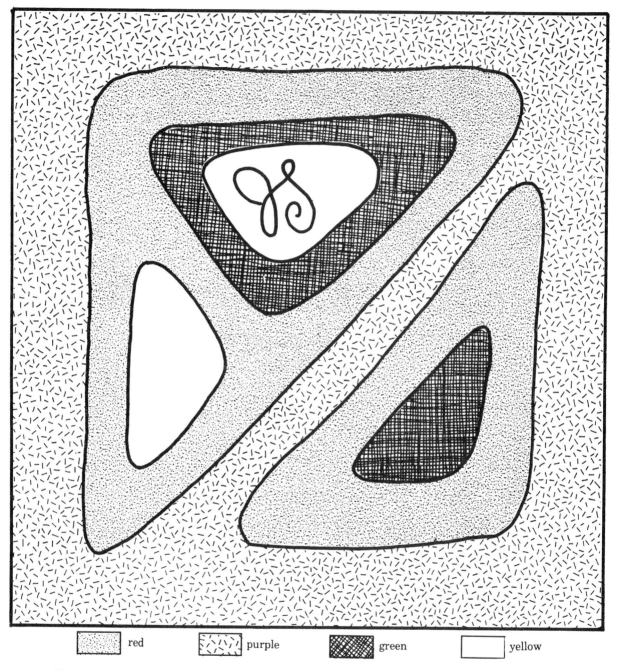

| red | purple | green | yellow |

Fig. 4.4 Geometric appliqué tote square; modified reverse technique.

way allows you to stitch on only one raw edge; it also eliminates the bulk of layering each piece and then cutting down to the colors beneath.

This design can be easily stitched because the curves are gradual. Using green thread, I began by stitching around the inside of green triangle. I then stitched around the inside of the red triangles using red thread and finished up the motif by satin stitching around the inside of the purple triangles with matching thread. The first pass will be set at stitch width 2, stitch length 0.6. Keep the satin stitches slightly open on the first pass. On the second pass, use a 3 width, 0.4 length satin stitch around appliqué. The 990 and 980 are programmed for use with Sulky thread. If you use another type of machine embroidery thread, you may have to shorten your stitch length to produce a close, smooth satin stitch.

Sew at a moderate speed. When your stitches begin to slant at the corners, stop with needle down at the inside corner. Lift the presser foot and turn the fabric, stitch one or two stitches or whatever it takes to keep the satin stitches straight. Continue stitching, remembering to always turn with the needle in the fabric. Finish the square as described in Chapter 12.

Blindstitching

A second way to attach appliqués to a background is with the blindstitch. Use the transparent appliqué foot. Prepare the appliqué according to Method E (see Fig. 4.3) and use monofilament thread on the top. Use your reverse blindstitch (2–7) mirror image; length and width are determined by you, but start with a stitch width 1 and a stitch length 2. Stitch around the appliqué, letting the straight stitches fall just outside the appliqué, with the bite of the zigzag catching the edge. You can set up the machine to give the look you want.

Do you want a wide bite? Then set the width to a higher number. The length of the stitch determines the closeness of those two stitches that go up and back, holding the appliqué in place. Find the right length by doing a sample. Use this method to attach patch pockets and to couch down heavy threads and cords. Usually monofilament is used on the top because it is almost invisible.

If you change the monofilament to a thread that will contrast with the fabric, this stitch gives the look of buttonholing by hand.

A line of blindstitching is used in the greeting card project in Lesson 4 (Fig. 3.9).

Edge stitching

To apply fabric with a straight edge-stitch, you will place the appliqué on the background as you did for blindstitching (if you are working with non-wovens like suedes or felt, don't press the edges under). Use the zipper E, or blind hem D foot. Set the straight stitch at a 2 length and stitch width at 0.

With the presser foot in place on the fabric, set the needle position to slightly within the appliqué. Stitch around the motif.

Project
Tote Bag Square (Edge-Stitch Appliqué)

This tote bag square (Fig. 4.5) uses straight stitching on felt.

Stitch width: 0; 1; preset for 990
Stitch length: 2; 1; preset for 990
Needle position: center or slightly left
Needle: #80/11–12 all-purpose
Feed dogs: up

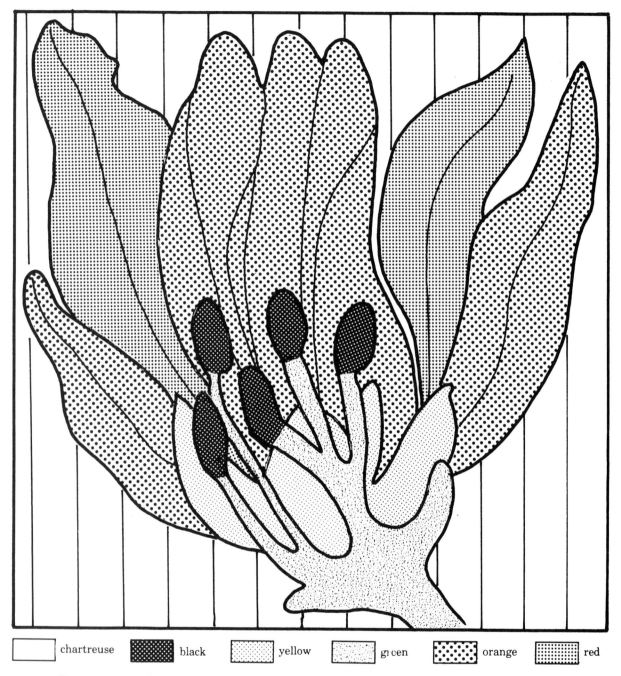

| | chartreuse | | black | | yellow | | green | | orange | | red |

Fig. 4.5 Flower design for tote bag square, edge-stitch appliqué technique.

Pressure: normal
Presser foot: zipper E, or blind hem D foot
Utility stitch: straight stitch; zigzag or tricot
Tension: *top*, normal; *bobbin*, normal
Fabric suggestion: 9″ (22.9cm) squares of
felt; one each of yellow, chartreuse, dark
green, Christmas red, pumpkin orange,
black
Thread: monofilament, black and red embroi-
dery
Accessories: Wonder-Under, empty ballpoint
pen, dressmaker's carbon, tracing pa-
per, water-erasable marker
Stabilizer: iron-on freezer paper

Press Wonder-Under behind each piece of felt, except chartreuse. That will be the background onto which you will appliqué the other fabrics. Within the 9″ (22.9cm) chartreuse square, draw a square 6¾″ (17.1cm).

Transfer the design in Fig. 4.5 to two pieces of tracing paper. Cut one pattern apart and place the appliqué shapes on the felt pieces, following the color suggestions in Fig. 4.5. Cut out petals and stamens. Iron freezer paper onto back of chartreuse felt. Using second pattern, trace outline of flower on background using dressmaker's carbon and empty ballpoint pen. Press hard. Remove the pattern. With water-erasable marker, draw vertical lines ½″ (12.7mm) apart on the chartreuse background. Stitch over lines with black embroidery thread using the tricot stitch on the preset setting (990) just inside flower outline. For other models, use a tiny zigzag on a 1 width, 1 length. The appliqué will cover the ends of the vertical lines.

Arrange your design within the 6¾″ (17.1cm) square. Place Christmas red petals on the background first. Press and stitch down the center and around each petal with monofilament thread. Note that the raw edge should guide by the inside of the right toe of the blind hem D or zipper foot. This thread does not hold a knot well, so I pushed the finishing button on my 990

at the beginning and end of each shape to eliminate tying off each thread.

On top of red petals, arrange the pumpkin orange petals. Press and stitch down the center and around each as pictured with red thread. Change back to monofilament thread. Place yellow base over petals. Press and edge-stitch. Place green stamen stems over yellow base, press and edge-stitch. Place black stamens in position, press and edge-stitch. Stitch as closely as you can. The foot helps to keep the stitching an equal distance from the edge of each appliqué.

Finish the square as described in Chapter 12.

Project
Tote Bag Square
(Straight Stitch)

The square in Fig. 4.6 also uses straight stitches to hold appliqués in place, but is otherwise quite different. I used pink and fuchsia fabric, plus all the tote bag colors on this one and layered several of the designs. The background is yellow.

Stitch width: 0
Stitch length: 2
Needle position: center
Needle: #90/14 stretch
Feed dogs: up
Presser foot: standard A or transparent appli-
qué foot
Utility stitch: straight stitch
Tension: *top*, normal; *bobbin*, normal
Fabric suggestion: light or medium-weight
closely woven cottons for appliqué
shapes, in aqua, purple, fuchsia, red, or-
ange and green; 10″ (25.4cm) yellow
square for background
Thread: yellow machine embroidery on top;
matching Zwicky cotton sewing thread
on bobbin

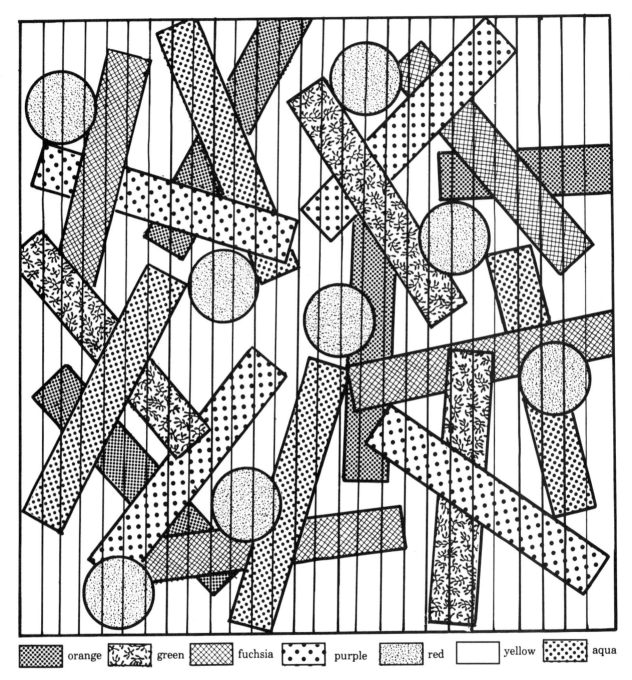

Fig. 4.6 Pattern for straight-stitch tote square. Use Wonder-Under or fusible webbing method to attach geometric shapes to the background fabric, then stitch evenly spaced lines of straight stitching to hold them.

66

Accessories: Wonder-Under; water-erasable or vanishing marker
Stabilizer: iron-on freezer paper

Apply Wonder-Under to all fabrics except the yellow background. Iron freezer paper to back of yellow background square.

Cut four rectangles each of aqua, fuchsia, orange, purple and green—3″ × ½″ (7.6cm × 12.7mm). Cut eight red circles ⅝″ (1.5cm) in diameter. I used the end of a Zwicky thread spool to trace my circles.

Work with one color at a time. I used orange first and arranged the four bars randomly on background fabric. Continue with the rest of the color bars. Your square may remind you of "Pick-Up Sticks." Put red circles on last. Press shapes onto background fabric.

With the water-erasable or vanishing marker, draw lines from top to bottom every ½″ (12.7mm) across the square. Starting at the top right corner, straight stitch to the bottom on the first line. Turn and stitch back, bottom to top, on the next line. Continue across the square.

Go back and stitch between those lines. You may be able to use the side of your presser foot as a measuring guide. Make one last pass and stitch between the lines again. There are now straight-stitch lines from top to bottom every ⅛″ (3.2mm).

Instead of row after row of straight stitches to hold appliqués in place, try satin stitches or use a double needle. Also try couching down metallics and thick cords. Finish the square as described in Chapter 12.

Cording edges

Corded edges give appliqués and decorative patches a neat, exact finish. Use a 7-hole foot if cord is fine enough to be threaded through it. You may also try a utility B, transparent appliqué, or raised seam foot F, or narrow hemmer to guide cord.

When finishing patches, sew the corded edges in two passes. Place the patch over typing paper or tear-away stabilizer. You'll need two pieces–one for each pass–and they must be large enough to extend past the edge of the patch.

On the first pass, apply the cord, sewing at a narrower stitch width, and with stitch length slightly longer than the final pass.

The final stitching is done with a close satin stitch, the needle stitching down in the fabric on one side of the cord, but stitching off the cord and fabric on the other side. Leave enough cord at the beginning and end to poke to the back and work into the stitches. Use a needle with a large eye to do this by hand. Or, when you reach the end of the first pass, cut the cord to slightly overlap the start. If you can cut it on an angle, the join will not be noticeable when the second pass is completed.

It is not necessary to cover the entire cord if the cord itself is decorative or is a color that adds to the effect you wish to achieve. When I had to appliqué dozens of velveteen crosses to a woolen ecclesiastical garment, I used a velour cord and an open zigzag, and sewed with a thread the color of the velour. When finished, the velour edges looked like an extension of the velveteen.

Lesson 11. Appliquéing with feed dogs lowered

In this lesson, the appliqués are sewn in place freely; sometimes edges are not completely covered.

Set up your machine by lowering the feed dogs and releasing pressure to between # and 1. Use either a hoop or iron-on freezer paper, and loosen the top tension slightly.

Blurring

What is blurring? Apply a fabric to another by starting to stitch within the appliqué. Then, following the shape of the appliqué, stitch around and around it, extending the stitching out into the background fabric. It's difficult to tell where one begins and the other leaves off. That is called blurring.

Although the sample here uses transparent fabrics, blurring can be done with any type of fabric. I chose to combine blurring with sheers and overlays to show you how to create pictures that look like watercolors. Thread color is usually the same as the appliqué, but never limit yourself. Use other colors as well.

When working with transparent fabrics, use pins to hold the appliqués in place. If possible, hold both in a hoop while sewing. Attach one layer at a time, sewing a straight stitch around the appliqué and then cutting back to the stitching. Blur the edges. Then stretch the next transparent fabric in the hoop, stitch and cut away excess, then blur the edges.

To blur edges, find any point inside the appliqué. Stitch round and round, in ever-widening circles, until the edge of the appliqué is reached. But don't stop. Keep stitching past the edge and into the background. Three transparent circles applied in this way, one overlapping the next, the third overlapping the others, makes a good sample (Fig. 4.7). Possibilities will grow from this one idea: try many colors, overlapping them to make other colors; give depth to a picture by overlapping so that the color becomes more intense as the layers are built up, and recedes where only one layer is used.

Project
Flower of Sheers and Overlays

Use this floral piece as a pillow top or slip it into your notebook. To do the flower sample (Fig. 4.8), set up the machine.

Stitch width: 0–5
Stitch length: 0–2.5
Needle position: center
Needle: #80/11–12 all-purpose
Feed dogs: lowered
Pressure: between # and 1
Presser foot: darning foot
Utility stitch: straight stitch
Tension: *top,* slightly loosened; *bobbin,* normal
Fabric suggestion: 9″ (23cm) square medium-weight white fabric for the background; ¼ yard (22.9cm) green transparent fabric; ⅛ yard (11.4cm) pink transparent fabric; 12″ (30.5cm) square off-white bridal veiling

Fig. 4.7 Blurring the edges of appliqués.

Threads: machine embroidery in yellow, green, and pink
Accessories: 7" (17.8cm) spring hoop with stabilizer or freezer paper without hoop
Stabilizer: tear-away or iron-on freezer paper

Use the circle and leaf shape to make the patterns. Cut out several dozen 1" (2.5cm) circles in pink transparent fabric. Also cut the same number of 2" (5.1cm) long leaf shapes from green transparent fabric. Patterns are provided in Fig. 4.9. You may not use all of these petals and leaves: It will depend upon how much they are overlapped and how large an area you're covering with the design. If using freezer paper, iron it to the background fabric.

Arrange and overlap the leaves in a circle on the background fabric, points toward the center. Plan so they will fit within the hoop (if you have chosen to work with one), keeping the leaves at least an inch (2.5cm) inside. If the presser foot gets too close to the edge, it will be difficult to sew around the appliqués without hitting the darning foot on the hoop.

Lay down the circles of color for the flower head, starting in the middle of the leaves. New colors pop out for the leaves and petals as you overlap, arrange and rearrange. Leave the center of the flower open. Don't pin down any of these small pieces.

After completing the arrangement of the sheers and overlays, cover with the piece of bridal veil to help hold them all in place. Pin the veiling down in several places near the center of the flower and at the edges of the fabric. If working with a hoop, lift your piece carefully from the table and place it in a hoop. Slip stabilizer under it.

Start by sewing around the petals of the flower. Use pink thread on the top, green thread on the bobbin. Stitch the petals very freely. Bring the stitching out past them, or inside, or make stitched circles between them. Stitch circles within circles.

Then change the top thread to green.

Fig. 4.8 Use bridal veiling to hold small pieces of appliqué fabric in place.

Fig. 4.9 Patterns for the flower design.

Stitch around the leaves in the same free-flowing way. Go up the centers and down, stitching in veins on some and leaving others without.

Now only the center is left to stitch. Change the top thread to yellow and set stitch width to a 4–5 width zigzag, stitch length 0, needle position to the left. Anchor your threads in the center of the flower. Stitch in the same spot at least a dozen times to build up a nubby "seed" (see Fig. 3.2). Anchor the threads again. Lift the presser foot and move to another place. Do another seed. There's no need to clip threads until all the seeds are completed. Keep building up the nubs and moving your needle from one place to the next until the flower center is to your liking. Then clip the threads between the zigzag areas.

Change the top thread back to green. Set stitch width back to 0, needle position center. Sew around the seeds. Go from one to another until all are outlined. When the picture is complete, take it out of the hoop if you've used one. Most of the stabilizer will drop away; the rest can be pulled off (or left on, since it won't show).

The bridal veil can be left as is. However, I often clip out areas to create color changes.

Scribbling

Scribbling is like darning over appliqués, but you will use both straight and zigzag stitches. It's a good way to lay in big areas of color without having to cover the areas with heavy embroidery.

The appliqué picture in Fig. 4.10 was placed on the outside of a tote bag. Use the patterns in Fig. 4.11 as a guide, enlarging or reducing to fit your purpose.

Stitch width: varies
Stitch length: 0–2.5
Needle position: center
Needle: #90/14 stretch
Feed dogs: lowered
Pressure: between # and 1
Presser foot: darning foot
Utility stitch: straight stitch
Tension: *top*, slightly loosened; *bobbin*, normal
Fabric suggestion: medium-weight cotton
Thread: machine embroidery on top; Zwicky sewing or darning thread on bobbin
Accessories: glue stick
Stabilizer: iron-on freezer paper

Fig. 4.10 This is part of a design that has been appliquéd to a tote bag, using free-machining to hold the appliqués in place.

Fig. 4.11 Use these patterns to create one element of the design shown in Fig. 4.10.

Apply the appliqués with a dab of glue stick and begin to stitch the edges down freely with either a straight or a zigzag stitch. Sew freely over the entire appliqué first to anchor it before embroidering the designs. Stitch inside and over the edges of the appliqués. If you can live with raw edges, then don't be too particular about covering them exactly. Here is a good place to blur edges. Add to the design by laying in different colors with the same free machining. Add as much stitching as you wish, but don't cover the entire appliqué, as that would defeat the purpose. Let most of the color show through. It's like sketching with colored pencils.

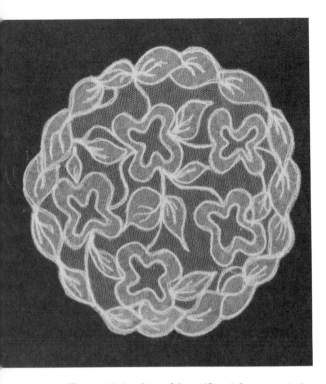

Fig. 4.12 Appliquéd lace (Carrickmacross), is made quickly using organdy and fine hexagonal net.

Stitching Carrickmacross

Carrickmacross is an Irish lace made with appliqués of batiste. Tiny pops, or eyelets, are embroidered in the fine hexagonal net which is used as the ground, and it has a picot edge. If hand done, this type of lace is very fragile, but our machine version is both beautiful and sturdy (Fig. 4.12).

Project
Carrickmacross Doily

Instead of batiste, we'll use organdy. I've used a polyester for the veiling, so my fabric will be the same. It will be white on white, typical of Carrickmacross lace.

Stitch width: 0
Stitch length: 0–2.5
Needle position: center
Needle: #80/11–12 all-purpose
Feed dogs: lowered
Pressure: between ⚏ and 1
Presser foot: darning foot
Utility stitch: straight stitch
Tension: *top*, slightly loosened; *bobbin*, normal
Fabric suggestion: white polyester organdy; fine white polyester hexagonal veiling
Thread: white cotton machine embroidery thread and white cordonnet (optional)
Accessories: 7″ (17.8cm) spring hoop; water-erasable or vanishing marker
Stabilizer: water-soluble

Copy the design in Fig. 4.13 onto the organdy, using a water-erasable or vanishing marker. Slip the net underneath the organdy and put them both into a spring hoop. If possible, always use a hoop large enough so you can do the entire design without having to move the fabric and net.

Set up your machine for free embroidery. Anchor threads and stitch on the lines around each motif at least three times. It may be necessary to stitch a fourth pass on some, but make it look consistent: Don't leave some lines with one pass, others with four. Plot the course of the needle ahead of time so there won't be too many stops and starts.

When the design is finished, take it out of the hoop and cut out all the areas that are to be free of organdy. Use sharp, fine-pointed scissors. The pair that comes with the 990 have curved blades, which help to lift areas away from the net. You may also lift organdy with the point of a seam ripper and then clip.

Should you cut the net, don't panic. Put it back under the needle and stitch a few lines of straight stitching over the cut, blending it into the other stitches already there. It will look like it was meant to be there all the time.

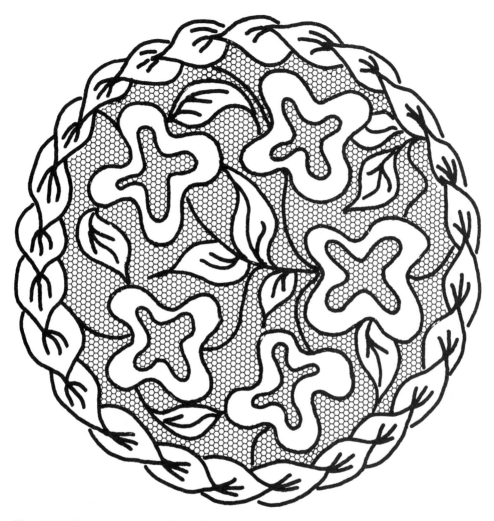

Fig. 4.13 The pattern for appliquéd lace.

When that is completed and looks great, decide whether to go on or to stop while you're ahead. You may go one step further, as real Carrickmacross lace always has a picot edge and small eyelets in the net, as shown in Fig. 4.14.

To stitch the eyelets, mark appropriate places on the organdy, such as the middles of the flowers. Lower feed dogs, remove presser foot and foot shank. Snap 4mm eyelet plate in place. Make a small hole through organdy and net with the point of embroidery scissors. Slip hole over eyelet plate. Use a zigzag stitch on a 2 width to make eyelet. Trim excess organdy from around eyelet.

Hand-worked Carrickmacross lace has a cord couched down around the appliqués to hold them in place. To do this by machine, stitch around the appliqués only

Fig. 4.14 Eyelets and picots in
Carrickmacross.

big. Try it for the edge of a bridal veil or for
the bodice and puffed sleeves of the wedding dress itself. Now that's what I call a
long-cut, but definitely worth it.

Layering transparent fabrics

Shadow work is my favorite. I love the
painterly effects of combining colors and
toning down with whites. It's done using
sheers and overlays. In the picture made in
the following project, the color does not
come from a colored cotton fabric layered
between organdies; instead, these flowers
are created only from transparent fabrics.

once before cutting back. Do not trim
around the outside edge. Put the piece
back in the hoop upside down. Use
cordonnet or pearl cotton in the bobbin.

Before beginning to outline the appliqués, dip the needle down and bring the
cord up to the top. Hold both threads to
one side as you take several stitches along
the design. In other words, don't anchor
the cord, as is usually done with thread.
Later go back and work the threads into
the stitches on the backside of the design.

Picots around the edge should be left until the rest of the stitching is completed.

Cut back to the edge. Use two layers of
water-soluble stabilizer. The topside of the
appliqué should be pinned against the stabilizer. Put all this into the hoop. First
stitch the cord around the leaves at the inside edge. Then, with a water-erasable or
vanishing marker, mark small dots every
⅛″ (3.2mm) along the edge to use as a
guide for the picots. Stitch in by following
the edge and making small loops at each
mark. Take it out of the hoop and wash the
stabilizer and marks out of the fabric.

What we've made is a small doily but, if
you're like me, you are not big on small
doilies. This is a fast technique, so think

Project Shadow Work Picture

In this project, I switch from feed dogs
up to feed dogs lowered, but most of the
stitching is done freely, so I've put it in this
lesson. This design (Fig. 4.15) will give you
an idea of what can be done with only
white, mauve and green organza.

Stitch width: 0–4
Stitch length: 0–0.5
Needle position: center
Needle: #70/9 all-purpose
Feed dogs: up, lowered
Pressure: normal; between ⁂ and 1
Presser foot: utility foot B, transparent appli-
    qué or darning foot
Utility stitch: straight, zigzag
Tension: *top*, preset (990, 980, 950), slightly
    loosened for other models; *bobbin*, nor-
    mal
Fabric: white, mauve, and green organza
Thread: green machine embroidery
Accessories: spring hoop; water-erasable
    marker
Stabilizer: water-soluble

Fig. 4.15 Layers of transparent fabrics give a painterly effect to shadow work.

Place the white organza over the design (Fig. 4.16) and trace it off with a water-erasable marker. Layer two mauves behind each flower on the white organza and pin them in place. Put this in a hoop.

With the machine set for free machining, without anchoring the threads, straight stitch around the flowers twice. Lift the needle and go to the flower centers. Stitch twice around each center, also: The lines should be next to each other, not on top of each other. Cut back to the stitching around the outside edge, but not too close.

Place the green organza behind the leaf areas and stitch in place with two lines of stitching. Cut back to the stitching at the edges.

Set up your machine for normal sewing. Put feed dogs up and use the transparent appliqué foot. Use stitch width 2, stitch length 0.5 or a setting that will produce a smooth satin stitch. Sew around the flowers and leaves. Be careful: sew too closely and the stitches will cut the fabric.

From the front of your picture, cut the white organza from one flower, the white and one mauve layer from another. Turn the hoop over. Cut out one layer of mauve from the back on another. Or from the back, cut out both layers of color, leaving only the white organdy and the flower center intact. Can you imagine the combinations and shades of mauve you can create?

The large leaf is divided into four sections. In the first section, cut out the top white layer and place a layer of green behind the remaining green layer to darken it. In the second area, cut out the white and leave just green. In the third, place white behind the section to make it three layers. The fourth is left as is, the white in front of the green.

Once you have finished the flowers and leaves, go back to the flower centers and blur them out by stitching spirals from the centers out to the edges. Or start at the edges and travel to the outside of the flowers. Leave some flowers with only the first stitching around the center.

Satin stitches should be sewn through at least two layers of fabric. Ordinarily, we'd add stabilizer, but tear-away could leave specks in the fabric that might show through. To prevent this, use green organza as a backing for the stems. The lines are satin stitched, then the stabilizing organza is cut back to the stitching.

Finish up with straight stitching. Set up again for free machining. Using water-soluble stabilizer behind the fabric, set the machine on stitch width 0, lower feed dogs, release pressure between # and 1 to sew in the accent lines.

Fig. 4.16 Shadow work design.

If one of the fabrics has pulled away from the satin stitches, don't give up. Layer a piece of transparent fabric underneath and stitch it on. Then cut away the original one. Or put a piece of organza underneath, use straight stitching or zigzags to sew in some lines, and pretend you wanted it that way. On the flowers, too: If by mistake you cut through two layers instead of one, leave it or layer something behind it. Sometimes blurring out more lines of stitching will attach and hide any mistakes.

Keep the stitching light and airy, with no wide satin stitches. There should be more fabric showing than stitching. When finished, wash out the stabilizer and pen marks.

This type of shadow work is quite fragile and I suggest using it for pictures or window hangings, rather than for clothing.

Project Stitching Three-Dimensional Appliqués

One of the prettiest dresses I've ever seen was at a fraternity dance back when we thought we had to wear yards of tulle and gobs of ruffles. This dress was a beautiful white organdy exception. Over the entire skirt were scattered lavender and

Fig. 4.17 Three-dimensional appliqué design.

peach pansy appliqués of organdy. They were attached only at the centers. It was a plain dress except for this scattering of flowers.

Detached appliqués do not have to have a heavy satin stitch edge, and I think you'll agree that straight stitching on fine fabric is easier and more beautiful. After all, that was a long time ago and I've never forgotten that dress.

Stitch width: 0
Stitch length: 0–0.4
Needle position: center
Needle: #60/8 or #70/9 all-purpose
Feed dogs: lowered; up

Pressure: between # and 1; normal
Presser foot: darning foot or no presser foot, special marking foot (optional)
Utility stitch: straight stitch
Tension: *top*, slightly loosened; *bobbin*, normal
Fabric suggestion: mauve and green organdy
Thread: machine embroidery thread to match
Accessories: spring hoop; water-erasable or vanishing marker
Stabilizer: water-soluble

Place a layer of water-soluble stabilizer between two layers of mauve organdy. Clip this into the spring hoop. Draw the design

Fig. 4.18 Pattern pieces for floral 3-D appliqué.

in Fig. 4.17 on it with a water-erasable or vanishing marker. You will copy the petal design twice. The small sample is done in pieces and combined later (Fig. 4.18).

Set the machine on moderate speed for accuracy. Free machine stitch three times around the edges with a straight stitch. Lines should be close together but not on top of each other. Use a colored thread that matches or is a shade darker than the fabric. Cut out the petals close to the stitching, but not too close.

The leaves should be worked in the same way on green organdy. Stitch only straight stitches as you follow the pattern. Go into the centers and stitch the veins as well. Cut out the leaves.

Place the flower petals on top of each other — stagger them so the petals underneath are not hidden by the top layer. Place this over the leaves and stitch them together with mauve thread by following the stitching in the center of the petals. You may go a step further and fringe the center. Using the special marking foot, green thread, stitch width 2 and stitch length 0.3, stitch in several places in the center of the flower. Finish by holding the flower under the faucet and rinsing out some, but not all, of the stabilizer. Shape the flower and leaves carefully and let them dry. They will be stiff, as if heavily starched, and will retain their shapes. How can you use these three-dimension appliqués? Add a band of them to a bodice of Carrickmacross lace. Make an utterly fake corsage or a flowered hat. Add the flower to a cord for a necklace.

Helpful Hints for Appliqué

If an appliqué bubbles, fix it by taking it out of the hoop and nicking the base fabric beneath the appliqué, which will then allow the base to lay flat.

Or slit the back a bit and fill the appliqué area with cotton. This is called trapunto. Hand whip the slit closed. Machine stitch on top of the appliqué to add to the design and hold the batting in place.

Another way to keep appliqué puckers from showing is to hide them by hand or machine embroidering over the appliqué.

When layering net, there is sometimes a moiré look to it that spoils the effect of your picture. To eliminate it, change the direction of one of the layers.

Don't limit yourself to fabric appliqués; thread appliqués are also effective. Work spider webs in another fabric, cut them out, and apply.

Work lace in space inside a small ring. Apply it to a background by free machining all around the inside edge of the ring. Then cut the ring from the lace.

Check out Lesson 6 on beads, baubles, and shishas.

Do pulled and drawn threads with the machine on one fabric and attach them to another background.

CHAPTER 5

Stitching Across Open Spaces

- **Lesson 12. Cutwork and eyelets**
- **Lesson 13. Free-machined needlelace**
- **Lesson 14. Battenberg lace**
- **Lesson 15. Hemstitching**
- **Lesson 16. Stitching in rings**
- **Lesson 17. Making Alençon lace**

People have been stitching in space for a hundred years; you can, too. However, if you are nervous about doing it, stitching on water-soluble stabilizer usually produces the same effects with even better results. Water-soluble stabilizer is so thin and pliable that placing multiple layers of it in a hoop, along with fabric, is no problem. Another reason I am sold on it is that, once the design is drawn on the stabilizer, it can be stitched exactly, as if stitching on fabric. That isn't possible when actually stitching in space. I use it for cutwork because it holds the cut edges in place while I stitch them and sometimes I use it on both sides of the fabric to give it even more stability.

I use stabilizer when stitching in rings, too. It keeps threads in place until they are anchored. There is no problem with slipping, as often happens when stitching in space.

This chapter includes cutwork, stitching in rings, creating needlelace, and stitching both Battenberg and Alençon laces. Hemstitching is included, as well. Be sure to keep all your samples in your notebook. You may not use an idea today or tomorrow, but maybe next year you'll refer back to your notebook and find just what you're looking for to make a special gift, or welcome a new baby. My notebook is especially valuable when I want to find machine settings for a technique I haven't used in weeks. No matter how well you know your Viking, you can't remember every detail of a method you've tried.

Lesson 12. Cutwork and eyelets

Cutwork

Cutwork is the forerunner of all needlemade laces. It was common as early as the sixteenth century. In handmade cutwork, part of the background fabric is cut away and threads are stretched from one side of the open area to the other. Bars of buttonhole stitches are worked over the stretched threads and the cut edges. Cutwork is done by using satin stitches in place of buttonhole stitches.

Project Cutwork Needlecase

When I wanted to do a cutwork project on the machine without dedicating my life to a large, time-consuming sailor collar or tablecloth, I found that the needlecase in Fig. 5.1 was exactly the right size. The single design can be used as a repeat pattern and it can be combined with embroidery, appliqué or shadow work.

I traced the pattern (Fig. 5.2) on paper two different times. On one pattern I add-

Fig. 5.1 The cutwork design on this needlecase can be used once, or as a repeat pattern.

ed lines where I wanted the thread bars, called "brides," to be.

Before you begin this or any project, practice, using the same fabric, needle and threads, stitch settings and stabilizers you will use on your finished piece. For this design, I practiced turning corners and satin stitching curves, as well as filling spaces with thread bars.

Cutwork is not usually backed by anything, but on this needlecase you can see that it is a necessity.

Stitch width: 0–2
Stitch length: 0–0.4
Needle position: center
Needle: #80/11–12 all-purpose
Feed dogs: up; lowered
Pressure: between # and 1; normal
Presser foot: darning foot; utility B or transparent appliqué foot
Utility stitch: zigzag
Tension: *top*, preset (990, 980, 950), slightly loosened for other models; *bobbin*, normal
Fabric suggestion: closely woven linen or kettlecloth
Thread: machine embroidery
Accessories: spring hoop; tracing paper; small, sharp embroidery scissors; pencil, water-erasable or vanishing marker, and permanent white marker
Stabilizer: water-soluble

Place the pattern without the thread bars on the back of the fabric and slip them both into a hoop. The topside of the fabric will be against the machine. Lower the feed dogs and put darning foot on. Release pressure between # and 1. Straight stitch around the outlines of the design two times with the same thread you'll use for the satin stitching. (Do not stitch the bars at this time.)

Take the fabric out of the hoop and peel off the pattern. Cut out the larger area. Put a piece of stabilizer over the topside and one underneath the fabric, and place all three layers in the hoop. Slip the second

Fig. 5.2 Cutwork pattern to copy.

pattern under the hoop. With a permanent white marker, trace the bars on the top stabilizer. Put the pattern aside until later.

With stitch width set to 0, freely stitch in the bars. Do the long, middle branching line first. Anchor the thread at the top by sewing in one place a few stitches, or by pushing the finishing button, and make a pass from top to bottom, then back again. As you sew from the bottom on that second pass, stitch the branches out and back as well.

Go back to stitch width 1. Stitch the first pass from top to bottom, moving the hoop quite quickly (remember the branches). Then, stitch back up from the bottom: This time move your hoop slowly. The

stitches will be closer together. Remember, you control this by how fast you move the hoop. The stitches will look like satin stitches in space. Anchor each branch by sewing at 0 width into the fabric just beyond the stay-stitching, or by pushing the finishing button. Zigzag to the top and anchor the thread.

Stitch the short bars at each side next. Anchor the threads at the top of the first bar, just beyond the two rows of straight stitching. Sew straight stitches across to the other side, anchor the threads again, and come back on the same line. Then begin zigzagging back across these threads with a 2 stitch width. When you reach the other side, stop, turn the width to 0 and follow the stay-stitch line to the next bar position. Sew across, back, and then zigzag as you did the first one. Complete all the brides on each side.

Cut out all three smaller shapes that are left in the design. Try to do this without cutting through the stabilizer on the back, but if you clip it, you can always slide another piece of stabilizer underneath. Put another piece of stabilizer on top and place all layers in the hoop. Using your pattern again behind the hoop, draw the bars on the stabilizer. Proceed with these branched bars as you did with the large cutout.

When you have finished all the bars, change the machine settings. Raise the feed dogs and set the machine on stitch width 2. Use the utility B or transparent appliqué foot. Change pressure to normal. Begin sewing at the point of the heart. Anchor the threads and proceed clockwise. As you travel around the curves, stitch very slowly, your machine set on moderate speed. To fill in the curves smoothly, stop with the needle down on the right side, lift the presser-foot lever, pivot the hoop, lower the presser foot, and stitch again. Repeat several times when negotiating curves.

Satin stitch around each cutout. Carefully pull away the stabilizer and rinse out any remaining pieces. Press the embroidery from the back.

Eyelets

There are 4mm and 6mm eyelet plates available for the Viking. Remember to mention the model number of your machine to the dealer when purchasing one. To use an eyelet plate, remove pressure foot shank, and snap eyelet plate over feed dog. Lower feed dogs. Place firmly woven fabric in a spring hoop and poke a small hole through it with an awl or sharp embroidery scissors. With right side of fabric up, slip hole over the tube in the eyelet plate. Lower presser bar. Set machine on a 2–4 width zigzag stitch. Dip needle into fabric and pull bobbin thread to the top. Push the finishing button or take a few straight stitches to lock thread ends. Zigzag around hole by moving the fabric around the hole as you sew. Push finishing button again or take a few straight stitches to lock off thread. Lift presser bar, remove work and clip thread at the fabric. Bring feed dogs up and take one stitch. The feed dogs move and pop the eyelet plate off. I've used eyelets in my embroideries, clumping them together for a center of interest, and one of my teachers uses them to decorate lovely bed linens.

Lesson 13. Free-machined needlelace

The terms *cutwork, lacy spiderwebs,* and *openwork* all describe a machine stitchery technique far removed from darning holes in socks or shredded elbows. But, like darning, they do entail stitching across open spaces.

Stitch width: 0
Stitch length: 0–2.5
Needle position: center

Needle: #80/11–12 all-purpose
Feed dogs: lowered
Pressure: between # and 1
Presser foot: darning or no presser foot
Utility stitch: straight stitch
Tension: *top*, normal; *bobbin*, slightly tightened
Fabric suggestions: any weight
Thread: one color, Zwicky cotton or polyester
Accessories: 6″ (15.2cm) wrapped wooden hoop; water-soluble stabilizer (optional)

Openwork is done in a hoop with the fabric stretched tightly. Place the hoop, fabric side down, on the machine bed. Draw a circle on the fabric: Circles are easier to control than the squares, crescents and paisley shapes you may want to try later.

Start stitching at the edge of the circle by bringing the bobbin thread to the top. Anchor the threads by sewing a few stitches in one spot or by pushing the finishing button. Guide the hoop slowly as you stitch around the circle three times (Fig. 5.3A). For a more stable area, cord the circle by zigzagging over a strand of pearl cotton; use the transparent appliqué foot, stitch width 2–3, length 1–2. Take the hoop off the machine and, without removing the fabric from it, cut out the circle close to the stitches. Replace the hoop and secure the threads once again at the edge of the hole.

Now you will begin to lay in a network of spokelike threads across the space. To do this, begin by stitching across from one side of the hole to the other side. If you elected to cord the hole, remember to remove the foot, drop the feed dogs, and release pressure before laying in the spokes. Move the hoop slowly, but run the machine moderately fast to strengthen and put a tighter twist on the spoke. When your needle enters the fabric again, move along the circle to another spot, secure threads, and sew directly across the hole again. Continue in this manner until you have as many spokes as you wish. On the last pass, go up to the center and backstitch right at the center of the wheel to strengthen the web. Starting at that backstitch, fill in the spokes by sewing in ever-widening circles around the center until the "button" is the size you wish it to be (Fig. 5.3B). Sew a few stitches into the button to lock the thread in place and again move to the outside to anchor the threads and complete that spoke.

Would you like a lacier filling? Sew one backstitch over each spoke after crossing it

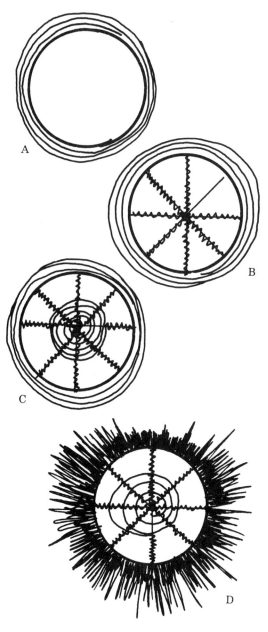

Fig. 5.3 Making needlelace. A. First sew around a circle three times. B. Cut out the center, embroider across the hole, creating spokes. C. Add circles of stitches around the center. D. Stitch radiating lines over the edge, into the fabric.

84

as you stitch around the center. This keeps the threads from slipping to the center. Travel around and around in wider circles till you reach the edge of the hole.

Although there are as many ways to finish off the edges of the spaces as there are ways to fill them with stitches, one of the softest looks is accomplished by straight stitching from the edge of the hole, out past it and back again, moving the hoop back and forth as if stitching sun rays (Fig. 5.3C). You can also use the widest zigzag and accomplish the same rays. Or, satin stitch around the edge and combine that with other embroidery. These are only a few ideas; try some of your own.

If you have used stabilizer, place your embroidery under a faucet and wash it out when your work is completed.

Create your own samples by placing a piece of medium-weight cotton in a hoop and drawing several circles on it. Stitch around one circle three times. Cut out the center. Stitch a spider web in the hole and finish it off on the edges. Go to the next circle and stitch both the center and the edges in a different way from your first sample. Then do another and another until you have many needlelace samples for your notebook. If you're pleased with the result and want to show it off, back with another fabric and use as a tote bag square.

Lesson 14. Battenberg lace

Battenberg lace was popular in the late 1800s. Straight, machine-made tape was shaped into a design and basted to stiff paper. Then the open spaces were filled with bars and embroidery stitches, which held the tape in shape. After the stitchery was completed, the paper was removed and the Battenberg lace could be used to decorate dresses, curtains or linens.

Project
Butterfly-shaped Lace

This lesson will teach you how to make one butterfly-shaped piece of Battenberg (Fig. 5.4). From there, you can go on to bigger projects, but let's see if you like Battenberg lacemaking by machine.

There is a variety of white, off-white, black, gold, and silver Battenberg tape to choose from. It's available by mail-order

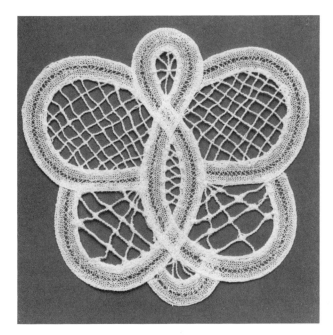

Fig. 5.4 Battenberg is embroidered after narrow tape has been shaped into a butterfly design.

(see Sources of Supplies) and from some needlework shops.

Should you create your own design, choose a tape that doesn't overpower the pattern. The one I used is ¼″ (6.3mm) wide. On each side of the tape is a thread that is thicker than the others. Pull gently to curve the tape into the shape you want.

Place two pieces of water-soluble stabilizer in a 7″ (17.8) spring hoop. Trace the outline of the design in Fig. 5.5 with a white permanent marking pen. Pull up the thread on the tape, pinning in the shape on the stabilizer as you go and using a glue stick to temporarily hold it in place. Hide ends as shown in Fig. 5.5. Baste down both sides of the tape to the stabilizer with wash-away basting thread if you have it or use fine thread in the same color as the tape. I find it more satisfactory to baste by hand than by machine.

Using white marker, draw in the stitching lines: Extend them by drawing dots onto the tape with water-erasable marker.

Fig. 5.5 Battenberg pattern.

At times the stabilizer may be cut out and these dots can be used for reference.

Set up your machine for free embroidery.

Stitch width: 0–1
Stitch length: 0–2.5
Needle position: center
Needle: #90/14 all-purpose or stretch
Feed dogs: lowered
Pressure: between # and 1
Presser foot: darning foot or bare needle
Utility stitch: zigzag
Tension: *top*, tightened to 6½; *bobbin*, tighten slightly
Thread: wash-away basting thread; #50 (ecru) machine embroidery
Accessories: 7" (17.8cm) spring hoop; water-erasable marker and white permanent marker; ecru Battenberg tape; glue stick; dressmaker's pins
Stabilizer: water-soluble, doubled, large enough for hoop

Start by straight stitching around both edges of the tape with machine embroidery thread. This prevents tape from curling. When you come to a place that joins a curve to the middle tape, stitch across to the other side and back again. After the design is attached, cut out the stabilizer in the center of the wings, body, tail and head. Set your machine on the zigzag stitch, width and length 0, for free embroidery.

For wing tops, follow the side of the tape (Fig. 5.6), straight stitch to the next mark and stitch across open space to the other side. Move hoop and needle quite fast. Follow the tape to the next mark to stitch in the next line. Then stitch around to the side and lay in the other rows of stitches that will cross the first ones. When those are done, zigzag at 1 stitch width over all straight-stitch threads. Repeat for other top wing.

To do the bottom parts of the wings (Fig. 5.7) stitch across wing from the body

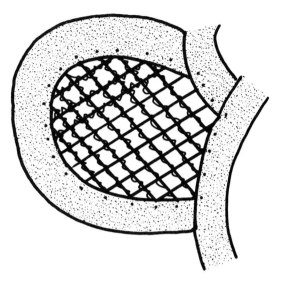

Fig. 5.6 *In the top part of wings, first a grid is stitched, then zigzagged at a 1 width over straight stitch threads, as indicated.*

down. Following the side of the tape with straight stitches, stitch the next branch from bottom of wing across the open space up to the body. Take a stitch into tape to anchor. Stitch another branch, fanning

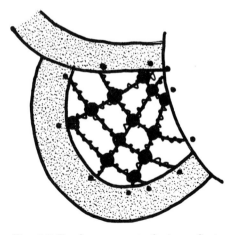

Fig. 5.7 *For bottom part of wings, first a grid is stitched, then circles are stitched around the crossed threads.*

from the body out to the edge of the wing. Following side of the tape again, walk needle over to the left side of wing. Sew across open space to the right side of wing. Repeat for other branches. When those are done, zigzag at 1 stitch width to each cross and stitch a small circle at the crossed thread. Go from one to the next until circles are complete.

Finish zigzagging over the branches, traveling up and back and to the next until they are all covered.

To make the spiderweb head (Fig. 5.8), lay in your threads, then zigzag over them.

To make the body (Fig. 5.9), straight stitch from one side of the tape to the other across the space, then zigzag back with stitch width 1. At the point where the stitches join the fabric and leave it again, zigzag several stitches over both threads to hold them together. Then travel over the next thread. Stitch down to the tape, then back over both threads with a few stitches before zigzagging over the next thread to the other side of the tape to complete the body.

For the butterfly tail (Fig. 5.10), stitch in the same manner, but with all threads

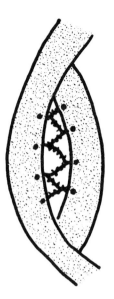

Fig. 5.9 Straight stitch, then zigzag, to create the body of the butterfly.

radiating from one point at top to create a fan effect.

After the lace is stitched, wash out the stabilizer and place the Battenberg between layers of toweling to press.

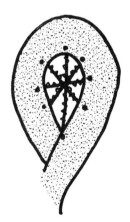

Fig. 5.8 The head is filled in with veins, called Sorrento bars.

Fig. 5.10 Radiating lines create a fan effect to complete the butterfly tail.

Lesson 15. Hemstitching

Hemstitching is a way of binding off groups of threads on a woven fabric with a line or two of small but distinct holes. I love the way my 990 hemstitches. I am able to duplicate hemstitching I've seen on heirloom lingerie, table linens and dresser scarves in a fraction of the time it took to do by hand. Use the single- and double-winged needles with the elastic straight stitch and the Trimotion stitches located on the top row of decorative cassette 2 (2–1 through 2–5). Single and double hemstitches are used to duplicate the hand *Point de Paris* hemstitch. The precise accuracy of the computer enables the needle to stitch into each hole at least twice, so it won't close up after many washings. Make a stitch sampler of your Viking hemstitches for your notebook.

Perfect this delicate technique by making the bonnet that follows. Then see Chapter 11 to stitch your own modern heirloom.

Set up your machine.

Stitch width: 0 to no wider than the needle plate opening when using a double-wing needle
Stitch length: varies
Needle position: center
Needle: single and double-wing needles; 2.0 double needles
Feed dogs: up
Presser foot: utility B or transparent appliqué foot, raised seam foot F
Utility stitch: zigzag
Tension: *top*, normal; *bobbin*, normal
Fabric: crisp fabric, such as organdy or linen
Thread: Zwicky darning thread (size #70 or #100); cotton machine embroidery thread

To thread two needles, follow instructions in the Viking Operating Manual. Remember to always thread your machine with the presser foot up.

Try hemstitching as described in your manual. Start with the single-winged needle and use a zigzag. Stitch a row of hemstitching. At the end of the first run, leave the needle in the hole at left, turn and return, poking into the same holes as on the first run.

You can make an all-over design, covering a large area with hemstitches. This is usually worked on the bias, then appliquéd to something else.

Now practice with the double-wing needle. Set up your machine in this way:

Stitch width: 1.5
Stitch length: 2
Needle position: center
Feed dogs: up
Pressure: normal
Presser foot: utility B or transparent appliqué foot
Utility stitch: zigzag

Make one pass, ending to the left. Lift the presser foot, turn the fabric and stitch the second pass.

Try this blindstitch with the double-wing needle:

Stitch width: 2–3
Stitch length: 2
Needle position: center
Feed dogs: up
Pressure: normal
Presser foot: utility B or transparent appliqué foot
Decorative stitch: reverse blindstitch (2–7)

Turn your hemstitching into shadow work as well. Cut back the piece of organdy underneath, clipping out both sides of the double fabric on either side of the blindstitches.

Project
Infant's Bonnet

I've combined hemstitching with utility stitches, decorative stitches and double needles to make the infant's bonnet shown in Fig. 5.11. Also included is a line of ribbon sewing. This can be made in the time it would take you to shop for a baby gift.

Nora Lou Kampe of LaGrange, Illinois, made this bonnet using embroidered eyelet fabric with a scalloped border — a way to make a baby gift in no more than an hour's time. I used her bonnet idea, but took the long-cut and embroidered the bonnet my-

self; it fits a newborn and you could make one for a christening. A gown can be done in the same hemstitching technique.

The finished bonnet is 13″ × 5¾″ (33.0cm × 14.6cm). Add to both width and length if you're adapting it for an older baby.

Stitch width: varies
Stitch length: varies
Needle position: center, right
Needle: 2mm twin needle; single- and double-wing needles
Feed dogs: up
Pressure: normal

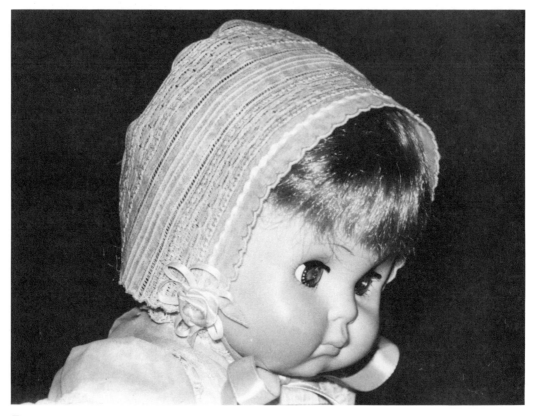

Fig. 5.11 Hemstitching, pintucking, and embroidery decorate the organdy bonnet for an infant or a doll.

Presser foot: utility B or transparent appliqué, narrow braiding, standard foot A, raised seam foot F and guide

Utility or decorative stitch: straight; reverse blindstitch (2–7); closed scallop (2–32)

Tension: *top*, normal; *bobbin*, normal

Fabric suggestion: white cotton organdy

Thread: light-blue, fine machine-embroidery thread; #5 light-blue pearl cotton; white cordonnet

Other supplies: pearl beads (optional); 1/8" (3.2mm) double-faced satin ribbon, approximately 1 yard (91.4cm); 1/4" (6.4mm) double-faced satin ribbon, 1/2 yard (45.7cm); 1/2" (12.7mm) double-faced satin ribbon, approximately 1 1/2 yards (137.1cm)

Accessories: water-erasable or vanishing marker, T-square

Begin with two pieces of organdy, each 18" × 9" (45.7cm × 22.9cm). I start with a much larger area than I need because I practice on the margin–running the decorative stitches so they will match when I do a mirror image.

Wash and iron the organdy. Mark the top fabric lengthwise, using a water-erasable or vanishing marker (Fig. 5.12). Start by marking lines 1" (2.5cm) apart from the front edge. Use a T-square for accuracy. Draw six lines. Then mark a line 1/2"

(12.7mm) from the last line, and another 1/2" (12.7mm) from that one; 7" × 13" (17.7cm × 33.0cm) is marked. Pin the two pieces of fabric together at the top of the lines.

Once you have learned how to hemstitch, the decoration is up to you. The following is only a suggestion: Thread the double-wing needle with light-blue thread. The first line of blindstitches are stitched 1" (2.5cm) from the front edge. Use the blue line as your guide and stitch on top of it. When you reach the end, turn and go back, cutting into the same hole you stitched on the first run. Sew slowly. If the needle does not hit exactly in the right place, stop and move the fabric by one or two threads. Continue.

Spread the fabric apart. The pintucking is done between the blue lines on the top piece only.

Change to the 1.6mm double needle. Use the raised seam foot F, light-blue #5 pearl cotton, feed dogs up, pressure normal, stitch length 2. Thread the raised seam guide with pearl cotton.

There are three lines of pintucking, so stitch the first line exactly in the middle, between the blue marker lines. Stitch the others on either side of this one, using the grooves in the foot as guides.

If you wish, stitch all four groups of

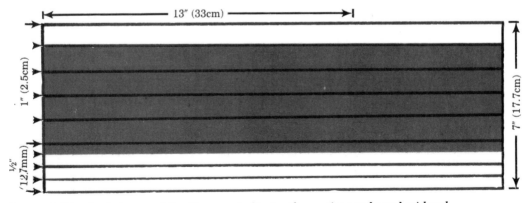

Fig. 5.12 The shaded area of the diagram indicates the portions to be embroidered.

pintucks between the blue lines at one time, then go back. Remove the raised seam foot F and guide. Change to the wing needle, transparent appliqué foot, and continue to hemstitch on the blue lines with the blindstitch. Remember, when you pintuck, work on one layer of fabric, but hemstitch on both layers.

Complete 4½" (11.4cm) of the bonnet (shaded area on Fig. 5.12) by filling in the empty spaces between the blindstitch pattern and the pintucks. Use the open effect of the single-wing needle, sewing in a straight line. Remember to come back again, punching holes in the same places where the first ones were. An even easier method is to use the elastic straight stitch on a 6 length. This way, you stitch one pass only because the stitch takes one stitch forward, two back, creating a nice-looking hole.

Should you still want more decoration, use the hemstitch of your choice. Sew down the sides of the lines of blindstitches. When you have decorated the fabric enough, straight stitch around the edge of the bonnet rectangle. Cut back to the stitching line. Put the piece you've practiced on into your notebook.

Fold the bonnet rectangle in half (Fig. 5.13). The fold will be the top of the bonnet. Pin the fabric together, matching decorative stitches so it is exact. Round off the front corners where the rosettes will be sewn (see Fig. 5.13). Open up and stitch ⅛" (3.2mm) in from the edges of the bottom and front.

Change to a closed scallop design (2–32) or satin stitch to stitch the front edge and the sides of the bonnet. Use a narrow braiding foot, or one that will guide the cord, size #80/11–12 needle, stitch width 4, stitch length 0.5 (or whatever works best for you to cover cord smoothly). Do a sample first.

Thread cordonnet through the clip in the foot. Place the foot with the thread hole on the line of stitching. Hold the cord

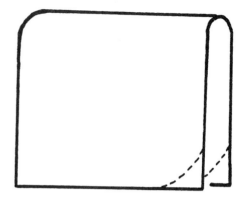

Fig. 5.13 When stitching is completed, fold the rectangle in half and round off the front corners, as shown.

up slightly as you cover it with stitches. When the scallop or satin stitching is completed, clip fabric back from the edge to the stitching, but not too close to the scallops.

Stitch down on the line ½" (12.7mm) from the edge (back of bonnet) and stitch another ½" (12.7mm) from that line. Fold the back under ½" (12.7mm), then again another ½" (12.7mm). Stitch across the first fold to make the ribbon casing.

Next, wind the bobbin with ⅛" (3.2mm) double-faced satin ribbon. Wrap the end onto the bobbin and begin winding by hand. Finish by winding slowly on the machine. Thread it through the tension spring of experimental bobbin case. Loosen tension screw so ribbon pulls through bobbin case with very little drag on it. Insert the bobbin into the machine and bring the ribbon to the top. Pull out at least 8" (20.3cm) of ribbon before beginning to sew. Set the machine for topstitching. Use a 4–6 stitch length.

Use the standard foot A, tension turned up to 6½–7, and needle position to the right. Place the bonnet front on the bed of the machine. The ribbon will be stitched from underneath, ½" (12.7mm) from the front edge. When you finish stitching, pull out 8" (20.3cm) of ribbon and cut it off.

Cut two ½" (12.7mm) satin ribbons,

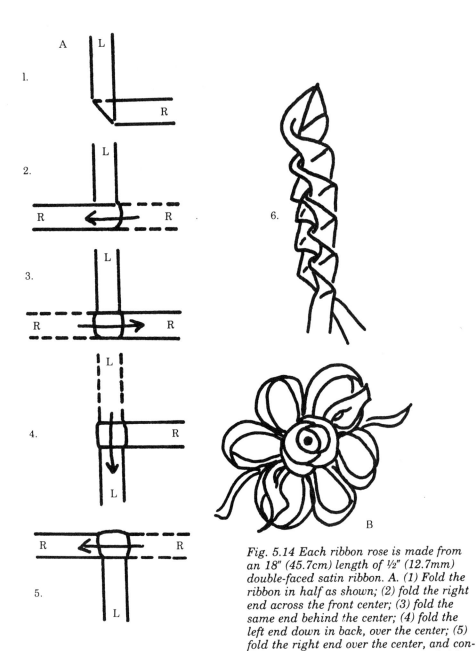

Fig. 5.14 Each ribbon rose is made from an 18" (45.7cm) length of ½" (12.7mm) double-faced satin ribbon. A. (1) Fold the ribbon in half as shown; (2) fold the right end across the front center; (3) fold the same end behind the center; (4) fold the left end down in back, over the center; (5) fold the right end over the center, and continue folding over the center until there are 30 folds between your fingers; (6) holding the last fold between your thumb and forefinger, release the rest of the ribbon, then pull on the ribbon end under the last fold to create the rose. B. By hand, stitch from the back to the center and back again to keep the rose from unwinding. Leave ½" (12.7mm) ends and cut each on a slant. Hold the loops in place with a small ribbon rose or tie small bows at the centers.

each 12″ (30.5cm) long, for the bonnet ties and attach by stitching several zigzag stitches in one place at the rounded corners under the ⅛″ (3.2mm) ribbon.

Make six loops from the 8″ (20.3cm) of ⅛″ (3.2mm) ribbon. Tack them by hand at the center on top of the ribbon ties. Make ribbon roses as shown in Fig. 5.14A, or tiny bows from the ½″ (12.7mm) ribbon and attach these over the loops by hand (Fig. 5.14B). Use double thread. Poke the needle up from the inside of the bonnet, through the ribbon ties, loops, and the center of the flower and a pearl bead. Then poke the needle back through the flower, loops, ribbon tie and bonnet. Do this several times. It's not necessary to go through the bead each time. Anchor the thread underneath.

Thread 18″ (45.7cm) of ¼″ (6.4mm) ribbon through the back casing on the bonnet and pull up to tie into a bow at the back (Fig. 5.15). Cut off at the length you prefer. There you have it—a priceless gift.

Fig. 5.15 Pull on each end of the back ribbon and tie into a bow to shape the crown of the bonnet.

Lesson 16. Stitching in rings

Stitching in rings is like making needlelace (Fig. 5.16). Instead of fabric surrounding a space, in this lesson the thread is attached to narrow gold rings. I selected rings about 2½″ (6.4cm) in diameter as an appropriate size for tree ornaments. See Sources of Supplies for ordering these rings.

Project Christmas Ornaments

A stabilizer isn't always needed when you sew in space. I used to make these Christmas ornaments without a stabilizer and it worked beautifully. But with water-soluble stabilizer underneath, you can stitch more intricate designs, and the thread will stay in one place, as if you were stitching on fabric.

Set up your machine.

Stitch width: 0–6
Stitch length: 0–2.5
Needle position: center
Needle: #80/11–12 all-purpose
Feed dogs: lowered
Pressure: between ∰ and 1
Presser foot: none (990, 980, 950); bare needle for other models
Utility stitch: zigzag

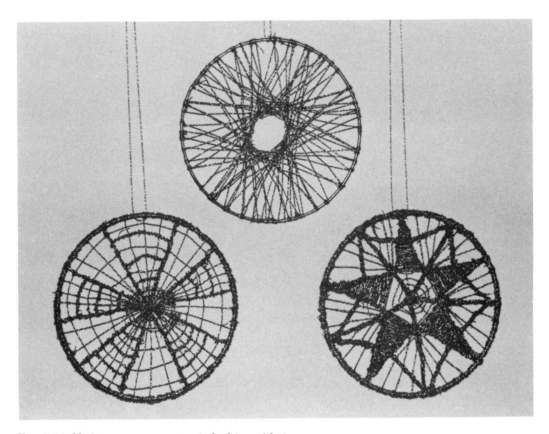

Fig. 5.16 Christmas ornaments stitched in gold rings.

Tension: *top*, normal; *bobbin*, normal
Thread: gold metallic on top and bobbin
Accessories: 2½" (6.4cm) gold ring; 7"
    (17.8cm) spring hoop; permanent white
    marker
Stabilizer: water-soluble

Double the stabilizer and put it into the hoop. Place the gold ring in the center. Draw a design in the ring. If you have a newer Viking, set your zigzag width at 6, all other models set width at 0. Hold ring down by putting foot shank on it.

Dip the needle down at the side of the ring and bring the bobbin thread to the top. Hold the threads to one side. If you

have a 6 stitch width, anchor the ring by zigzagging needle over ring a few times. I sew one stitch at a time, being careful that needle clears the ring. For other models, anchor the ring by hand-walking the needle from the outside to the inside of it. Set width to 0. Stitch from one side to the other several times. Hold onto the ring and stitch across to the other side. The chain of stitches will be tighter if you sew fast but move the hoop slowly. Anchor the thread on the other side by sewing over and back on the ring as you did at first.

Work back across and anchor on the other side. Keep doing this until you have laid in the spokes of the design. Remember,

95

with water-soluble stabilizer you can change direction when stitching in open spaces. After the last anchoring stitches, go back into the ring and finish the piece. It can be symmetrical or not. I feel that the lighter the look, the better. Stitching it too thickly will be a detraction, but you may want to zigzag over threads, as in cutwork, to add variety to the design.

Anchor the last stitches and take the ring out of the hoop. Cut back the stabilizer, then dissolve it by holding the ring under running water. Hang it from your Christmas tree with a cord.

Lesson 17. Making Alençon lace

Alençon lace took its name from the French town. The lace was developed there and was so expensive it was rarely seen, except in shops with a wealthy clientele, where it was sold as yardage and used as trimming for lingerie, dresses, and household items.

On the fine, mesh net background is a heavy design, so closely woven it is almost clothlike. Characteristic of Alençon lace is the heavy thread that outlines the design.

Project
Alençon Pincushion

Our Alençon is made on a single layer of bridal veiling. The design is freely embroidered by machine, then outlined with pearl cotton or cordonnet (Fig. 5.17).

Stitch width: 0
Stitch length: 0–2.5
Needle position: center
Needle: #80/11–12 all-purpose
Feed dogs: lowered
Presser feet: darning foot and utility B or transparent appliqué foot
Utility stitch: straight stitch
Pressure: between # and 1
Tension: *top*, normal; *bobbin*, normal
Fabric suggestion: bridal veil, 36″ × 5″ (91.4cm × 12.7cm); pink satin, 4½″ × 11″ (11.4cm × 28.0cm)

Thread: Zwicky #100 or #120 fine white sewing thread; #8 pearl cotton or cordonnet on bobbin to match
Accessories: 7″ (17.8cm) spring hoop; permanent white marker; 2 cups of sawdust
Stabilizer: tear-away and water-soluble

Prepare a sample of your stitching to be sure it looks like you want it to. I like a slight bubbly look to the pearl cotton, but

Fig. 5.17 Alençon lace pincushion.

you may want a tighter stitch. If so, tighten the top tension.

Put the water-soluble stabilizer in the hoop. Place it over the design and copy it with the permanent marker (Fig. 5.18). Then place the veiling over the stabilizer in the hoop.

Thread with fine thread in the top and bobbin. Bring the bobbin thread to the top and hold both threads to one side. After stitching a few stitches, clip these ends off. I don't anchor the threads as they will be sewn in anyway. Outline the design first with straight stitches.

When completed, go back and stitch in the petals and leaves. Sew a line next to the outline, then another within that and another, and so on until you have filled it in. If some of the lines overlap, don't despair, as this will happen. Just try to keep from building up heavy stitching lines.

It's not necessary to cut the thread as you complete one section and start another. Loosen the top thread by lifting up on the presser foot and turning the handwheel or tappng the foot pedal if necessary. Slowly pull or push the hoop to the next place. There's no need to bring up the bobbin thread again, as long as it is still connected to the fabric.

When finished stitching, go back and clip threads between motifs. Bring long threads to the back to be clipped and dotted with a drop of Fray-Check. Use tweezers to pull out loose threads on the back.

Change the bobbin to the one containing pearl cotton. I use the experimental bobbin case, pearl cotton through bobbin tension. Loosen bobbin tension so cord pulls like normal sewing thread. Tighten upper tension to 7. Take the veiling out of the hoop and turn it over. The topside of the lace

Fig. 5.18 Lace pincushion design.

will be underneath. Double check the tensions by sewing on another piece of veiling in another hoop. The pearl cotton should lay flat underneath without pulling; yet it should not be so loose it looks loopy.

Dip the needle into the veil and bring the pearl cotton to the top. Hold it to one side as you begin: Don't anchor it. Outline the design. It is very important to keep from going over lines too many times. You want it to be thick, but not ugly.

When you complete outlining, cut off the pearl cotton, bringing any long ends to the back. Work those under a few stitches on back by hand and clip them off. Put your lace, still in the hoop, under the faucet to wash out the stabilizer.

Measure the top of the pincushion. The finished size will be 4″ × 5″ (10.2cm × 12.7cm) so add ½″ (12.7mm) to each measurement; 4½″ × 5½″ (11.4cm × 14.0cm). Cut two pieces of pink satin this size. Stitch the lace to one of the rectangles. Seam allowance is ¼″ (6.4mm).

Cut a piece of veiling 36″ (91.4cm) long (twice the perimeter of the pincushion), and 5″ (12.7cm) wide. Cut a piece of tearaway stabilizer the same length and 2″ (5.1cm) wide. Pin the cut edges of the veiling together to hold it in place. Slip tearaway under the fold. Set your machine to satin stitch or use the closed scallop stitch (2–31 or 2–32).

With feed dogs up and the right edge of the B or transparent appliqué foot placed just within the edge of the fold, stitch width 4, length at 0.4 (or whatever would give you an attractive stitch), sew down the length of the veiling and cut back to the stitching. Wash out the stabilizer.

To gather the ruffle, zigzag over cordonnet (see Lesson 4). Stitch the length of the cut edges (stitch length 2, stitch width 2). Use the cord to gather the ruffle.

Join the two ends of the ruffle by placing one end over the other about ½″ (12.7mm). Using a 2 stitch width, and 0.4 length, satin stitch down the width of the piece of veiling. Cut back to the line of stitching on both sides.

Gather the ruffle, placing the seam at a corner. Corners should be heavily gathered to make sure they lay beautifully when completed. Distribute the ruffles around the edge of the pincushion. Remember that the embroidered edge will be toward the *center* of the pincushion. Stitch in place. It's not necessary to remove the cordonnet.

The last step is to sew the back of the pincushion to the lace. Place right sides together, and work all the net ruffles inside as you pin around the edge.

Sew within the stitching line on front. Leave a large enough opening so you can turn the pincushion to the outside. When turned, fill it very tightly with sawdust (or use another filler, if you prefer). Stitch the opening shut by hand.

Do you like making lace? Try other variations by using utility stitches, satin-stitch or Pictogram star flowers, or bands of intertwined cordonnet at the edges.

CHAPTER **6**

Drawing Threads Out of Your Fabric

■ **Lesson 18. Needleweaving**

To create an area of free, lacy openwork called needleweaving, first draw threads out of a fabric, then stitch over the remaining threads. On this long-cut, I used exactly the same color thread on the top and bobbin as that of the dress; I'm constantly being asked how it was stitched. The solution to the mystery follows.

Lesson 18. Needleweaving

Because needleweaving is worked in a straight line, I chose to decorate the sleeves of a summer dress (Fig. 6.1). I knew this dress would be washed many times, so I chose a polyester sewing thread for durability. I matched it perfectly, both spool and bobbin, with the fabric.

First do a small sample of needleweaving for your notebook. The openwork is 1″ (2.5cm) wide. Pull out a horizontal thread at the top and the bottom where the openwork will be. Straight stitch across those lines. Then pull out the horizontal or weft threads in that space.

Project
Openwork
on Sleeves

You will machine stitch over the vertical or warp threads, drawing them close together as you zigzag. To arrange threads into groups, use the rickrack (2–1) stitch on the longest stitch length, 4.5. Place fabric under transparent appliqué foot so half of the stitch falls into the pulled thread area and the other half of the stitch falls onto the fabric. This makes it easier to zigzag stitch the bars (Fig. 6.2).

Stitch width: 0–6
Stitch length: 0–0.5
Needle position: center
Needle: #80/11–12 all-purpose
Feed dogs: lowered, up
Pressure: between # and 1; normal
Presser foot: transparent appliqué; darning, or no presser foot
Tension: *top*, normal, loosened; *bobbin*, normal
Utility stitch: zigzag
Fabric suggestion: loosely woven
Thread: Zwicky polyester
Stabilizer: tear-away, or construction paper to match thread; water-soluble (optional)

Take off the regular presser foot and use the darning foot. Try working without a

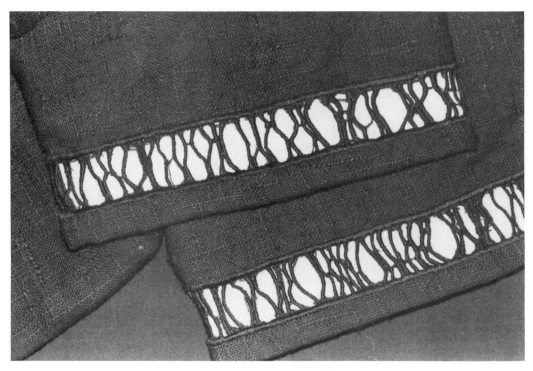

Fig. 6.1 Needleweaving decorates the sleeves on a summer dress.

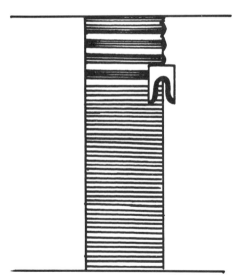

Fig. 6.2 Use rickrack stitch to arrange threads into groups.

hoop on this project. The stitching goes fast and a hoop would only slow you down.

You may stitch with water-soluble stabilizer behind your work, but that is optional. Prepare your machine for embroidery by lowering the feed dogs. Release pressure to between # and 1. Be sure the presser bar is down before you start to stitch. Dip the needle down and bring the bobbin thread to the top. Anchor the threads. Set the machine on stitch width 4–6 and normal tension.

Using both hands, grasp the top and bottom of the fabric between your fingers, stretching it slightly as you stitch. Keep the fabric as close as you can to the needleplate, and keep tension on the warp threads.

Begin to move from just below the stitched line at the bottom to just over the stitched line on top. Move the fabric slowly, but sew at a comfortable speed, catching several warp threads together as you zigzag to the top.

When you reach the top, move sideways to the next several warp threads and begin stitching those together. About halfway down, move the fabric to the side and catch a few stitches into the previous group of zigzagged threads (Fig. 6.3). Then move back and continue to the bottom of the threads. Finish all the warp threads in the same manner, satin stitching up and down, while at the same time catching threads from the previous run in one or two places. This adds interest and strength to your openwork and is an integral part of your needleweaving.

After finishing, remove water-soluble stabilizer and pull the piece back into shape while damp. Press.

If you did not use stabilizer, then spray with water to enable you to pull it into shape. Press.

Draw two horizontal lines (one inch apart and as long as your needleweaving) across a piece of construction paper or tear-away stabilizer. Place your needleweaving on top of this, using the drawn lines as guides to keep the open area straight.

Set up your machine for straight stitching with feed dogs up and the transparent appliqué foot on. Sew a line of straight stitches across the top and bottom on the same guidelines you stitched at the beginning. This will hold the needleweaving in place and stabilize it for the final stitching.

Set the machine to a wide zigzag, feed dogs still up, stitch length 0.4–0.8 (or whatever will result in a perfect satin stitch). The upper tension on the 990, 980, and 950 loosens automatically. For other models, loosen tension slightly and satin stitch over those lines, covering the edges in two passes — the first narrower and more open than the second. This takes longer, but the results are more profes-

Fig. 6.3 Pull out warp threads from the fabric and zigzag freely over the remaining wefts. Then finish the edges on each side with satin stitching.

101

sional-looking. The stitching will fall just to one side of the fabric and will catch the fabric on the other side to neatly finish the edge of the needlelace. Tear off the stabilizer and steam press the embroidery carefully.

If the stabilizer can still be seen behind the stitches, it may be possible to remove it by dampening it, then using a tweezers to remove it. Or use this trick: if you can find a permanent marker the same color as the thread, dab in the color where necessary.

Try needleweaving across the yoke or pocket of a blouse, or down the middle of sleeves, or combine two rows of this with lacy spiderweb circles scattered between.

If you don't like the see-through look, or if you want to add another color, back the open area with another fabric.

You are more than halfway through *Know Your Viking.* Do *you* know your Viking?

CHAPTER 7

Layering Fabrics: Quilting

- ■ **Lesson 19. Quilting with feed dogs up**
- ■ **Lesson 20. Quilting with feed dogs lowered**
- ■ **Lesson 21. Trapunto**
- ■ **Lesson 22. Italian cording**

I've always taken time to make handmade gifts for special people. But if I make a crib quilt, for example, I'd like to know that the baby won't be twice as long as the quilt by the time the gift is presented. If I'm sewing clothes, I'm realistic: I want the garment to be in style when the recipient opens the box.

So, although I love hand quilting and hand sewing, they often take too long. Machine quilting, on the other hand, is speedy and sturdy. You can use heavy fabrics like corduroy, as well as thick batts, and you will have no trouble stitching them together. If machine quilting is done properly, it can be as fine as handwork.

In this chapter I've included quilting with the feed dogs lowered and in place, trapunto, and Italian cording.

Remember several things when doing any type of quilting. The first is to pre-shrink all fabrics. I usually use cotton poly-ester blends for my quilts so they stay new-looking for a long time. Sheets are excellent backing materials. They come in a myriad of colors and prints, can be of excellent quality, and they won't have to be pieced. When I make a quilt, I use a sheet that is larger than the top.

I usually quilt with a polyester sewing thread. Most brands come in a wealth of colors. Should I want to emphasize the stitching line, I will double the thread. But when I sew on a patterned material or a fabric that changes color throughout, I choose a monofilament. I may or may not use monofilament on the bobbin, depending upon the samples I do first.

Using safety pins instead of hand basting is my favorite method of holding the fabrics and batt together before I quilt. I don't use dressmaker's pins because many of them fall out before the quilt is completed—and those that don't usually stab me.

Lesson 19. Quilting with feed dogs up

Instead of a regular presser foot, I use the dual feed foot when I sew lines of straight quilting stitches. It minimizes puckering on the backing fabric, as the top and bottom fabrics are fed through at the same speed with no slipping.

Before I had one of those helpful accessories, I grasped the quilt in both hands and kept it taut as it fed through the machine. As I progressed, I stopped and looked underneath to be sure I had a smooth lining. I must admit I became an expert at sewing without puckers. It may take a little longer, but the lack of a dual feed foot should not deter you from starting your first quilt experiment.

Can you imagine how fast you could make a quilt using striped fabric or a striped sheet for the top? Use the stripes as quilting lines. If you use stripes for garments, keep in mind that the more rows of quilting, the smaller the piece becomes. I either quilt the fabric first and then cut out the pattern, or I cut my pattern larger than necessary, do the quilting and then lay the pattern back on it when finished. I recut the pattern where necessary.

If you piece a quilt and decide to machine quilt it by using stitch-in-a-ditch, you may prefer using the blind hem D or buttonhole C foot. Stitch-in-a-ditch is done on top of the quilt by stitching in the seam lines (the ditches). With the C or D foot, it is easy to stitch exactly in the ditch because the inside edge of the right toe and the needle positioning can be set for accuracy.

Project
Tote Bag Square (Appliqué and Quilting)

This quilted sample can be used as a square for the tote bag in Chapter 12. It includes appliqué, satin stitches, and sewing with feed dogs up (Fig. 7.1).

Stitch width: 0–4
Stitch length: 0–2.5
Needle position: center
Feed dogs: up
Pressure: normal
Presser foot: transparent appliqué foot
Utility stitch: zigzag
Needle: #80/11–12 all-purpose

Tension: *top*, slightly loosened; *bobbin*, normal
Thread: Sulky or Zwicky cotton in green, yellow and dark purple to match fabrics
Fabric: one 9″ (22.9cm) square of Christmas red cotton for background; three 9″ (22.9cm) squares in green, yellow and dark purple; 10″ (25.4cm) square of fleece
Accessories: water-erasable or vanishing marker; Wonder-Under or fusible webbing and Teflon pressing sheet; tracing paper and pencil
Stabilizer: iron-on freezer paper

There are five fabrics used in this quilted square. Iron freezer paper to back of red 9″ (22.9cm) square. Back green, yellow and dark purple with fusible web or Wonder-Under following manufacturers instructions (or see Chapter 1).

Trace the design in Fig. 7.1 and cut apart. Place each piece on fabric and draw around it with a water-erasable marker. Have you noticed how butting pieces of appliqué next to each other usually leaves gaping areas, no matter how careful you are? To prevent this, plan to overlap adjacent pieces by ¼″ (6.4mm) so you don't have two raw edges to sew over. Decide ahead of time which side of each piece will have a seam allowance that can be slipped under the corner fabric next to it. If you use this method, you'll have only one edge to cover with satin stitches. Cut appliqué shapes and fuse them to red background. I fused the green first, then the yellow, and finished with the purple.

Set your machine to satin stitch, a hair narrower and longer than the numbers you will use on the second and final pass. On the second pass, use a stitch width 4 and close satin-stitch length 0.4. Sew at a moderate speed and always turn with the needle in the fabric.

When you have finished satin stitching the fabric in place, back the piece with fleecy Pellon, slightly larger than the

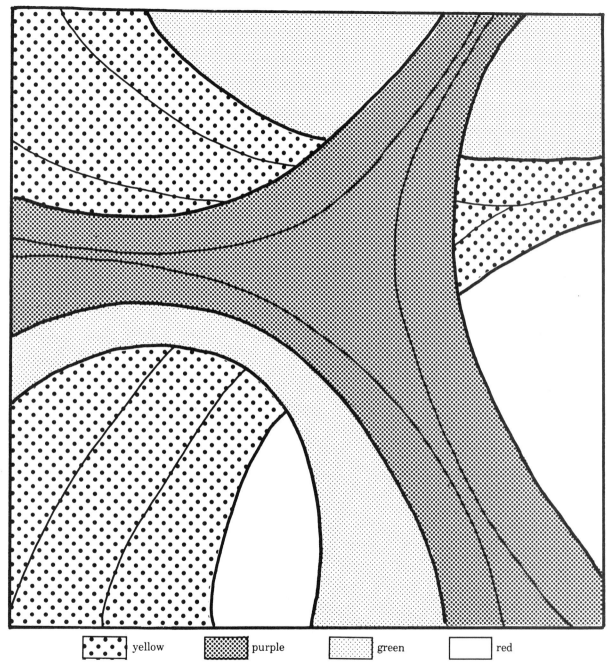

Fig. 7.1 Appliquéd and quilted tote bag square.

square, and under that slip a piece of tear-away stabilizer. Go back and stitch (stitch width 0, stitch length 2) down each side of the satin stitches. This not only adds to the quilted look, but it gives the satin stitches a clean finish.

Then echo quilt the square on a 2.5 stitch length, using a color that matches each fabric (or use monofilament thread).

Finish the square as described in Chapter 12.

Lesson 20. Quilting with feed dogs lowered

As you can tell from the lesson title, this will be free-machine quilting. The machine setting will not control the length of the stitches; you will. If you move the fabric fast, the stitches will be longer than if you move it slowly. Not working in a hoop, you must use a darning foot to prevent skipped stitches. And no hoop means you must hold the fabric taut while stitching.

Stitch width: 0
Stitch length: 0–2.5
Needle position: center
Needle: #90/14 stretch
Feed dogs: lowered
Pressure: between # and 1
Presser foot: darning foot
Utility stitch: straight stitch
Tension: *top*, normal; *bottom*, normal
Fabric suggestion: medium-weight cotton; fleece or quilt batting
Thread: machine embroidery
Accessories: air-soluble or water-erasable marker

One of the easiest ways to learn free quilting and to practice control at the same time is to quilt around the motifs of a printed fabric as shown in Fig. 7.2. Even the underside looks terrific: you may like the looks of the lining better than the printed side. If so, it makes for a stunning reversible jacket.

When quilting any fabrics with feed dogs lowered, don't place the stitching lines too closely together, unless you want to emphasize the area that *isn't* stitched. Closely stitched, it will be too stiff and you'll lose the contrast of light and dark shadowing that makes this type of machining so effective.

Fig. 7.2 Cotton print, batting and velveteen are quilted together by stitching the butterfly design.

Lesson 21. Trapunto

In trapunto, two pieces of fabric are stitched together, following a design. Then the quilter selects the areas of the design to be stuffed with fiberfill. Usually trapunto is done from underneath the fabrics.

Layer two pieces of material together and use the felt flower design in Fig. 4.5 (Lesson 10). Transfer the design to the top fabric. Place both fabrics in a hoop. Stitch in the design, using machine embroidery thread the same color as the fabric, with your machine set up for free-machine embroidery or feed dogs up and embroidery foot on. Stitch in the design. Make small slits in the backing fabric behind the petals, leaves, or stamens—or all three.

Add fiberfill, poking it in with a tool that is not sharply pointed. Whip stitch the slits closed by hand.

You can trapunto from the top by appliquéing on top of a base fabric. Slip filling inside the appliqué before you've attached it all the way around. You may want to add stitches over the surface of the appliqué to hold the stuffing firmly and to embellish the design.

Lesson 22. Italian cording

Italian cording is often mistaken for trapunto. The difference is that the area to be stuffed in Italian cording will be the space between two stitching lines. Instead of using fiberfill, thread a cord of appropriate size through the double lines of stitching.

It's also possible to create the look of Italian cording in one pass of the machine, on one layer of fabric when stitching with a double needle. Thread gimp or pearl cotton through the raised seam guide and it will be caught between the lines of stitching by the bobbin thread.

Project
Tote Bag Square (Italian Cording)

This square (Fig. 7.3) was done using a single needle.

Stitch width: 0
Stitch length: 2–2.5
Needle position: center

Needle: #80/11–12 sharp or all purpose
Feed dogs: up
Pressure: normal
Presser foot: transparent appliqué
Utility stitch: straight stitch
Tension: *top*, normal; *bobbin*, normal
Fabric suggestions: lightweight cotton for top; stiffer cotton for backing
Thread: Sulky or Zwicky machine embroidery cotton
Cord: appropriate-size acrylic yarn or cable cord
Accessories: hand-sewing needle; large-eyed hand-sewing tapestry needle to thread cord through the design; water-erasable or vanishing marker

Draw your design on the fabric with a water-erasable or vanishing marker, indicating where the lines will cross and which ones cross over, which under.

When you are stitching the lines, don't anchor threads when the lines cross. Instead, pull several inches of thread out of the needle. Hold the thread to one side. Skip over the intersection; then begin

Fig. 7.3 Italian cording tote bag square.

108

stitching again. When finished, go back and clip the threads in the middle. Thread up a sewing needle and poke all the top threads through to the back and work them in. Finish up by working the cord through the design by hand.

It's difficult to turn corners with cording and make those corners look sharp. Poke the needle out of the back fabric at a corner, and then back in again in the same place, leaving a small loop of the cord out in back.

When working with a double needle, turn corners in three steps. Stitch to the corner. Stop. Needles should be grazing the fabric. Lift the presser foot. Half-turn the fabric. Lower the presser foot and turn the wheel by hand to make one stitch. Raise the needles and again bring the needle points down to barely touch the top of the fabric. Lift the presser foot again and complete the turn. Lower the presser foot and continue stitching.

Directions for finishing the square are in Chapter 12.

Look for inspirations for Italian cording in books on Celtic designs or bargello borders.

CHAPTER **8**

Adding Interesting Seams to Your Fabric

■ **Lesson 23. French handsewing by machine**
■ **Lesson 24. Seaming with feed dogs up and lowered**

In previous chapters, the emphasis was on decorative stitchery. In Chapters 8 and 9, the focus is on sewing. The chapters are so closely related that at times they even overlap. Included in Chapters 8 and 9 are many of the sewing long-cuts I mentioned in the Preface and Chapter 1. But now, instead of decorating a garment by embroidering or appliquéing on it, you'll learn to make the garment unique by changing the seams, hems and edges.

Let's face it: seams are not always interesting. Most of them are hidden and it's not necessary that they do anything but hold two pieces of fabric together. On the other hand, seams can be the focal point of your creation. This chapter includes seams for the finest lace to the heaviest canvas — seams purely practical and those that combine decoration with practicality. Stitch up samples of all of them for your notebook. You'll discover that knowing your sewing machine is a joy.

The project in this chapter is a wedding handkerchief (Fig. 8.1). After learning how to accomplish French handsewing on the machine, work this project. It can also be used as a pillow top.

Lesson 23. French handsewing by machine

When I first heard about the type of clothing construction called French handsewing, I thought it was something new—until Marcia Strickland, a friend from Birmingham, Alabama, showed me her daughters' dresses. They were made of laces, with pintucks and embroidery, entredeaux and hemstitching, and looked like our family's christening gown. I knew French handsewing; I just hadn't been acquainted with the term. We'd always called it "sewing by hand" and I had agonized over it years ago, when I was sure I'd be struck blind by the tiny stitches before I made it through junior high school. It was hard for me to believe that I could accomplish the perfection of Marcia's clothing on my sewing machine (called "French handsewing by machine" or "French machine sewing").

It's possible to find lace and tucked blouses, skirts and dresses in any department store today. Because this feminine look is expensive in ready-to-wear, if you learn the following hand-sewing techniques by machine and sew them yourself, you will save money and have a lot of fun besides.

Fig. 8.1 French handsewn wedding handkerchief stitched on my Viking.

First, I had to learn basics before I could stitch collars or dresses. Marcia taught me that if I apply fabric to lace, one of the rules of French handsewing is that I must always have entredeaux between.

Entredeaux literally means "between two." It is purchased by the yard in fabric shops or you can make your own (see next section). The fabric on either side of the ladderlike strip down the center is trimmed off before it is attached. I also learned that the holes in entredeaux are never evenly spaced, no matter how expensive it is.

Marcia suggested size 100 pure cotton thread and #70 needle for sewing. She uses an extra-fine thread because the batiste fabric used is extremely lightweight, and stitches are visible when attaching lace and entredeaux or stitching pintucks. And she suggests using cotton thread for heirlooms because it will last a long time.

When handsewing, Marcia chooses cotton batiste because it is easier to roll and whip the edges of cotton. Polyester or cotton/polyester blends have minds of their own. It's hard to roll them as they keep unrolling while you try to whip them in place.

But French machine sewing can easily

be done on blends, so I often choose a cotton/polyester for fabric (and thread), as it doesn't wrinkle like pure cotton.

I learned so much from Marcia, I filled a notebook with samples, ideas, and short-cuts. When you stitch up samples for your own notebook, if a technique can be done several ways, do them all and then decide which works best for you. The following techniques are all you need to learn for French machine sewing.

Making entredeaux

Entredeaux is quite expensive when purchased by the yard. However, you can make your own with the double-wing nee-dle and one of the utility stitches on your Viking.

Stitch width: 0
Stitch length: 3.5
Needle position: center
Needle: double-wing
Feed dogs: up
Pressure: normal
Presser foot: utility B or transparent appliqué
Utility stitch: elastic straight stitch
Tension: *top*, normal; *bobbin*, normal
Fabric suggestion: cotton organdy
Thread: white or ivory Zwicky darning thread #60/2 or #70/2

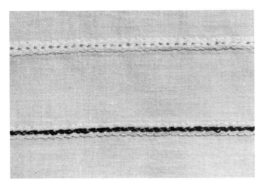

Fig. 8.2 Entredeaux made on my Viking from a strip of cotton organdy.

Cut a strip of cotton organdy *across* the grain, 1″ (2.5cm) wide. On a single layer, stitch the length of fabric strip down the middle. The needle takes two stitches for-ward, one back, so the hole poked by the wing needle is bound open and will with-stand washing or dry cleaning. Remove your work and press strip flat. Turn strip around and guide it so the wing needle tracks back in the large holes created by the first row of stitching (Fig. 8.2). In a few minutes, you can stitch all the entredeaux you'll ever need.

Sewing French seams

French seams are used on lightweight, transparent fabrics to finish the seams beautifully, disguising raw edges. They are also found on smocked garments as a fine finish.

The seams are accomplished in two dif-ferent operations (Fig. 8.3). Begin with fabric pieces wrong sides together. If you have a 990, stitch the seam, using a #70/9 needle, fine sewing thread and the tricot stitch on the preset setting. For other mod-els, use a straight stitch, length 2, or tiny zigzag 1 width, 1 length. Open and press seam to one side. Cut back the seam allow-ance evenly, to ⅛″ (3.2mm). If you have used the tricot stitch or tiny zigzag, trim fabric very close to the stitch. Turn the fabric back over the raw edges, press again (the seam will be at the edge), pin, and stitch again, enclosing the ⅛″ (3.2mm) seam allowance. By trimming close to the zigzag stitches before the fabric is folded back over the seam allowance, no madden-ing wispy threads poke out to ruin the per-fect French seam.

Stitching rolled and whipped edges

Rolled and whipped edges (Fig. 8.3) are always used in conjunction with French handsewing because each piece of fabric must have a finished edge before it is at-

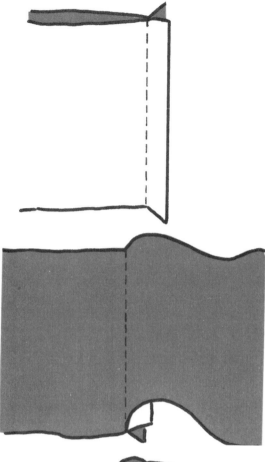

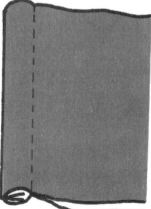

tached to lace or to entredeaux. When working by machine, sometimes you can finish the edge at the same time you attach it to the lace. These edges can be worked several ways and everyone seems to have her own favorite.

Settings for both the standard A and narrow braiding foot follow:

Stitch width: 1
Stitch length: 0.4
Needle position: center
Needle: #70/9
Feed dogs: up
Tension: *top*, normal; *bobbin*, normal
Fabric: Cotton batiste
Thread: #100 cotton
Utility stitch: zigzag

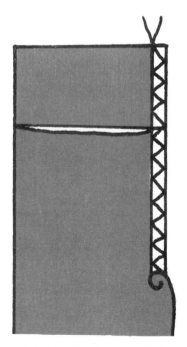

Fig. 8.3 To construct French seams, place fabrics wrong sides together, stitch the seam, trim to ⅛" (3.2mm), then fold the fabric back over the seam allowance and stitch down outside the allowance.

Fig. 8.4 Rolled and whipped edges, started by stitching first on a piece of scrap fabric, then placing the good fabric directly in front of the scrap to begin the roll and whip at the edge.

113

Start the edge so even the first thread in the fabric will be rolled and whipped: Feed a small piece of scrap fabric—about 2″ (5.1cm) long—under the foot. Use the same fabric you will be sewing on. The edge should be placed to the right of the center of the standard A or narrow braiding foot.

Stitch, holding the threads from the top and bobbin until the fabric begins to roll. As it rolls and as you approach the end of the scrap fabric, butt the good fabric up to it (see Fig. 8.4). It will also roll, beginning exactly at the edge. Later you will cut off the scrap fabric.

I also like working a rolled and whipped edge with the raised seam foot F.

Stitch width: 4
Stitch length: 1
Needle position: center
Tension: *top*, 8; *bobbin*, normal
Pressure: normal
Fabric: batiste, work with wrong side up
Presser foot: raised seam foot F
Utility stitch: zigzag

When first starting, guide raw edge against the inside of the right toe. Hold threads to the back. The toe helps curl fabric and the space between the toes keeps fabric curled before it is stitched.

Gathering rolled and whipped edges

Before you roll and whip, thread top and bobbin with normal sewing thread. Loosen top tension slightly. Straight stitch (stitch length 2) along the edge of the fabric. Instead of anchoring your threads, leave several inches (centimeters) of thread at the beginning and end of the stitching. Rethread top and bobbin with fine thread and return tension to normal. Starting at the top again, overcast the edge as you did for rolling and whipping (Fig. 8.5A). The straight stitching must not be caught in these zigzags.

Hold the thread ends at the beginning of your line of straight stitching to keep them from slipping through as you gather. Pull on the bobbin thread at the other end of the line of straight stitches and evenly distribute the ruffling (Fig. 8.5B). *Hint:* If you use an off-white thread in bobbin for gathering stitches, it is easier to find later.

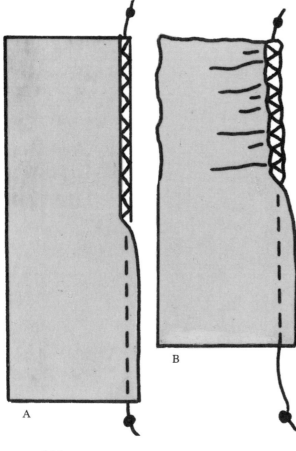

A

B

Fig. 8.5 Gathering a rolled and whipped edge. A. Sew a line of straight stitches along the edge of the fabric, then roll and whip over the line of stitching. B. Gather the material by pulling on the bobbin thread from the line of straight stitches.

114

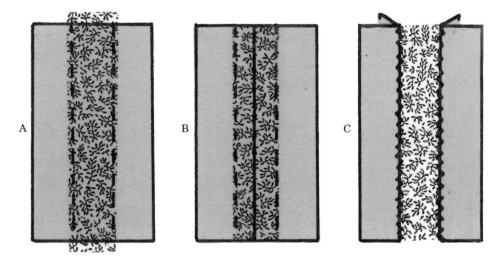

Fig. 8.6 A. Sew lace insert to fabric by straight stitching down each side of the lace. B. Cut through the fabric behind the lace from top to bottom. C. Turn back the seam allowances on both sides and zigzag down the edges of the insertion. Trim the seam allowances back to the stitching.

Applying insertion

Insertion is lace with two straight sides. It is easily applied by machine (Fig. 8.6). Draw two lines the width of the lace on the fabric. Pin the lace inside the lines. Machine straight stitch down both sides of the lace to hold it in place. Cut straight down the fabric behind the lace. Fold the seam allowances back and press.

Then zigzag over the edges of the lace and the straight stitching to attach the lace and finish the edges simultaneously. Cut the seam allowances back to the stitching.

Apply scalloped lace as an insertion by placing it on the fabric and basting it down both sides. Zigzag closely over the edge, following the scallop. Cut away the fabric underneath. This method can also be used for straight-edge insertion, but the join will not be as strong as folding back the seam allowance and stitching over the doubled fabric.

Joining scalloped lace

Find the most heavily patterned place in the design to join scalloped lace. Overlap two identical patterns, and stitch a fine zigzag (stitch width 1, stitch length 0.8) with feed dogs up. Follow the edge of the design as shown in Fig. 8.7. Trim back to the line of stitching.

Using entredeaux

Entredeaux is used between fabric and lace. Only the ladderlike strip of stitching down the center of the entredeaux is attached.

Stitch width: 2 or adjust
Stitch length: 1–1.5
Needle position: center
Needle: #70/9 all-purpose
Feed dogs: up
Pressure: normal
Presser foot: buttonhole C or transparent appliqué foot

115

Fig. 8.7 Join two pieces of lace together by overlapping the design at each end, zigzagging the "seam," then cutting back the surplus lace to the stitches.

Utility stitch: zigzag
Tension: *top*, normal; *bobbin*, normal
Fabric suggestions: batiste
Thread: #100

Measure the length of entredeaux you will need and cut off the fabric on only one side. Attach that side. Place the topside of the entredeaux to the topside of the rolled and whipped edge, the entredeaux on top, as shown at left in Fig. 8.8. Be sure the edges touch. Hand walk the machine through the first couple of stitches to be sure the needle is clearing the edge on the

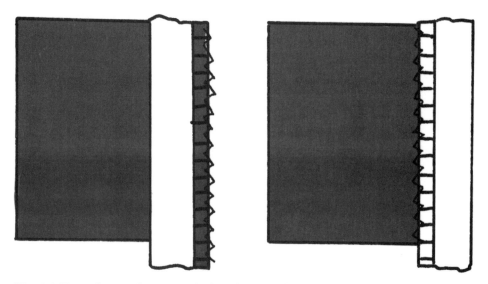

Fig. 8.8 To apply entredeaux to rolled and whipped edges, place it on the fabric, right sides together. Zigzag into each hole and off the edges. Then press open.

116

right side and falls into the holes of the entredeaux on the left (Fig. 8.8). Don't worry if the needle skips a hole in the entredeaux once in awhile, because it won't show. Sew with your Viking set on moderate speed. When finished, pull the entredeaux to the side away from the fabric and press (at right in Fig. 8.8). Repeat for the other side.

Gathering lace edging

There are several threads at the edges of lace. Use a pin to find the one that gathers the lace and then pull up the thread. Hold onto both ends of this thread, or you might pull it all the way through when gathering the lace. Evenly space the gathers.

Attaching straight-edged lace to rolled and whipped edges

Place the topside of the lace against the topside of the fabric (Fig. 8.9). Be sure the edges are even. Use a zigzag at a setting of stitch width 2 and length 1. The needle should stitch within the edges of lace and

fabric on the left, and stitch off of them on the right swing (Fig. 8.9). Flatten out and press.

Attaching entredeaux to lace insertion

Stitch width: 2, or adjust
Stitch length: 1, or adjust
Presser foot: buttonhole C or standard foot A
Utility stitch: zigzag

Trim fabric from one side of the entredeaux. With topsides up, place the trimmed edge of the entredeaux up next to the edge of the lace.

Zigzag the edges together so the needle barely catches the lace and goes into each hole of the entredeaux (Fig. 8.10). Start by using a 2 stitch width and 1 stitch length, but make adjustments in these figures if you find they are needed.

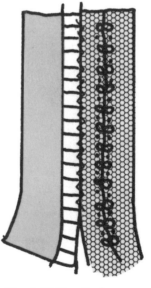

Fig. 8.10 To attach entredeaux to lace insertion, place edges next to each other and zigzag together.

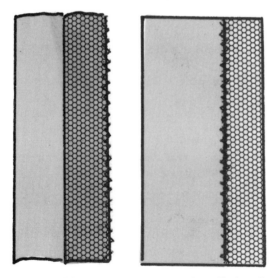

Fig. 8.9 Place insertion on top of a rolled and whipped edge; zigzag to attach. Press open.

117

Sewing lace to lace

Stitch width: 2–3
Stitch length: 1–2
Presser foot: standard foot A
Utility stitch: zigzag

Use the standard A foot and butt the edges of the two laces together, right sides up. Use stitch width 3, stitch length 2. Sew the length of the lace.

Fagoting

There are times when we need different detailing on a bodice, sleeve or skirt. It may not be called for in the pattern, but it's a way to make that garment our own, so we choose to take a long-cut and add a creative touch of our choosing to the original pattern.

Fagoting is one way to change a seam or add one. With your Viking, you need only a special marking foot, since it's like making fringe.

Stitch width: 2–3
Stitch length: 0.8
Presser foot: special marking, standard A or transparent appliqué foot
Utility stitch: zigzag

Make a sample first. Loosen the top tension on your machine to 4 and put the special marking foot on. Place two pieces of fabric with right sides together. Stitch along the seam line. When the line is completed, pull the seam open to reveal the stitches. Change to the transparent appliqué foot. Choose a decorative stitch or even straight stitch to sew each side of the fabric close to the fold. You may need stabilizer underneath your work on finer fabrics.

Go even further with fagoting and bundle the stitches: Put on standard A foot. Use the elastic straight stitch, length 3 or 4. Test to see which you like better. Center foot over fagoting and sew. The stitch automatically groups fagoting into little bundles (Fig. 8.11).

Fig. 8.11 Fagoting and bundling stitches for an open seam.

Use fagoting above the hem of a skirt or pocket, around a sleeve or square collar.

Special marking foot techniques

The special marking foot has a lot of decorative applications. It can be used for floral or circular motifs to create chenille-type texture, or it can be cut through the middle and used as a fine fringe trim or border. Here's how.

Stitch width: 4–5
Stitch length: 0.6–0.8
Needle position: center
Needle: #80/11–12 all-purpose
Feed dogs: up
Pressure: normal
Presser foot: special marking foot; transparent appliqué

118

Utility stitch: zigzag
Tension: *top*, preset (990, 980, 950), slightly
    loosened for other models; *bobbin*, nor-
    mal
Fabric suggestions: firmly woven cotton or
    terrycloth fingertip towel
Thread: two Zwicky cotton threads through
    needle, bobbin threaded normally;
    thread to contrast with fringe
Accessories: water-erasable or vanishing
    marker
Stabilizer: tear-away

Before stitching your notebook sample, test-sew fringe on a scrap to fine-tune tension and stitch length. Threads should stand away from the fabric and be close together without bunching up. Depending on background fabric, it may be easier to use stabilizer under your work.

Draw motif on background fabric or fingertip towel with marker. Stitch over line with fringe, turning fabric to make curves and circles. Push finishing button at the end of design to knot off threads.

Fig. 8.12 Special marking foot fringe motif and border.

For fringe trim, sew a straight row of fringe, cut it open and press. It is important to anchor thread so fringe will not pull out, so use one contrasting thread through the needle with a closed decorative stitch. Use the stitch on a 4–5 width, and sew down the middle of opened fringe (Fig. 8.12). Great to decorate pocket tops on children's clothing or a fingertip guest towel.

Project Wedding Handkerchief

Many of the techniques you have learned for French machine sewing will be used to make the handkerchief (see Fig. 8.1). You will need: 5″ (12.7cm) square of fine batiste; ½″ (12.7mm) lace insertion; 1″ (2.5cm) beading; entredeaux; lace edging; ⅛″ (3.2mm) double-face satin ribbon, about 6 yards (5.5m); a ruler and water-erasable marker.

How to figure exact amounts of lace and entredeaux is included in the directions below; the width of your lace will determine the length you will need. Use a #70/9 needle and #100 sewing thread.

For the center of this handkerchief (Fig. 8.13), I rolled and whipped a 5″ (12.7cm) square of batiste. Use the method you prefer. Entredeaux was added to the edges; do one side of entredeaux at a time, cut and overlap the openings of the entredeaux at the corners.

Stitch the beading (the lace with holes for threaded ribbon) and lace strip together before attaching them to the entredeaux. Together, the strip of lace is 1½″ (3.8cm) wide.

Estimate how much lace you'll need for your wedding handkerchief by first measuring around the center square of batiste

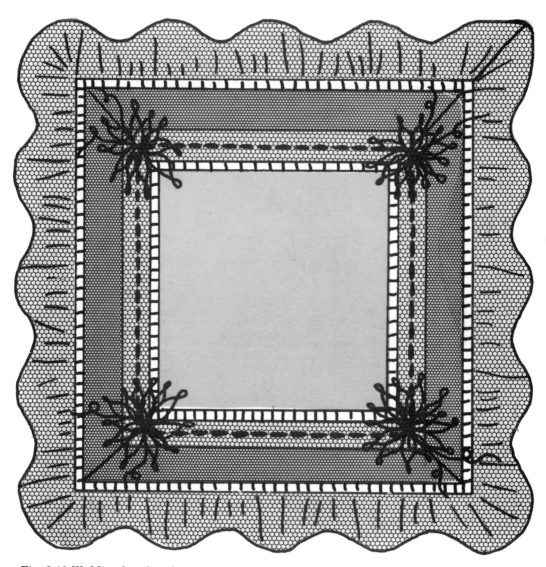

Fig. 8.13 Wedding handkerchief pattern (see also Fig. 8.1)

and entredeaux; the example is approximately 20″ (50.8cm).

Double the width measurement of the strip of lace you've made when you stitched the beading to the lace insertion: 1½″ × 2 = 3″ (3.8cm × 2 = 7.6cm). Multiply 3″ × 4 = 12″ (7.6cm × 4 = 30.5cm) to

arrive at the number of inches (cm) needed for the corner miters.

Add the distance around the center square (20″ or 50.8cm) to the corner miters (12″ or 30.5cm). Exact measurement of the lace needed is 32″ (81.3cm). Add 2″ (5.1cm) more for safety.

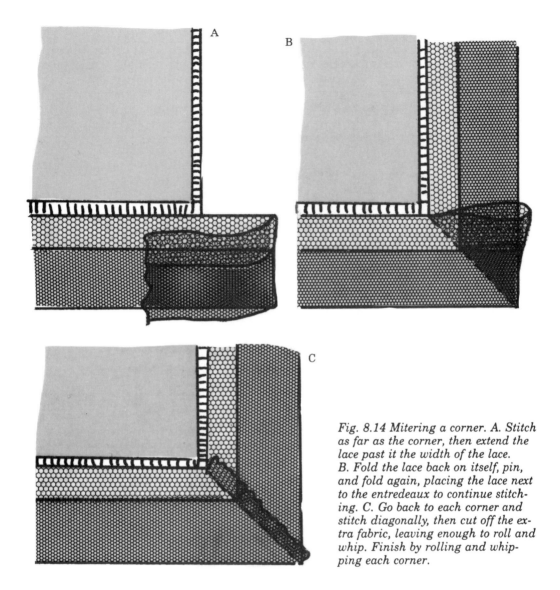

Fig. 8.14 Mitering a corner. A. Stitch as far as the corner, then extend the lace past it the width of the lace. B. Fold the lace back on itself, pin, and fold again, placing the lace next to the entredeaux to continue stitching. C. Go back to each corner and stitch diagonally, then cut off the extra fabric, leaving enough to roll and whip. Finish by rolling and whipping each corner.

Leave 2″ (5.1cm) of lace at the corner before you begin attaching lace to the entredeaux (Fig. 8.14). Trim the entredeaux. Place the edge of the lace strip next to the entredeaux so the edges touch (see Fig. 8-14A). Stitch along the first side, ending with needle down at the corner, extending the lace 1½″ (3.8cm) beyond the

corner (this is the width measurement of the strip of lace I used). Raise the presser foot. Fold the lace back on itself by the same measurement, 1½″ (3.8cm) or the width of your lace. Pin the lace together at the corner and then fold the lace so it will lie at the edge of the entredeaux on the next side you will stitch (Fig. 8.14B). Turn

121

your work to continue stitching, and put the presser foot down. Hand-walk the first stitch to be sure it catches the lace. Continue stitching slowly to the next corner. Attach lace to the other sides as you did the first.

After the strip of lace has been attached, go back to each corner and fold the lace diagonally to miter it. Check carefully that the corners will lie flat. Pin each one. Mark with a ruler and water-erasable pen where the line of stitching will be (Fig. 8.14B). Sew down the line with a straight stitch before cutting back, leaving enough lace to roll and whip by machine (Fig. 8.14C).

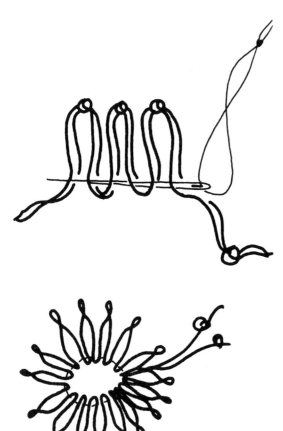

Attach entredeaux to the edge of the lace, overlapping the holes of each piece at the corners, as done previously.

Measure around the outside edge. Double this for the gathered lace measurement. Sew the ends of the lace together by overlapping and, at the same time, matching the designs top and bottom. Sew a narrow zigzag along the design and cut back to the line. Place this seam in a corner.

Gather the lace edging by pulling the correct thread and attaching it to the entredeaux. Pin the gathered lace to the entredeaux first to adjust the gathers. Keep the corners of the lace ruffle quite full. Next, stitch the lace to the entredeaux. This can be done in two ways: (1) Place entredeaux on top of the gathered lace, topsides together. Line up the edges and proceed as if attaching the entredeaux to rolled and whipped edges; or (2) Place gathered lace next to the entredeaux, topsides up, and zigzag stitch as you did in "Attaching Entredeaux to Lace Insertion."

Thread ⅛" (3.2mm) double-faced satin ribbon through each of the four sides. Leave 3" (7.6cm) tails at each end. Tie overhand knots at the ends. Stitch the tails in place by hand to keep the ribbon in place.

Make rosettes for each corner (Fig. 8.15): First tie an overhand knot every 2½" (6.4cm) along a length of ribbon until you have 16 knots. Leave long ends. Use a double-threaded needle. Make loops on the needle by arranging the ribbon with knots at the top (Fig. 8.15). Sew back through all of the loops again. Pull up and attach the rosettes to the corners of the handkerchief. Tie knots at the ends of the ribbons.

Fig. 8.15 To make a rosette, tie overhand knots in the ribbon every 2½" (6.4cm). Fold the ribbon into loops with knots at the top. Sew through each loop, then pull into a rosette.

Lesson 24. Seaming with feed dogs up and lowered

Using a narrow hemmer

Why is this foot called a hemmer when it can be used as a seamer? And why is it so infrequently used? It sews seams that are used for strength and decoration. Using this foot makes a seam that looks good on both sides (Fig. 8.16).

Use a narrow hemmer (5mm seam) for shirt-weight material. The seam will be 5mm. If you want a wider seam for denim weights, use the narrow hemmer to turn the top seam allowance over for topstitching.

To use the narrow hemmer, pin two pieces of fabric together so the fabric underneath projects ⅛"–¼" (3.2–6.4mm) beyond the top piece (Fig. 8.16A). Fold the extension over the top piece and sew a few stitches (8.16B). Leave the needle in the fabric. Lift the hemmer so you can slide the fabric into it. Stitch the seam. Guide the fabric carefully so it feeds evenly.

Press seam. Open up the fabric. Again put it into the hemmer. Pull gently away from the seam on both sides as you guide the seam through the presser foot for the second time. The second line of stitching finishes the seam so it will lie flat (Fig. 8.16C).

Sewing a fake lapped seam

If you don't have a narrow hemmer, then sew a ⅝" (15.9mm) seam and press the fabric to the left (Fig. 8.17A, B).

With right side up, use the blind hem D foot and place the inside of right toe in the ditch or seam line. Adjust needle position so needle enters fabric about ⅛" (3.2mm) from the ditch. Stitch.

For the second run, place the outside

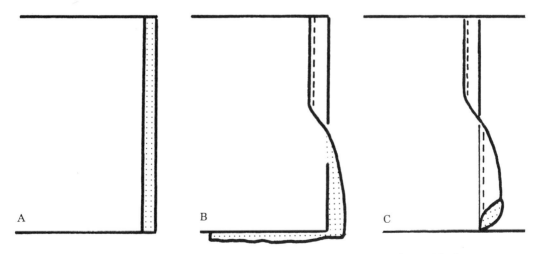

Fig. 8.16 Constructing a lapped hem. A. Place two pieces of fabric together, with the underneath fabric extending beyond the top. B. Use the narrow hemmer to stitch the first seam, overlapping the top fabric. C. Open the fabric for the second pass, which will hold the seam in place.

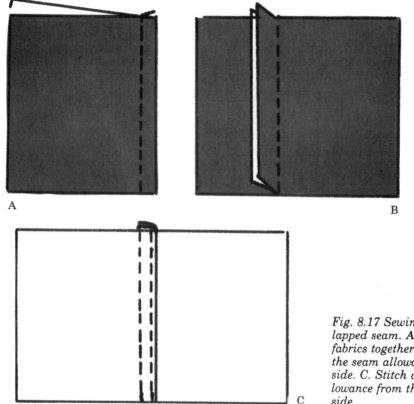

A   B

Fig. 8.17 Sewing a fake
lapped seam. A. Seam two
fabrics together. B. Fold
the seam allowance to one
side. C. Stitch down the allowance from the right
C   side.

edge of right toe on the first stitched line, needle to the left, and sew a fake-felled seam (Fig. 8.17C).

Of course, you can stitch fake lapped seams with just the standard A or straight stitch foot. It's possible to use the edge of some presser feet as a measure. Or, mark the stitching lines with a water-erasable marker.

Seaming with a side-cutter

The side-cutter is wonderful for cutting fabric and overcasting it in one operation (it's a little like turning your sewing machine into a serger). I didn't think I needed one until it was given to me as a gift. Now I use it constantly. You'll want to use it with many of the practical stitches, such as

overlock, double overlock and zigzag. One limitation is the type of fabric it will accept. I could not sew the canvas tote bag with it—it doesn't like tough, tightly woven fabrics.

Stitching over yarn on knits

No more stretched-out seams on knits and jerseys when you use this method.

Stitch width: 2–5 or preset
Stitch length: 1–4.5 or preset
Needle position: center
Needle: #80/11–12 all-purpose
Feed dogs: up
Pressure: normal
Presser foot: narrow hemmer, narrow braid-
        ing or transparent appliqué foot

Utility stitch: zigzag or flatlock
Tension: *top*, normal; *bobbin*, normal
Thread: polyester sewing
Accessories: baby yarn, pearl cotton, narrow twill tape or ⅛" (3.2mm) ribbon

Thread baby yarn, pearl cotton, twill tape, or ribbon under foot, through curl or clip, from front to back. Be sure to have 2"–3" (5–7.5cm) tail behind foot. Stitch over the yarn with a zigzag or other join-and-overcast stitch to stabilize the seam. The foot guides yarn, pearl cotton, etc., automatically. For a seam that is stable, yet still able to stretch, stitch over a strand or two of elastic thread.

Imitating hand piecing on quilts

Here is a seam shown to me by a quilter. After stitching two quilt pieces together, run a 2 width, 2 length zigzag over the line of straight stitches (Fig. 8.18). When the seam is pressed open, it gives the impression of perfect hand piecing. Why not skip

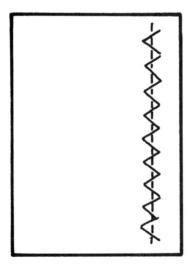

Fig. 8.18 To create the look of hand piecing, zigzag over a seam of straight stitches. Then press the seam open.

the first step of straight stitching? Because the two passes will make the quilt seams sturdier, and the line of straight stitching is an excellent guideline for the zigzagging.

Joining veiling with a scallop stitch

What kind of a seam can be used on veiling? In Lesson 17, a straight seam is stitched on Alençon lace, using a close zigzag stitch. A more decorative seam is stitched with the closed scallop stitch (2–32). Overlap the edges, stitch, then cut back excess material on each side to the scallop.

Using utility and decorative stitches

Don't overlook the flatlock and honeycomb (2–15) stitches on your machine. They are sewn from the top of the fabric. You may have avoided using them when sewing ribbing onto sweatshirts or for top decoration if you experimented on thick fabric and had an uneven look to your stitches. But now you can elongate the stitches on most Vikings. If you have a 990, 980 or 950, use a sample of the same fabrics and push the stitch length button to find the correct setting for a perfect decorative stitch.

A number of stitches on cassette 2 can be sewn between two pieces of fabric to create an open, interesting seam (Fig. 8.19). The bridging stitch (2–6) is one that works beautifully, as does the feather stitch (2–19). The feather stitch is one of my favorites. I use it on quilt tops to stitch the layers together.

I also used the bridging stitch on a Bermuda bag I made from Ultrasuede scraps. Using a commercial kit, I cut the scraps into squares and rectangles—enough to cover the pattern. I used the Teflon presser foot and polyester thread to stitch the scraps together. To do this, I lifted them in pairs from the pattern and sewed the hori-

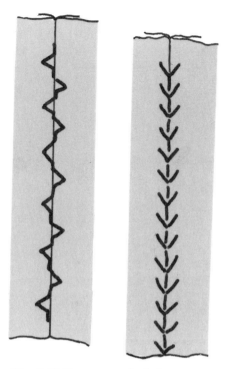

Fig. 8.19 Decorate and stitch a seam
with either the bridging stitch, 2–6
(left) or feather stitch, 2–19.

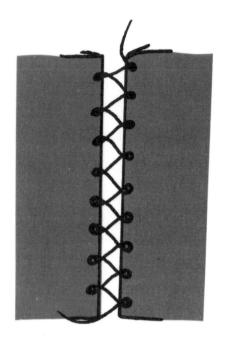

Fig. 8.20 Stitching a decorative seam
using free machining.

zontal seams first. Then I went back and
sewed the vertical seams. When the stitching was completed, I placed the pattern
over the Ultrasuede and cut off fabric pro-
jecting beyond the edges. After that, I was
able to finish the bag according to the kit
directions.

Creating seams with feed dogs lowered

If you use a similar seam with fabric instead of Ultrasuede, fold under seam allowances at least ⅝″ (15.9mm) and press.
Move the two pieces of fabric about ⅛″
(3.2mm) apart, topsides down. If the fabric
is washable, you may want to slip water-

soluble stabilizer under it and baste the
fabric ⅛″ (3.2mm) apart. Use size #8 pearl
cotton in the bobbin. Tighten top tension
slightly. Lower the feed dogs, release pressure to between # and 1, and use the
darning foot. Sew freely from one side of
the fabric to the other, making loops as you
enter and leave it (Fig. 8.20). When you
finish, change to regular bobbin thread.
Put utility foot B on, bring feed dogs up
and pressure to normal. Topstitch down
along the folds. Then cut back underneath
to the stitching.

These techniques only scratch the surface of interesting seams for your fabric.
New seams are introduced every time a
new utility or decorative stitch is incorpo-
rated into a machine. They are welcome, of
course, but in the meantime there is no
lack of beautiful and practical work you
can do.

CHAPTER 9

Adding Hems and Edges

- **Lesson 25. Turning hems once**
- **Lesson 26. Blind hemming**
- **Lesson 27. Sewing narrow hems**
- **Lesson 28. Using bias tape**
- **Lesson 29. Zigzagging a narrow edge**
- **Lesson 30. Covering wire for shaped edge**
- **Lesson 31. Cording edges**
- **Lesson 32. Making thread fringe**
- **Lesson 33. Piping edges**
- **Lesson 34. Topstitching**

I remember when "good clothes" didn't mean "clean jeans." There were puffed sleeves, sweetheart necklines—always braided, piped, or embroidered in some way. We wanted to dress like movie stars. Dresses were molded to them and then decorated creatively. Designers always took many long-cuts.

The more you know about your machine, the more inventive you can become: no more boring clothes! You may not think you'll ever use all the decorative hems and edgings in this chapter, but make samples for your notebook anyway. You may be surprised.

With the range of fabrics and styles now available, and the variety of effects we want to achieve, choosing the appropriate hem or edge is not always easy. Before sewing a hem or decorative edge on anything,

ask yourself these questions: What type of fabric? What type of garment? Who is the garment for? Will it be worn forever? How decorative is it to be?

I have my favorite ways to hem and finish edges. I've also learned hems and edges I will never do again. What makes the difference? Appearance, of course, and ease of stitching. I think I have tried every imaginable variation, and those that follow are the ones I prefer because they are useful and good-looking.

Stitch samples of each and put the results in your notebook for reference. Include your own favorites as well. Write the machine settings on each one, along with comments such as what fabrics work well, where you would use them, whether they were long-cuts with happy endings or more trouble than they were worth.

Lesson 25. Turning hems once

I used to cringe at the thought of hems turned only once—all those raw edges! But I have changed my way of thinking.

Using double needles on knits

My favorite hem for T-shirts and other casual knits is turned once and stitched in place with a double needle. The two stitching lines share one bobbin thread, giving the stitches the stretch they need.

Stitch width: 0
Stitch length: 2.5–3
Needle position: center
Needle: double, at least 2mm
Tension: *top*, normal; *bobbin*, normal
Fabric: knit
Presser foot: standard A, utility B or transparent appliqué foot
Utility stitch: straight stitch
Thread: polyester

It is simple to fold up the hem and sew with a double needle from the topside of the fabric. Rest presser foot and stitch on a double layer of fabric. *Tip:* If the fabric puckers, shorten the stitch. If it waves out of shape, lengthen the stitch.

When finished, trim the fabric back to the stitching underneath. The three-step zigzag can be used for variation. Remember to push the double needle symbol or hand-walk the needle through the first few stitches to be sure the stitch clears the needle plate opening.

Hemming with a double needle on sheers

Use a double needle for sheer fabrics, too. When a narrow hem would be neither suitable nor attractive, fold up a 4″ (10.2cm) hem on lightweight fabrics and sew across. Lightweight garments hang better with the weight of a deep hem and it's also more attractive when the hem of the underskirt isn't visible underneath.

Of course you can add more rows of stitching, evenly spaced from the first. Cut back to the top of the stitching.

Hemming with utility or decorative stitches on front

The next hem for delicate fabrics is much the same, but uses a single needle and the scallop stitch (2–32).

Stitch width: 4
Stitch length: 0.3–0.4
Needle position: center
Presser foot: utility B or transparent appliqué
Pressure: normal

For hemming on sheers, use one or more rows of scallops, evenly spaced from the first. Cut back to the top of the stitching.

Stitch width: 0; 6
Stitch length: 3
Needle position: center
Needle: #110 jeans
Presser foot: utility foot B

To hem heavy, canvas-type fabrics with a machine that will do an elastic straight or rickrack stitch (2–1), first find the cor-

Fig. 9.1 Use light flannel between hem and skirt, then quilt the hem with lines of straight stitching.

rect width and length by practicing on a piece of the same fabric you will use for the finished article. Set up the machine for a rickrack (2–1) or elastic straight stitch. This is an extremely strong stitch. Use it for anything from deck furniture canvas to jeans.

Refer back to the stitch samples you did in Chapter 2. You may prefer other decorative stitches to those mentioned here. Experiment with different fabrics and stitches, keeping all your samples in your notebook.

Quilting a hem

Another single-fold hem can be done on heavy materials such as wool or velveteen. Use a dual feed foot. Allow about 8″ (20.3cm) for the hem of the skirt. Put light batting, such as flannel sheeting, inside and pin in place. Sew four or five rows of straight stitches, one line at a time, to quilt the hem (Fig. 9.1). Space the lines of stitching as you wish or use edge guide so spacing is even. Try quilting a long Christmas skirt or an evening skirt using metallic thread.

Or turn the skirt inside out and put pearl cotton on the bobbin to contrast with the skirt. The topside will be against the bed of the machine. Stitch rows, then cut back to the last line of stitching. This can be done around sleeve bands or down jacket facings as well.

Create a quilted effect by turning a hem up at least 3″ (7.6cm). Press it in place. Sew 3 to 5 rows of pintucks using a 3.0 double needle. Trim away excess hem fabric up to the stitch.

Lesson 26. Blind hemming

I remember when most of the hems I put in garments were blind hems worked by hand. Times have changed, but that doesn't mean I've given up blind hems. The only difference is that I do them more quickly now—by machine.

To begin the hem, decide first if you can live with a raw edge. If you can, then leave it as it is, but if you hate that unfinished edge, then attach a lace edging over it or stitch around the edge with the three-step zigzag or flatlock stitch before you proceed.

Turn up the hem 1½″ to 2″ (3.8cm to 5.1cm) and pin very closely around it, about an inch from the top. If the fabric slips, the hem will be a mess, so don't try to save time by not pinning a lot.

Or use Tami Durand's method. Baste the hem and skirt together, by machine, ¼″ (6.4mm) from the edge of the turned-up hem. There will definitely be no slip-

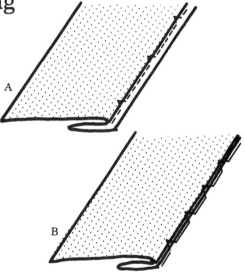

Fig. 9.2 Blindstitching. A. Fold over the hem, then fold the skirt back, letting ⅛″ (3.2mm) show beyond the edge; stitch on the edge of the fabric. B. Or fold the garment back even with the edge, and stitch off the fabric, the left swing stitching the fold.

ping. Fold back and proceed as you do with the pinned hem. When finished, pull out the basting.

Set your machine up.

Stitch width: 3
Stitch length: 1.5
Needle position: center
Feed dogs: up
Pressure: normal
Presser foot: blind hem foot D
Utility stitch: blindstitch
Tension: *top*, loosened; *bobbin*, normal
Thread: sewing
Accessories: dressmakers' pins

Fold the garment back on itself, leaving ⅛" (3.2mm) of hem at the edge to stitch on (Fig. 9.2A). Put the fold of the fabric against the inside of the right toe of the blind hem D foot (refer to your manual). Stitch on the edge of the fabric and let the needle catch about 2 threads of the fold. The Viking blind hem foot enables you to stitch almost invisible blind hems. However, you may have to check the settings on scrap fabric first to determine the correct stitch width and length for thick fabrics.

I made a fine batiste bishop dress with yards of blind hemming, but the stitching pulled too tightly. Despite the fine thread, loosened tension, and a #60 needle, I didn't like the looks of it. The answer? I sewed from off the fabric. I folded the fabric back so the fold met the finished edge exactly. Then I stitched outside the fabric and the left bite held it together with no pulling (Fig. 9.2B). I've tried it on several heavier weights of fabric as well, and it works beautifully.

Lesson 27. Sewing narrow hems

Next to wing needles, the most unused accessories are the narrow hemming presser feet. I think I know why: few stitchers ever take time to practice with them. They're great time savers, but I had to learn to use them, too. Now after yards of hem samples, I can't do without them.

Set up your machine, read the directions, and reread as you work. Before you begin to hem a garment with one of the hemmers, cut back the seam allowances that have to be sewn over. Then learn to start the fabric. I hated starting a hem because of those first problem inches until I tried Gail Brown's method, which follows.

Straight stitching

Practice with a 2 or 3mm hemmer at first, because it is easier to use when learning. Also needed are lightweight cotton to hem and a 3" (7.6cm) square of tear-away stabilizer.

Overlap the piece of tear-away stabilizer with the fabric about ¼" (6.3mm) and sew them together. Start rolling the stabilizer into the scroll of the hemming foot. By the time the fabric is introduced into the hemmer, the hem is being sewn down starting on the first thread of the fabric.

Guide the fabric by holding it taut and lifting it slightly as it rolls through the foot. The edge of the fabric must be vertical. As long as you pay attention, guiding and holding the fabric correctly, the machine does the rest.

Sewing on lace

This method is simple and it does save time.

Stitch width: 3–4
Stitch length: 1–1.5
Pressure: normal
Needle position: center

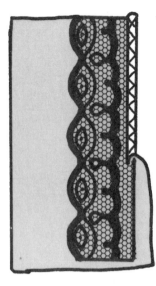

Fig. 9.3 Lace is attached with a finished edge in one step.

Presser foot: standard A, raised seam F or narrow braiding foot
Utility stitch: zigzag
Fabric: lightweight cotton, lace edging
Thread: fine sewing thread to match

Place the lace on top of the fabric, topsides together, the edge of the lace ⅛″ (3.2mm) from the edge of the fabric.

The fabric is usually placed to the right of the middle of the presser foot but practice first with the presser foot you choose. As you sew, it will roll and be whipped over the heading of the lace (Fig. 9.3).

See other methods of sewing lace to fabric in Lesson 25, "French handsewing."

Attaching scalloped lace

Apply scalloped lace to fabric, topsides up, by overlapping it to make a hem (Fig. 9.4). Let the fabric extend well past the curve on top of the lace. Baste lace to fabric. Zigzag along the edge, following the scallop. Cut back the fabric underneath to the stitching line.

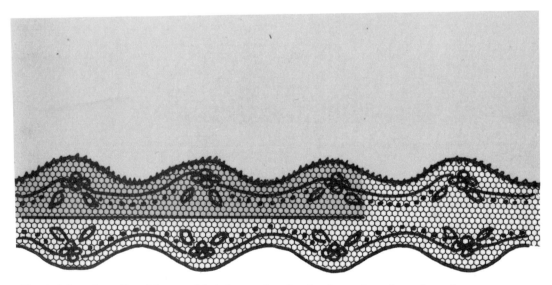

Fig. 9.4 Attach scalloped lace to fabric by overlapping it, zigzagging along the scalloped edge, then cutting the fabric back to the stitching line.

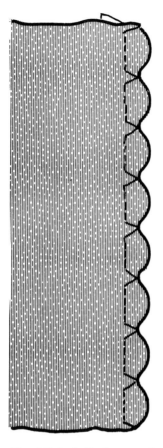

Fig. 9.5 A shell edge on tricot, stitched with the reverse blindstitch (2–7).

Stitching shell edging

This is a good hem and edging for lingerie (Fig. 9.5). Or use it to decorate ribbon and tucks.

Set up your machine:

Stitch width: 6
Stitch length: varies
Needle position: center
Feed dogs: up
Pressure: normal
Presser foot: standard foot A
Utility or decorative stitch: overcast stitch, reverse blindstitch (2–6) or arch stitch (2– 8)

If you are going to cross a seam when hemming, then cut back the seam allowances that will be sewn over.

The foot rests on the fabric for this one; you do not feed fabric into the foot. Fold the fabric under ½″ (12.7mm) and place the folded edge to the right. Stitch, letting the right swing of the needle sew over the edge, creating the shell pattern. To make a corded shell tuck, lay a strand of pearl cotton next to the folded edge. Guide the fabric so the needle stitches over pearl cotton when it swings to the right. At the end, cut back to the stitching underneath.

Roll and shell hemming

The 3mm narrow hemmer not only makes a narrow, straight-stitch hem, but will also roll and shell as shown in Fig. 9.6, if the machine is set on zigzag. Usually it's the finish of choice when hemming tricot, as it decorates and hems in one operation. It's impossible to turn square corners on these hems, so round off any corners before you begin to stitch. Because tricot rolls to one side, hem with the right side up. If you will stitch over a seam while hemming, first cut back the seam allowances you'll cross so the fabric will feed in without a problem. As the fabric is rolled into the foot, it will curl and be sewn into a narrow, puffy roll.

Stitch width: 4–6
Stitch length: 2–4.5
Needle position: center
Feed dogs: up
Pressure: normal
Presser foot: 3mm narrow hemmer
Utility or decorative stitch: zigzag or reverse blindstitch (2–7)
Tension: *top*, 6½–7; *bobbin*, normal

It's important to keep the fabric straight ahead of the presser foot and raise it a bit to keep it feeding easily. The needle goes into the fabric at the left, then off the edge of the fabric at the right and pulls up a shell.

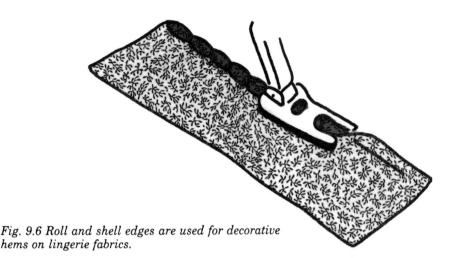

Fig. 9.6 Roll and shell edges are used for decorative hems on lingerie fabrics.

Lesson 28. Using bias tape

I must admit, I equate bias tape with the edges of Grandma's apron, but now that I can apply it so easily, I'm finding new ways to use it. I especially like it for toddlers' sunsuits and dresses.

This is the only method I use; what I like best about it is that the tape is sewn on almost invisibly. You don't need the bias binder accessory.

Stitch width: 0
Stitch length: 2–3
Feed dogs: up
Pressure: normal
Presser foot: buttonhole C, overcast J foot
Utility stitch: straight stitch
Needle: #80/11–12 all-purpose
Needle position: left
Thread: monofilament
Fabric: lightweight cotton, double-fold bias
    tape
Accessories: glue stick, pins

Look at the bias tape: One side is wider than the other. The wide side will be on the back of your work. Open the bias tape and place the narrow side on top, the cut edge of the tape along the cut edge of the fabric. If there is a ⅝″ (15.9mm) seam, cut it back to fit the width of the bias. Pin in place.

Adjust the needle position so the crease in the tape is guided at the inside of the long toe of buttonhole foot. Stitch along the crease.

Fold the tape over the edge. I sometimes dab the underside with glue stick between tape and fabric. Pin if you wish, or baste by hand.

Press the bias and check that the underside of the bias extends slightly beyond the seam line on the topside.

From the topside, stitch in the ditch of the seam so long toe of buttonhole foot or metal guide of overcast J foot butts up against the tape. Again, adjust the needle position to enable you to sew exactly in the ditch. The stitching catches the edge of the bias underneath. I've decided I can't sew without the buttonhole or overcast feet.

133

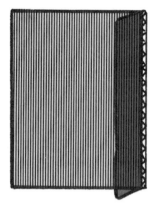
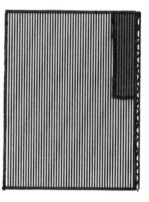

Fig. 9.7 From the top of the fabric, sew a narrow, close zigzag down the folded edge (left). Cut back the fabric underneath to the stitching line.

Lesson 29. Zigzagging a narrow edge

This is only one of several methods to produce a strong, finished hem or edge of tiny, tight zigzag stitches. Use it to finish ruffles, napkins and scarves.

Stitch width: 2
Stitch length: 0.5–0.8
Needle position: center
Presser foot: utility B or transparent appliqué
Utility stitch: zigzag

Fold the fabric under about ½" (12.7mm) and guide the fold of the fabric exactly in the middle of the foot.

Stitch on the fabric with the left swing of the needle, the right swing stitching just off the right side of it (Fig. 9.7). After stitching is completed, cut the fabric back to the stitched edge, as partially done below.

Lesson 30. Covering wire for shaped edges

In a bridal shop I saw yard goods that included nylon filament at the edges of chiffon and organdy ruffles. It was an attractive finish for the ruffles that can be applied to skirt and sleeve hems or across the drop-shoulders of wedding gowns and formal wear.

A case displayed dozens of headpieces using the same nylon filament to keep bows perky and ribbons from wilting. You are invited to create your own, combining filament and sheer fabrics, beads and silk flowers.

I could also see many Halloween costume possibilities here. Use the filament at the bottom edge of a long, filmy skirt or, if you want to make an angel costume, use heavy gauge filament for floppy wings.

Nylon filament is available by the yard at stores that sell bridal lace and fabrics. But I found that it is much easier to buy 25-pound-test fishing line in a sporting goods store. Cheaper, too. I've used both and I don't think there's a difference. There are different weights to fishing lines, which means they come in different thicknesses.

For super-thick costume fabric, you can use weed-trimmer line. It comes in a 50-foot length and the diameter to use is .05mm. This fits in the clip of the narrow braiding foot. Use the same foot or experiment with your buttonhole foot. Use the same method to apply any of the nylon filament mentioned.

Stitch width: 4
Stitch length: 1
Presser foot: narrow braiding
Utility stitch: zigzag

I've used the transparent appliqué foot also. The settings will be different, so experiment.

I placed the filament about ¼" (6.4mm) from the edge of the fabric (the needle should stitch off the edge of the material on the right swing). As you sew, the edge of the fabric will roll over and enclose the line (Fig. 9.8).

Milliner's wire or florist's wire is available already covered with thread. Both of these can be stitched into the edge of fabric

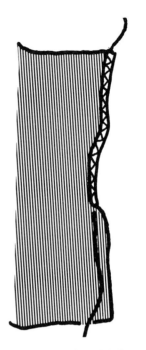

Fig. 9.8 Rolling fabric over nylon filament or wire creates a rigid, finished edge.

in the same way as nylon filament. They both come in different gauges. Unlike the nylon edge, the wire can be bent into any shape you might want. Buy milliner's wire at bridal shops and florist's wire at craft shops. Make flower petals and leaves using wire.

Lesson 31. Cording edges

Covering cords

Covered cord produces one of the finest, prettiest edges to use on table linens, on scarves, collars, wherever you want a delicate but very strong edge.

Stitch width: 2–3
Stitch length: 0.6–0.8
Needle position: center
Presser foot: narrow braiding foot
Utility stitch: zigzag

Thread: Zwicky machine-embroidery or sewing thread; #5 pearl cotton

Thread pearl cotton through the clip in the narrow braiding foot. Place the foot a presser-foot's width from the edge of the fabric and stitch (Fig. 9.9). Cut back to the stitching when it's completed. For a cleaner, more stable edge, satin stitch over edge again with a slightly shorter (0.4–0.5) stitch length.

To create a thicker edge, stitch over two strands of pearl cotton with a wider zigzag. Stitch and finish as described above.

If you use this method to finish the edge of a collar, you won't need to turn the collar. Instead, sew with wrong sides of upper and under collar together to eliminate the bulk of a turned-in seam allowance.

To make a delicate edging for a bridal veil, cord the edge.

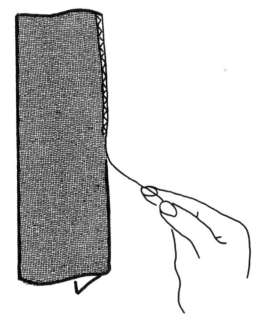

Fig. 9.9 Zigzagging over cord produces a strong corded edge.

Stitch width: 2
Stitch length: 0.5–0.8
Needle position: center
Presser foot: narrow braiding foot
Utility stitch: zigzag
Thread: fine sewing thread to match veil; #8 pearl cotton to match veil

Without folding the veiling, place it so the edge extends past the presser foot on the right. Slip #8 pearl cotton in the clip of the narrow braiding foot. Sew over the pearl. Cut back to the pearl for a fine finished edge. (Try a corded scallop stitch, 2–31 or 2–32, too.)

Creating crocheted edges

This decorative edge is used to finish shirt plackets and collars. It's a delicate, lacelike finish that lends itself to feminine clothes and baby items.

Stitch width: 6
Stitch length: 0.4
Presser foot: narrow braiding or transparent appliqué foot
Decorative stitch: closed scallop (2–32)
Fabric: medium-weight cotton
Thread: color to contrast with fabric; gimp or #5 pearl cotton the same color as the thread
Accessories: tear-away stabilizer or colored paper to match thread

Thread the narrow braiding foot with pearl cotton, or lay the pearl under the transparent appliqué foot, to do a corded edge using the scallop stitch (2–32). Place stabilizer underneath and far enough to the right to be under the stitches, as shown in Fig. 9.10. The fabric should be doubled; the fold is placed just to the left of the clip in front of the presser foot. Stitch at the edge. The scallops will catch the fabric, but most of the stitches will be off the edge onto the stabilizer (Fig. 9.10). Carefully tear off the stabilizer when you finish.

Try other decorative stitches at the edges of fabrics. I like the small, undulat-

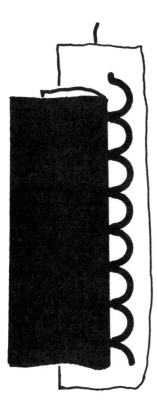

Fig. 9.10 Make a crocheted edge with the scallop stitch (2–32).

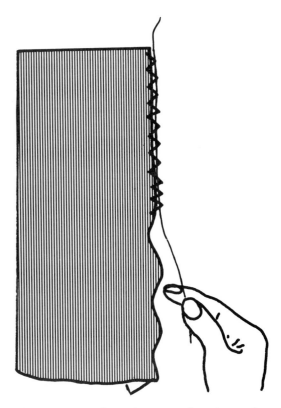

Fig. 9.11 Keep knits from stretching by stitching over an elastic thread.

ing scallop (2–31), too. Use it on the edges of plackets or sleeves and decorate collars with it. Sew on doubled fabric, then cut back to the stitching. The edge of the baby bonnet in Fig. 5.12 was worked this way.

Reshaping knits with elastic

Elastic can be used to keep stretchy edges in shape, or to reshape them.

Stitch width: 2
Stitch length: 2–3
Presser foot: narrow braiding or transparent appliqué foot
Utility stitch: zigzag

Thread the elastic though the clip in the narrow braiding foot or under appliqué foot. Keep the elastic at the edge of the knit and sew down the fold (Fig. 9.11).

Lesson 32. Making thread fringe

How many machine owners use a special marking foot for tailor tacking? I can't find one. Most of the time the special marking foot is used for fringing, fagoting, or for sewing on buttons.

To make a fringed edge, you will need

137

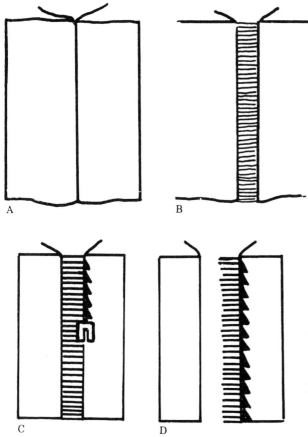

A　　　　　　　　　B

C　　　　　　　　　D

Fig. 9.12 Making thread fringe. A. Butt two pieces of fabric together. Stitch down between folds with zigzag stitches over the special marking foot. B. Open up the stitching and pull out the bobbin thread. C. Topstitch, using decorative stitch whose edge is even with the fold. D. Pull off other fabric piece.

Thread: machine-embroidery
Fabric: medium-weight cotton
Stabilizer: tear-away

Don't overlap, but butt the fabric folds next to each other. Hold them together as you sew down between them (Fig. 9.12A). Pull the bobbin thread out, then *very carefully* pull the fabrics apart, but leave them connected by the stitching (Fig. 9.12B). Care can make or break your work as the fringe wants to jump out of the fabric until you accomplish the next step.

Return upper tension to normal. Place a stabilizer under the fabric. Put transparent appliqué foot on. On the side that will retain fringe, place fringe under foot so fold is even with the slit in the foot (at the left). Stitch a line of decorative stitches. Use one where the straight edge of the stitch is even with the fold (Fig. 9.12C) to anchor the fringe in place. Carefully pull off the other piece of fabric (Fig. 9.12C, D).

If you look closely at the eyelashes of the denim doll in Fig. 3.18, you will see thread fringe. As you get to know your machine, you'll see more and more ways to use it to make the simplest tasks even simpler. On to the next lesson.

two pieces of fabric. Both pieces will be folded under about 5/8" (15.9mm), but one piece of fabric will be eliminated later.

Loosen the top tension to 3.5–4.

Stitch width: 2; varies
Stitch length: 0.3; varies
Presser foot: special marking; transparent appliqué
Utility or decorative stitch: zigzag; decorative stitch of choice

Lesson 33. Piping edges

Miniature piping is especially pretty and colorful on the edges of children's clothing. Use a #3 or #5 pearl cotton and a piece of bias fabric twice the width of the seam allowance. I may not use bias fabric at all. It seems to make little difference, and though held sacrilegious, you can save fabric by cutting on the straight, so try it for yourself. Cover the pearl with purchased bias tape by laying it inside the fold. Use a presser foot with a narrow groove, such as the narrow braiding foot. Straight stitch narrow piping by snugging stitch up next to the raised edge. The foot has a groove in which to fit the covered pearl while stitching it. Adjust the needle position to sew at the edge of the cord.

To cover thick cord for upholstery, use the piping foot. Forget what you've learned about always using a zipper foot for this procedure. The wrapped cord fits into the groove of the piping foot and never slips. I sewed over 100 yards of that one day and it couldn't have been easier. Attaching covered cording to a pillow is also a breeze with this foot.

Lesson 34. Topstitching

There is nothing richer-looking on a coat or suit than an even line of topstitching.

When you need a narrowly spaced double line, use a double needle. For topstitching a heavy fabric, I use a topstitching needle with two sewing threads, eliminating the fraying of buttonhole twist. Sew the second line of stitching in the same direction as the first.

When topstitching on lapels, the roll line indicates where the top threads will go to the underside. For this reason, if you use two threads on top, you must use two threads on the bobbin as well. Wind the bobbin with two threads at one time instead of using only one. Then treat the threads as if they were one.

Instead of anchoring threads, leave a long enough thread at the beginning and the end to work in later invisibly by hand.

Use orange thread and the elastic straight stitch, length 4.5, to stitch on denim, creating the look of commercial topstitching on jeans.

How can you keep topstitching straight? You have several choices. Use tape along the edge of the fabric and sew next to it. Using the blind hem D foot is my first choice because the distance from the edge of fabric to the stitching line can be set with Viking's variable needle positioning.

If using lightweight material, set the stitch length for 2–2.5. If using medium-weight fabric, a longer stitch looks better. If you have a 990, let your Sewing Advisor decide the proper stitch length for topstitching your fabric. Stitch samples on scraps of the same material to see what stitch length setting you prefer.

I think there is hope for more decorative dressing. Have you noticed how Joan Crawford's clothes don't look so funny anymore?

CHAPTER **10**

Machine Tricks: Adding Threads to Threads

- Lesson 35. Making cord
- Lesson 36. Making tassels

For nine chapters, we've used fabric and thread for sewing and embroidering. I'll bet you know your sewing machine pretty well by now, but there's more: In this chapter, I'll show you how to make cords using your machine. Some will be used for practical purposes, such as belt loops and hangers for pendants, but we'll make other cords for decoration, bunching them together into tassels.

Lesson 35. Making cord

Twisting monk's cord

Monk's cord is made from several strands of thread or yarn held together and twisted to make a thick cord. The cord may be used in many ways—as a finish around pillows, as a handle for handbags, and as thick fringe in tassels.

On the Viking, monk's cord is made using the bobbin winder. If your bobbin is all metal or all plastic, the cord size is limited, as you will slip the cord down through the center of the bobbin and seat the bobbin on the winder. Pearl cotton (#5) is the thickest that will seat properly. (However, there is a way to get around this. You can tie dental floss—it doesn't slip—around the center of a thick cord, leaving long enough ends to seat the floss into the middle of the bobbin winder. Then you are able to wind monk's cord of any thickness.)

If you are working alone, you will also be limited by the length of cord you can use and still reach the machine's foot pedal. To make a very long cord, for a belt for example, get a friend or family member to work the foot pedal while you hold the end of the cord. For a shorter cord, use a 2 yard (1.8m) length. Fold this in half, knot the two ends together, and slip the loop through the center of a bobbin. Bring the two ends together at the other end, and tie. Of course you can tie the cord onto the bobbin around the center and work with one cord, not two. If you do work with one cord, tie a loop at the end of the cord to slip your finger through before you begin to twist the cord.

Next, push the bobbin down into place on the pin (Fig. 10.1). When clicked into place, the bobbin will hold the cord securely. Put your index finger in the loop of cord at the other end and stretch the cord to keep tension on it. Step on foot pedal.

Keep winding the cord until it is so tight the blood supply to your finger is threatened. Work your finger out of the loop and, still holding it tightly, find the middle of the cord with your other hand. Hold onto that spot while you place the loop from your finger over the spool pin, if it is close

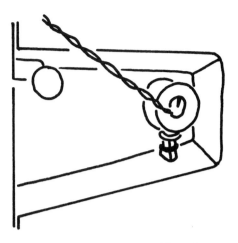

Fig. 10.1 Make monk's cord by poking a
doubled pearl cotton thread through
hole in the bobbin on the bobbin winder.

keep the cord smooth. At this point you
will see that it is more successful if you
work with a partner.

When the cord is twisted as tightly as it
will go, take it out of the bobbin and off the
spool pin. Tie an overhand knot to hold the
ends together until you actually use it.

I use this cord to make thick fringe for
tassels, sometimes slipping washers, bells,
beads or a spacer to the middle of the cord
after I have twisted it and before I double it
and make the final twists (Figs. 10.2 and
10.3).

These quick cords can be used for belt
loops, button loops, ties for clothing. Or
twist up a batch to tie small packages.

enough. Otherwise, keeping tension on the
cord, bring both ends together and very
carefully let it twist to make a monk's cord.
Work down the twists with both hands to

Fig. 10.2 Machine-made
monk's cord is used to make
this tassel.

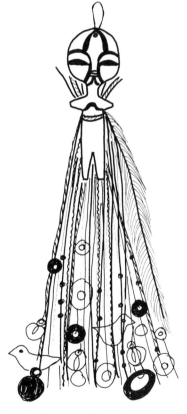

Fig. 10.3 A doll tassel made
with monk's cord.

Stitching belt
and button loops

Belt loop cords can be made by pulling out the bobbin and top threads and folding them over to make about six strands. Use a zigzag stitch width 4–6. Set your machine for free machining, with feed dogs down and pressure released to between # and 1. Use a darning foot or no presser foot at all.

Hold the threads tightly, front and back, as you stitch. You will feed the threads under the needle and determine the stitch length. These tiny cords work well for corded buttonholes.

You can also zigzag over thicker cords and hold them together. If you add a contrasting thread color, you can make interesting tassels (see the next lesson).

Lesson 36. Making tassels

I'm drawn to tassels. I sketch them when I see them in museums or books, and I have a notebook full of ideas cut from magazines. I've labored over a few myself, using hand embroidery, even tiny macramé knots. Sometimes they look like fetish dolls—another weakness—and so I play them that way.

How can my Viking help me make tassels? First of all, I make monk's cord using the bobbin winder. I combine those with other cords, sometimes stringing beads or bells on them (Figs. 10.4 and 10.5).

I can also use a braiding foot or transparent appliqué foot to make colorful cord. Holding several pearl cotton cords together, I place them in the groove on the bottom of the presser foot and zigzag stitch over the pearl with a contrasting color. I choose a stitch width 6 to enclose the cords, and a stitch length 1 to let some of the cord show through.

Fig. 10.4 Monk's cord is used for the tassels at left *and* center. *A collar, stitched by machine, was used for the one at* right.

142

Project
Tassel Collar

Several ways to make tassels by machine involve using water-soluble stabilizer. The first method is for a collar of stitched cords to wrap around the main tassel cords.

Stitch width: 6
Stitch length: 0.5
Needle position: center
Needle: #80/11–12 all-purpose
Presser foot: transparent appliqué
Utility stitch: zigzag
Feed dogs: up
Pressure: normal
Tension: *top*, normal; *bobbin*, normal
Cord: 16 yards (14.5m) rayon cord (available at fabric shops) for the collar; #5 pearl cotton to match cord; many yards of string, thread or yarn for main part of tassel (the more yarn used, the plumper and more attractive the tassel), cut into 16" (40.6cm) lengths
Thread: Sulky embroidery to match rayon cord
Accessories: water-soluble stabilizer

First fold the 16" (40.6cm) lengths of yarn in half to find their centers. Use one yarn piece to tie the lengths together there. Knot tightly. Then tie an overhand knot with the ends of that cord to make a hanger for the tassel.

Cut six dozen 8" (20.3cm) lengths of purchased rayon cord. Place a piece of water-soluble stabilizer on the bed of the machine and lay these cords next to each other across the stabilizer (in horizontal rows as you are looking at them). Starting ½" (12.7mm) in from the right side, place a strand of #5 pearl cotton perpendicular to and crossing all the cords (Fig. 10.6). Satin stitch over the pearl cotton and the rayon cords. Sew down several more rows of

Fig. 10.5 More tassels stitched by machine.

143

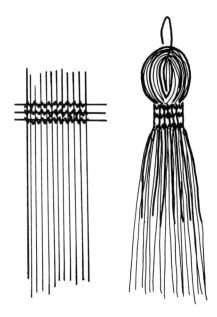

Fig. 10.6 Make a collar for the tassel by placing cords next to each other, then zigzagging over cords laid at right angles across them.

Project
Covered Wire Tassel

Cover 18″ (45.7cm) of milliner's wire with stitches for the next tassel (Fig. 10.7).

Stitch width: 6
Stitch length: 0.5
Needle position: center
Needle: #80/11–12 all-purpose
Feed dogs: up
Pressure: normal
Presser foot: transparent appliqué
Utility stitch: zigzag
Tension: *top*, normal; *bobbin*, normal
Thread: Sulky embroidery
Accessories: tweezers
Stabilizer: water-soluble (optional), cut into
    long strips 1″ (2.5cm) wide

pearl, lining up each pearl cord next to the one stitched before it. When completed, cut off the ½″ (12.7mm) rayon threads protruding from the top of the collar. Zigzag over the edge, which will give the top a smooth finish. Remove water-soluble stabilizer by dipping or spritzing it with water. Press collar between two terrycloth towels.

Wrap the collar, inside-out, 1½″ (3.8cm) down from the fold of the tassel cords. Pin the collar tightly around the cords. Remove it from the tassel and machine stitch the ends of the collar together. Cut back to the stitching line and zigzag over the edge. Turn right side out, then pull the yarn tassel cords from the bottom through the collar to complete it. The collar should fit snugly.

You could embroider the same basic collar in an almost endless variety of ways for your tassel collection.

Fig. 10.7 Cover milliner's wire with stitches and twist the wire around cords to make a tassel.

Set up your machine and place water-soluble stabilizer under the wire if you wish. Sew over the wire. If the wire doesn't feed well, then use a longer stitch length and go over it twice. The milliner's wire is covered with thread and this keeps the rayon stitches from slipping.

Make 45 thick cords for the tassel by zigzagging over two 12″ (30.5cm) strands of #5 pearl cotton for each one. *Hint:* Stitch two 15-yard-long (14m-long) cords together and cut them into 12″ (30.5cm) pieces.

To use the wire for the tassel, first fold the 12″ (30.5cm) long cords in half. Slip an end of the wire through the fold, extending it past the cord 2″ (5.1cm). Bend the wire back 1″ (2.5cm) at the end and twist it around itself to make a loop for hanging (the loop will enclose the cords).

With the other end of the wire, wrap the tassel around and around till you reach halfway down the length of it. Hold the end of the wire with the tweezers. Wrap it around the point of the tweezers to make a decorative coil at the end (Fig. 10.7).

Project
Doll Tassel

The fertility doll tassel is a combination of several dozen 10″ (25.4cm) cords, including linen, jute and monk's cords (see Fig. 10.3) all tied to a small African doll. I placed the bundle of cords on the bed of the machine, letting it extend 1″ (2.5cm) to the right of the presser foot and flattening it with my fingers to allow me to stitch over the cords. The machine was set up for free-machining, with feed dogs lowered, pressure released between # and 1, and a darning foot in place. Using the widest zigzag, I stitched forward and back across the cords. When I finished, I spread glue from a glue stick across the stitching on one side of the bundle and placed this at the back of

the doll, wrapping and tying it in place with a linen cord.

To decorate the tassel, I slipped a long feather under the linen wrapping cord, and strung some of the tassel cords with beads, brass bells and metal washers. Overhand knots held the objects in place at different heights on the cords. There's a hole in the top of the doll, so I added a loop of cord there to hang the tassel.

Project
Making
Two Tassel Tops
by Machine

Tassel tops are made on the sewing machine for the two tassels shown in Fig. 10.8C and 10.9. Put a 7″ (17.8cm) square of felt in a 5″ (12.7cm) spring hoop. Draw half a circle and embroider this, using decorative and utility machine stitches. Take it out of the hoop and cut out the half-circle (Fig. 10.8A). Cut out a wedge from the side of the half-circle (Fig. 10.8B). Fold the larger piece in half, topsides together. Straight stitch the cut edges. Turn to the right side.

Cut six tassel cords, each 18″ (45.7cm) in length, from rayon cord or machine-made monk's cord. Find the center and tie them together at the middle with a cord 8″ (20.3cm) long. Thread that cord through a large-eyed needle and push it up from inside through the top of the cone. Tie a knot at the end and hang the tassel.

The second tassel is also made of felt, with a machine-stitched top (Fig. 10.9).

Stitch width: widest
Stitch length: varies
Needle position: center
Needle: #90/14 topstitch
Feed dogs: up

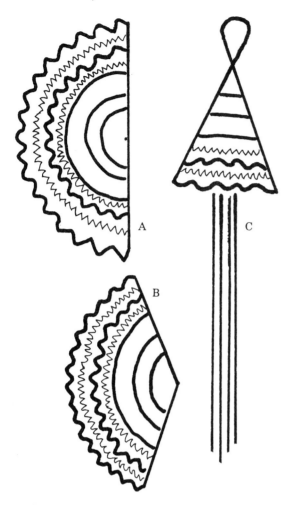

Fig. 10.8 Making a machined tassel.
A. Embroider a half-circle of felt.
B. Cut a wedge from it, and sew up
the sides to form a cone. C. The
cone becomes the top of the tassel.

Fig. 10.9 A tassel made of satin
stitches on felt.

Pressure: normal
Presser foot: overcast J, narrow braiding, or
    raised seam F; utility B or transparent
    appliqué
Utility stitch: zigzag
Tension: *top*, loosened; *bobbin*, normal
Fabric suggestion: 9″ (22.9cm) square of felt
    (tassel top will be completely covered
    with stitches)

Thread: Sulky embroidery—I chose red, yel-
    low and blue; #8 red pearl cotton; #5
    blue pearl cotton (optional)
Accessories: 7″ (17.8cm) spring hoop, small
    bells, glue stick, fine-point marker
Stabilizer: tear-away

The finished size of the tassel top is 2″ ×
2″ (5.1cm × 5.1cm). I worked with a 9″
(22.9cm) piece of felt so it would fit in the

7" (17.8cm) spring hoop. This allows enough room for the presser foot without hitting the edge of the hoop, as you will stitch both sides of the tassel top area—2" × 4" (30.5cm × 10.2cm)—at once.

Trace the pattern from Fig. 10.9. Cut around the tracing and lay this on the felt. Draw around the pattern with a marker (it won't show when tassel is completed).

Begin by carefully stretching the felt in the hoop. Use the overcast J foot for this top or use corded (#5 pearl cotton) satin stitches with the narrow braiding or raised seam foot. Starting on the right side, place one line of close, smooth satin stitches. Add another row next to the first, and continue, changing colors as you wish. Now sew between the satin stitches, using a contrasting color and the elastic straight stitch. You may prefer using a double thread in a topstitching needle, with a straight stitch.

Cut out the stitched design; then cut it in half. Place wrong sides together.

Cut about five dozen lengths of pearl cotton, each 12" (30.5cm) long. Fold them in half. Place the folds inside the felt pieces along the straight edge. Pin the felt together or use a dot of glue stick to hold everything in place as you stitch. Zigzag across the straight edge of the felt to keep the pearl cotton in place. Zigzag around the curve as well. Then go back with a satin stitch and stitch around it again with a 6 stitch width, stitch length 0.5. Add bells to each side and a hanger at the top. Clay or metal found objects also work well as ornaments.

I agree, making tassels is a nutty thing to do (but it's fun). Use them to decorate your tote bag, for key chains, zipper pulls, decorations on clothing, curtain tiebacks. I confess that I hang them all over my sewing room.

147

Chapter **11**

Decorative Stitches

by JAN SAUNDERS

- ■ **Lesson 37. Stitches**
- ■ **Lesson 38. Decorative motifs and Pictograms**
- ■ **Lesson 39. Machine accessories used with decorative stitches**

I have spent a lot of time waiting in line in airports, grocery stores, and post offices. I can always tell when someone joins the line who has a new sewing machine. How? Decorative stitches cover almost all of the person's garment!

I love my Viking 990, but it's always a challenge deciding where to use those beautiful stitches in a classic, tasteful way, without looking like I've been embroidered from head to toe. I'll share some of my successes with you in this chapter, but I also hope you'll want to find more ideas for yourself. So where does the inspiration come from?

I have been keeping an idea file since college consisting of designs torn out of mail-order catalogs, the newspaper, craft and decorating magazines, coloring books and calendars. I also save advertising flyers and greeting cards with interesting graphics.

I like to include something special on every garment I make. It may be a custom embroidery or pocket design, a topstitch, a hem or seam finish. I have been sewing since I was seven, so these garments have mounted up. I'd like to keep every successful project I've made, but the house is not big enough for everything. So I take photographs of the out-of-style or outgrown projects before retiring them to Good Will.

I also keep a stenographer's notebook with stitch samples, notes taken from sewing seminars and fashion shows, and sketches of ready-to-wear details I hope to incorporate in my work someday.

The lessons in this chapter show you how to use collected ideas in creative ways. The first lesson is designed for someone without a lot of time, and contains ideas you may not have thought of for stitching rows of decorative stitches. We'll make plaids out of stripes and stitch beautiful borders. Then, I'll offer great ideas to pique your children's sewing interest by creating secret codes, messages and nametags. You will also learn how to preserve part of an old quilt by making and decorating an easy-to-sew Christmas stocking.

Lesson 38 shows how to translate a picture into stitches using your Viking Pictogram feature. We'll start by perfecting single motifs and framing them in covered buttons or earrings. You'll learn to create more involved motifs on pockets, collars, or cuffs, then translate an outdoor scene into Pictogram stitchery. Finally, you will make a Viking crest with your monogram to add to your ever-growing collection of tote bag squares.

The third lesson combines use of Viking accessories with decorative stitches. You'll probably love the long-cuts in this lesson. The 7-hole foot is used with a host of decorative Viking stitches to bring an old denim vest up-to-date. You will see the beauty of hemstitching on a handkerchief linen blouse, and make a detachable collar by transforming linen scraps into something beautiful.

Fig. 11.1 Stitch a row or two of open embroidery stitches above shell tuck. Trim away excess fabric on back to the line of stitches.

Lesson 37. Stitches

Using rows of decorative stitches

You have a lot of decorative stitches, letters and numbers on your Viking. If you are like most folks, you have probably experimented by writing every family member's name, maybe even stitching your favorite Lotto numbers. I made nametags for twenty kids coming to a birthday party. But there are many other ways to use these stitches in a decorative and practical way.

I will be referring to decorative stitches in this chapter as "open" and "closed." With a "closed" stitch, the beauty is in stitching it close together (stitch width 4–6, stitch length 0.3–0.5), like the satin stitch or ball stitch (2–28). "Open" stitches, such as the three-step zigzag, blindstitch or overlock, are usually sewn at a stitch longer than 1.

The most obvious way is to use rows of decorative stitching on hems and edges. Whenever I line a skirt, rather than blind hemming or straight stitching the hem in place, I decorate the hem edge. Fold lining hem up about 2" (5cm) and press. Shell tuck the hem, using the reverse blindstich 2–7) on the widest width, stitch length 2. For a more pronounced shell, tighten the upper tension slightly. To finish hem, run a row or two of open embroidery stitches about 1½" (3.8cm) above the shell tuck. If the presser foot rests on a double layer of fabric, it feeds evenly and the stitches look better. One of my favorite open decorative stitches on the Viking 990 is the scallop with the loop in the middle (2–9). Program the first motif on the preset setting; the second motif is the same stitch, mirror-imaged and programmed on a 3 width (Fig. 11.1).

After decorating the hem, trim excess lining away to the stitches. Even if the fabric ravels, the decorative stitch prevents the hem from pulling out. Voilá! Your own designer touch.

For growing children or changing fashion, let a hem down by pressing it with a half white vinegar, half water mixture on your press cloth. If the crease will not press out or has discolored the fabric, cover the hemline with a row or two of decorative stitching. You can even create a border print by using one of the suggestions in Fig. 11.2. You don't want it to look as if you are covering a hemline crease, so repeat your decorative border somewhere else on the garment: sleeve hems, pocket tops, suspenders, front tab or waistband. You may like the garment better after adding the decorative touches.

Cablestitching with a double needle

Double-needle cablestitching texturizes a fabric with raised rows of stitching resembling a machine-knitted cable stitch. Do not confuse double-needle cablestitching with "cabling" described in

149

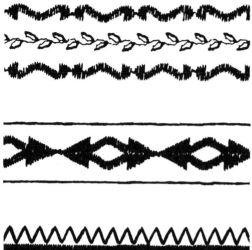

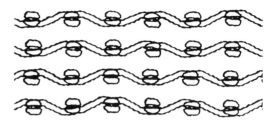

Fig. 11.3 Use 2.0mm double needles, matching thread to fabric; sew rows of open embroidery stitches on your Viking.

Fig. 11.2 Create a border print using decorative stitches. Here are three possibilities.

Chapter 2; although the two techniques sound similar, you will discover they are quite different.

I have found this decorative effect works best on knits like wool jersey, cotton interlock, velour and stretch terry. Although you may want to cablestitch your fabric before cutting out the pattern pieces, I've found that it isn't always necessary if using one of the fabrics mentioned. If in doubt, test it first on a scrap.

Use 2.0mm double needles, matching thread color to the fabric; sew rows of open embroidery stitches on your Viking. My favorite stitch is one of the scallop variations with the point or loop in the middle (2–8 or 2–9). See Fig. 11.3; note that I've used black thread on white fabric throughout this section so that stitch details show clearly.

On a single layer of fabric, right-side-up, mark where the center row of stitching will be sewn. Remember to push your double-needle button, so the stitch and nee-

dles clear the presser foot. Stitch the first row of double-needle cablestitching on the center mark, from top to bottom. Turn fabric around, and sew the next row of cablestitching from the bottom up, a presser foot width away from the first row. Alternating the stitch direction prevents fabric from pushing off grain. If you have chosen one of the asymmetrical stitches, use the Viking mirror image feature so rows of stitching look the same, regardless of the direction you stitch. Continue this process, sewing from the center mark out, until you

Fig. 11.4 Sew from the center out with double needles until you have five to ten rows of cablestitching.

150

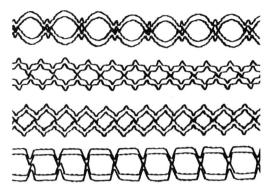

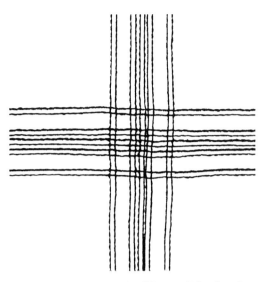

Fig. 11.5 Match rows of cablestitching, back-to-back or point-to-point.

Fig. 11.6 Create a "plaid" on solid-colored fabric using double-needle pintucks.

have five to ten rows of cablestitching (Fig. 11.4). Cablestitches look great down a sleeve or on the center front of a sweatshirt. You can also use them to create the effect of ribbing on a cardigan or jewel neckline. Make a companion fabric for cuffs, collars, front or back yoke this way. For a slight variation, match a stitch, back-to-back or point-to-point, using the arch stitch (2–8), the three-step zigzag, bridging stitch (2–6) or reverse blindstitch (2–7). See Fig. 11.5.

Creating plaids and stripes

I created a plaid on a solid fabric simply by crossing rows of double-needle pintucks (Fig. 11.6). Again, mark the center row of tucks. Start stitching from the center row out. Because the tucks are spaced so close together, the raised seam (pintucking) foot will enable you to keep the rows straight and evenly spaced.

Make a plaid out of striped fabric with double needles and a straight, blind hem or bridging stitch (2–6). Thread needles with silk twist or two threads through the same needle, matching the stripe colors found in your base fabric. If your spool pins cannot accommodate two spools of thread at once, place a drinking straw over the spool pin for an extension (Fig. 11.7). Use your Viking edge guide, and sew straight rows of

stitching at an angle, or perpendicular to the stripes in the base fabric. The edge guide enables you to keep rows of stitching perfectly straight and evenly spaced (Fig. 11.8).

Note: Your 4.0mm double needles are useful in another way unrelated to plaids and stripes. Topstitch jeans pockets using 4.0 double needles to simulate Calvin Klein's popular pocket design.

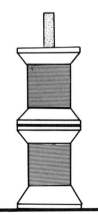

Fig. 11.7 Place a drinking straw over spool pin to create an extension.

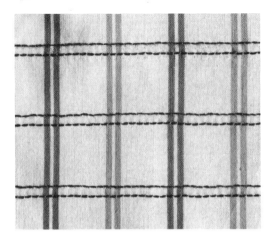

Fig. 11.8 Rows of stitching sewn perpendicular to fabric stripe will create a custom plaid.

Project Decorative Messages

When a friend comes to visit my stepson, Ryan, the first thing they do is run up to the sewing room and make nametags on my 990. This exercise is fun, entirely Ryan's idea, and has helped build his spelling skills. We've also made nametags for my in-laws; written out our name, address and phone number; and practiced Ryan's spelling list on fabric. I used to supervise, but now that Ryan knows how to use and program the machine, he and his friends entertain themselves by decorating their work with favorite stitches. I'd like to share some of this childhood creativity with you. You never know when you'll need to keep your children busy on a rainy day. This project is for the Viking 990 and 980.

Stitch width: 6
Stitch length: preset
Needle position: center
Needle: #80/12 or #90/14 all-purpose

Feed dogs: up
Pressure: normal
Presser foot: utility B or transparent appliqué foot
Decorative stitches: letters on lettering cassette (programs 3 and 4); decorative stitches of choice
Tension: preset
Fabric suggestion: closely woven broadcloth or denim
Thread: Sulky or Zwicky cotton thread in a rainbow of colors
Accessories: pinking shears; buttons; beads; construction paper; glue stick (optional); ruler; vanishing marker
Stabilizer: adding machine tape or tear-way stabilizer

Ryan prefers making nametags on a piece of broadcloth cut 3″ × 6″ (7.5cm × 15cm), folded over into a 3″ (7.5cm) square. When using denim, cut a 3″ (7.5cm) square.

Program your name, a friend's name, your secret code or word-for-the-day into your Viking. Draw a straight line from one side of the fabric to the other in the middle of nametag with ruler and vanishing marker. If you are using broadcloth, place a strip of adding machine tape or tear-away stabilizer under your work. Stitch name on the fabric, centering it on the line. If you have chosen script lettering, clip threads between letters. For both script and block lettering, clip threads at the end of the word. Tear off stabilizer. Pink the edges. Voilà! A nametag, great for identifying your room or your friends at a birthday party.

For more interest, program your favorite decorative motif before and after the name. Or create a border. Ryan's favorite border is the train with the engine, coal car and caboose (2–21, 22, 23), shown in Fig. 11.9.

One Father's Day, we used a glue stick to place pieces of tissue paper from a birthday piñata in a colorful arrangement on a

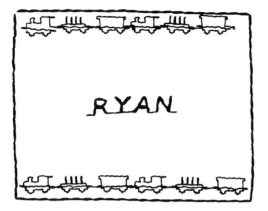

Fig. 11.9 Child's nametag stitched with engine, coalcar and caboose motifs (2–21, 22, 23).

fabric background. Then Ryan stitched through the paper with the word "Daddy." My husband was so pleased, he wore his nametag to a business meeting (oh, what we won't do for our children!).

I'm sure you and your children will come up with many more ideas. Add buttons, beads, glitter or fabric paint to your creations. They are fast and easy, and if you make a mistake, it's easy to start over.

Sewing, pleating, and folding paper

A few years ago, I bought a small wall hanging by Vicki Herrick at a craft fair. She called her piece *Transparent Folds*. She used artist's tracing paper, ripped one edge, then colored it with various shades of pink, purple and blue pastels. The paper is pleated and stitched through the folds, so

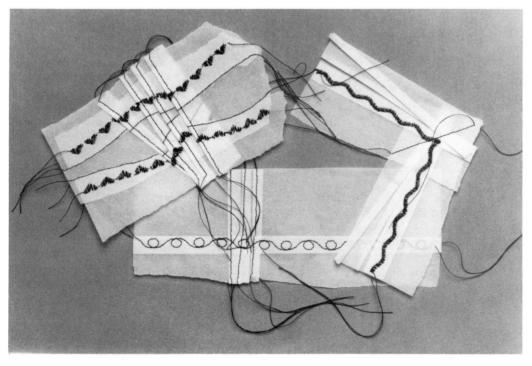

Fig. 11.10 Paper stitching, folding and pleating.

the thread ends trail off the paper. It is mounted under glass, so the thread tails become a part of the picture. All this is done on a piece of paper no larger than 5″ (12.5cm) square.

Vicki's work inspired me to try my hand. Instead of using pastels, I used straight and decorative stitches on a double layer of tracing paper. I used different colors of top and bobbin threads, with the darker color on the bobbin (Fig. 11.10).

Try it yourself. It's fast and whimsical. After stitching the paper, fold, pleat and stitch the folds — some with, some without thread in the needle. The needle holes in the paper give an unusual texture. Because you are working with a double layer of paper, you can trim or rip the underlayer away from some of the stitching for a shadow effect. There is no right or wrong way to do this, and it is so fast. If you don't like what you've made, rip some more tracing paper and start again.

Project Heirloom Christmas Stocking

I am always rushing around during the holidays trying to finish making gifts and decorate the house. An easy, fast way to accomplish both is to turn an old, almost worn-out quilt into Christmas stockings, a teddy bear, throw pillows (heart-shaped, square or round) or clothing, like a belt, vest or jacket. If a quilt has been in the family for some time, chances are that the sentimental value has prevented you from getting rid of it. So let's turn it into an heirloom. If you don't want to use your quilt, look for one at garage sales, flea markets or resale shops. Even a quilt in poor condition will have some areas that will

work well for your project. I chose to make everyone new Christmas stockings this year. Here's how you can do the same.

Use an old stocking for the pattern. Trace pattern on a piece of large tracing or tissue paper. It's important to draw your pattern on something translucent so you can see the quilt through it. Mark cuff area. Remember to add ¼″ (6.4mm) seam allowances. Lay paper pattern on old quilt and move it around until you see an interesting area, not too badly worn. Remember that the top 3″–5″ (7.5–11.5cm) will be hidden by a cuff, so you don't want the most interesting part covered.

Cut stocking back and cuff from unbleached muslin. For a more elegant treatment, use satin, velvet or taffeta.

Cut cuff double the finished depth, plus ½″ (12.7mm) for seam allowances. For example, the stocking I made had a 3″ × 7½″ (7.6 × 19.1cm) finished cuff, so I cut the cuff 6½″ (2 × 3″ = 6″, plus ½″ = 6½″) (2 × 7.6cm = 15.2cm, plus 12.7cm = 16.4cm) by 7½″ (19cm).

Three rows of grosgrain or satin ribbon at the top of the cuff carry a holiday message (Fig. 11.11). I used ribbon in the predominant quilt colors — red, light blue and tan. Before stitching ribbon, test your spelling on a scrap. If you misprogram, you may end with a message you don't want. Don't use stabilizer under ribbon. It's too hard to pick out and some ribbons may not take to being dipped in water. After stitching holiday messages (Fig. 11.12), press ribbons flat from the underside.

To attach ribbon to cuff, set your Viking as follows:

Stitch width: preset 990; 1 other models
Stitch length: preset 990; 1 other models
Needle position: center
Needle: 4.0mm double needle
Feed dogs: up
Presser foot: utility B or transparent appliqué foot; edge guide
Utility or decorative stitch: tricot stitch; count-

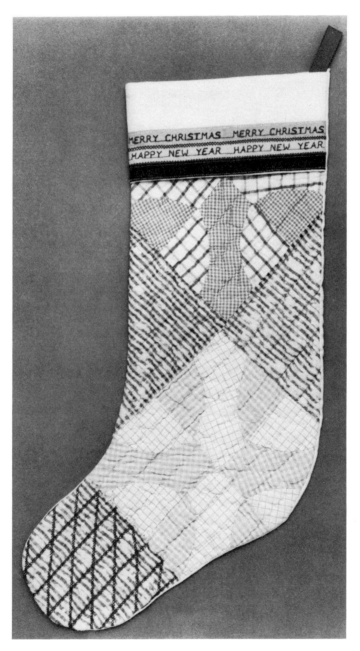

Fig. 11.11 Christmas stocking with three rows of ribbon carrying a holiday message.

Fig. 11.12 Detail of stitching on ribbons.

ed cross-stitch (2–16); tiny zigzag; decorative stitches of choice

Tension: *top*, normal; *bobbin*, normal

Fabric: old quilt; muslin, taffeta, satin or velvet; two or three colors of ribbon to match quilt, 12″ (30.5cm) each

Thread: silver metallic, red machine-embroidery and off-white Zwicky cotton thread

Accessories: glue stick; beads and lace (optional); large sheet tracing or tissue paper; water-soluble marker

To establish a guideline, fold cuff in half lengthwise, wrong sides together, and press. Open cuff. On a single layer, place the bottom edge of ribbon at fold and pin or glue stick in place. If you want a ruffle trim, sandwich it between ribbon and cuff fabric. Using the tricot or tiny zigzag stitch, guide so left needle stitches into bottom of ribbon, while right needle stitches into cuff fabric and/or trim.

Butt the next ribbon against the first, and guide so one needle stitches on one ribbon, and the other needle stitches on other. Repeat for third ribbon (Fig. 11.13). Be-

cause double needles are almost ¼″ (6.4mm) apart, I used the counted cross-stitch (2–16) between the double row of decorative stitching for more definition between the messages. Fold cuff in half along the bottom edge of ribbon. Press.

To define the front of the stocking, stitch over existing quilting lines with the

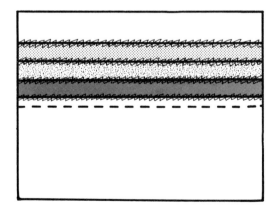

Fig. 11.13 Butt second ribbon against the first; guide so that one needle stitches on ribbon, the other needle on ribbon next to it.

counted cross-stitch. The hand-quilted stitches were difficult to see, so I used the edge guide to keep rows even (Fig. 11.14). I also requilted a number of areas using decorative stitches and metallic thread. Add beads, ribbons or lace. Be creative.

Place right side of cuff to wrong side of stocking front. Slip a ribbon loop between cuff and stocking front at the top corner for the hanger. Stitch cuff to stocking front at top (see Fig. 11.12). Turn cuff to right side. Press.

Roll a ¼" (6.4mm) hem to the inside on the top of stocking back. Press and stitch. Place front and back of stocking with right sides together. Sew around stocking with a ¼" (6.4mm) seam allowance. Turn stocking right-side-out. Press.

Since our family is getting bigger, I have a number of stocking fronts cut out, ready to sew. I've given them as wedding gifts, then, when the first child is born, Junior gets a customized stocking that looks just like Mom's and Dad's.

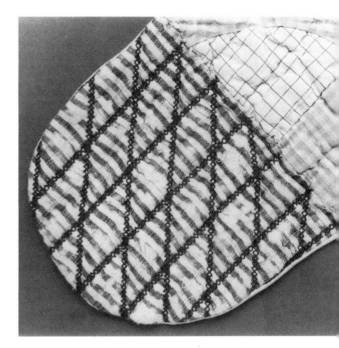

Fig. 11.14 Stitch over existing quilting line on toe of stocking with counted cross-stitch (2–16).

Lesson 38. Decorative motifs and Pictograms

Computers are a part of almost everything these days. And, as with many of you, they scare me . . . or at least they did until I got my Viking 990.

The Viking computer does almost everything but cut the pattern out. By combining Satin Elements, you can create original single motifs, small Pictogram embroideries, borders and design lines. In this lesson, I will show you some basic motifs and ways to combine them. You will make Pictogram covered buttons for your first project. Then, you will create small Pictogram embroideries that can be used to make a pair of earrings.

To perfect your skill in guiding the fabric while making a Pictogram design line, I'll show you a way to practice the same line stitched in many shapes and directions to create a three-dimensional look on an iris appliqué.

We'll also make a tote bag square that interprets an outdoor scene with Pictogram stitchery. It's almost like having a paintbrush and skilled artist built into your sewing machine.

The other tote square for this chapter is a Viking crest done with Pictograms in colors that match the tote bag.

Project
Pictogram Motif Buttons and Earrings

The best way to perfect your skill in making Pictograms is with practice. Let's make a Pictogram motif over and over again, then use our needleart for covered buttons. Next, we'll be ready to turn a small Pictogram embroidery into a pair of earrings.

The completed designs for buttons and earrings are shown in Fig. 11.15.

Stitch width: 6 (preset)
Stitch length: 0.4 (preset)
Needle position: center
Needle: #80/11 all-purpose, or #90/14 stretch needle
Feed dogs: up
Pressure: normal
Presser foot: transparent appliqué foot

Tension: preset
Fabric suggestion: light- to medium-weight, tightly woven white fabric
Thread: Sulky or Zwicky cotton thread in favorite color for buttons; fuchsia, turquoise and green for earrings
Accessories: size #30 covered button forms; size #45 covered earring forms (see Sources of Supply; seed pearls or small beads (optional); hand needle and embroidery floss; vanishing marker; 5"–7" (12.7–17.8cm) spring hoop; hand-embroidery floss (optional)
Stabilizer: tear away

Stretch your button fabric in spring hoop. Trace pattern in Fig. 11.16 onto fabric with the vanishing marker, tracing both circles. Put tear-away stabilizer under circles.

The Satin Element setting for the Pictogram for the size #30 covered buttons is 2–34, 38, 38, 35, 34, 38, 38, 35 preset:

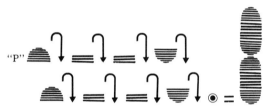

Place presser foot over the line of the inside circle and begin stitching at medium speed. You will be making two petals in the first pass.

For the second pass, turn your work clockwise 90 degrees, place presser foot over the line of the inside circle again, and stitch. You should have four petals that meet in the middle. Make two more passes so the Pictogram looks like Fig. 11.16. Repeat for as many covered buttons as you'll need. Once flowers are cut out, stitch a French knot with floss or sew seed pearl in the center of each. Cover your button forms.

Study the finished earrings in Fig. 11.15; the pattern is provided in Fig.

Fig. 11.15 Covered buttons and embroidered earrings.

158

11.17. You'll want to use Sulky rayon or Zwicky cotton machine embroidery thread in fuchsia, turquoise and forest green, as I did, or select your own color combination.

To set your machine for the Pictogram berries, use Satin Elements 2–34, 35, width 3:

For Pictogram leaves, use 2–34, 38, 35, preset:

For Pictogram branch, set machine using 2–43, width 2:

For the stem, use elastic straight stitch, preset.

Draw concentric circles, using the size #45 earring pattern in Fig. 11.17 for the circle. Draw Pictogram embroidery pat-

Fig. 11.17 Pictogram motif for embroidered earrings, shown in Fig. 11.15.

tern in inner circle with vanishing marker. Stitch fuchsia berries first, turquoise leaves next, green stem and branch last. I find that using the same color thread on top and bobbin works best.

To finish buttons and earrings, remove fabric from hoop and tear off stabilizer. Cut out each embroidery ¼" (6.4mm) *outside* the larger circle. Run small gathering stitches by hand around the outside circle, then draw fabric and stitches up around button or earring form. Work fabric into the teeth so the outside edges are smooth. The Pictogram should come just to the edge of the button/earring form. Snap the back of the button/earring in place. You will find it easier to push the back on over a spool: place button/earring back so the shank or post is centered in the hole on the top of the spool. Snap embroidered front to the back by pushing down on the spool.

Satin Element design lines

The inspiration for the back of the jacket shown in the color insert came from old calendar art. The iris shown in the detail here (Fig. 11.18) looks vibrant and alive because colors you normally think of as

Fig. 11.16 Pictogram flower for covered buttons, shown in Fig. 11.15.

Fig. 11.18 Pictogram design lines give dimension to iris (see jacket in color section).

clashing were used next to each other. To create this three-dimensional vibrancy, I fused the base color of each petal to the background fabric, as described in Chapter 4. The fabrics used were silks, rayon and moiré taffeta. The background is hunter green cotton upholstery velvet. The iris petals are fire-engine red, fuchsia, royal blue, purple and orange. *Note:* When I fused the appliqué to the velvet, I used light pressure on the iron and a napped press cloth so the nap of the velvet was not crushed.

I used Satin Elements 2–37, 43, 39, preset to program the line on both the regular setting and mirror image to contour each petal:

Remember to program the end of each line with the finishing button; this way, you always start at the beginning of the program. The stitch locks itself off at the end, so you don't have to tie off each thread. Thread colors I used were shades of red, fuchsia, purple and blue. For a subtler effect, use a palette of pastels for appliqué and design lines.

There is no right or wrong way to do this technique. The stitch, when programmed in the regular setting, tapers out from right-needle position. Therefore, I used it on all outside edges where the straight edge was on my right. The stitch tapered *into* the appliqué, while finishing the edge at the same time.

Rather than constantly turning the fabric, I used the mirror image feature to make lines that tapered from the left *into* the appliqué. The same setting was used to create the line for all contouring. The variation is done by the way you turn the fabric to stitch each line. I use my fingers like the center point of a compass for sharp curves.

Don't cover the entire appliqué with contour stitches—that defeats its purpose. Instead, use a 2 width satin stitch to finish edges. To create veins in the leaves, use the elastic straight stitch on a 3.5 length, or program your own line of satin stitching. You've just created your own wearable art.

Project
Tote Bag Square (Landscape Pictogram)

The most difficult part of this project was finding the source of inspiration. I looked at calendar art and photographs to come up with the idea for the design in Fig. 11.19. After that, the stitching was easy.

Stitch width: varies
Stitch length: varies
Needle position: center
Needle: #80/11 all purpose or #90/14 stretch
Feed dogs: up
Pressure: normal

Pictogram: varies
Tension: preset
Fabric suggestions: 9″ (22.9cm) square of firmly woven cotton or felt in light green; 9″ (22.9cm) square firmly woven cotton in white
Thread: Sulky rayon or Zwicky cotton machine embroidery thread in dark green, yellow green, sunshine yellow, orange and fuchsia
Accessories: embroidery scissors; water-erasable marker; dressmaker's carbon; empty ballpoint pen; tracing paper
Stabilizer: iron-on freezer paper; Wonder-Under

Iron freezer paper to wrong side of white background fabric. Fuse Wonder-Under to wrong side of light green fabric. With dressmaker's carbon and empty ballpoint pen, trace and cut light green foreground in Fig. 11.20. Fuse it to background.

Stems and leaves are made on background, using the tricot stitch, preset width and length; and open heart, 2–25, width 6, stitch length 2.5–4.5.

Mark background with a line every ½″ (12.7mm), using water-erasable marker. Stitch every other line in dark green thread with the tricot stitch (also used for cattail stems, so don't make all your tricot stitches the same length). Stitch remainder of lines in yellow green with the open heart stitch (2–25).

Trace and transfer flowers to foreground, marking the centers of each flower for placement. Mark centers with either a line or circle. A line gives you a flower that looks like it is a three-quarter view, a circle gives you a straight-on view.

Program flower petal shapes using 2–36, 38, 35, width 4, length preset:

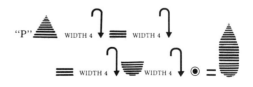

Fig. 11.19 Pictogram embroidered tote bag square.

Remember to program the finishing button at the end of the petal.

For petal placement, start from the center and work out. Make first petal, then turn fabric around and make second petal opposite the first (Fig. 11.21). The third is placed 90 degrees to the right of the second petal, the fourth is 90 degrees to the right of the first. The next four petals fill in between the first four (Fig. 11.21). Stitching petals this way, the flower does not look "crowded." Make six yellow and five orange flowers.

To make round centers, program the Satin Elements using 2–34, 38, 35 preset, this way:

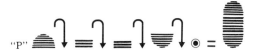

To make oblong centers, program 2–34, 38, 35 preset:

162

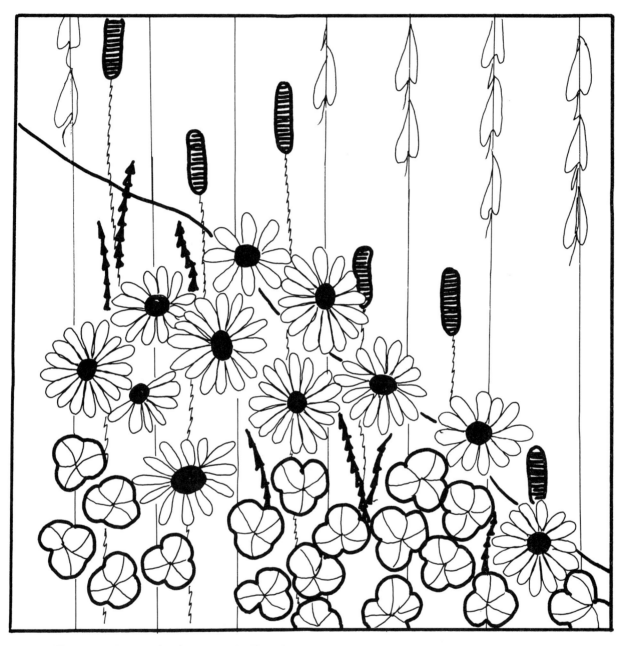

Fig. 11.20 Pattern for the square in Fig. 11.19.

Fig. 11.21 Sequence for stitch-ing the eight petals: the sec-ond group of four fills in be-tween the first four.

For a very solid center, thread your ma-chine with two threads through the same needle, or stitch over center a second time. Centers are stitched with fuchsia thread.

To make a clover leaf, use dark green thread and program the Satin Elements using 2–42, 44 preset:

This makes a half-circle. Stitch the first half-circle, pivot fabric 180 degrees, then stitch second half-circle so stitches are ex-actly next to each other. Pivot fabric about 60 degrees to make a second clover leaf, as described above. Pivot again, another 60 degrees to make third clover leaf.

To put on the finishing touches, stitch short rows of triangles (2–36) on a 2 width or use single open embroidery motifs such as the daisy pattern (2–5).

To make cattails, use brown thread and program Satin Stitch Elements using 2–34, 43, 35 preset. Push finishing button.

164

Project
Tote Bag Square
(Viking Crest)

This handsome crest in Fig. 11.22 com-bines Pictograms, decorative and utility stitches, and monograms in the same project.

Stitch width: varies
Stitch length: varies
Needle position: center
Needle: #80/11 all-purpose or #90/14 stretch
Feed dogs: up
Pressure: normal
Presser foot: transparent appliqué foot
Tension: preset
Fabric suggestion: 9″ (22.9cm) light- to medi-um-weight firmly woven cotton in white or bright yellow

Fig. 11.22 Viking crest tote bag square.

Thread: Sulky rayon or Zwicky cotton machine-embroidery thread in red, forest green, spring green, purple and royal-blue

Accessories: dressmaker's carbon; empty ballpoint pen; tracing paper; vanishing or water-erasable marker

Stabilizer: iron-on freezer paper

For the flowers, use closed hearts 2–27 on preset, stitching with red thread. Following are the other decorative stitches, Satin Elements, and thread colors used. Flower centers: blue, 2–34, 35, preset:

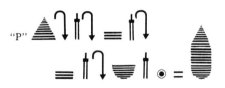

Branches: spring green satin stitch, width 1, length 0.4–0.6

Large leaves: forest green, 2–41, 38, 35, preset:

Small leaves and fronds: forest green, 2–36, 38, 35, width 3, preset:

Frond branches: spring green, straight stitch, length 2.5

Horizontal boxes: purple, *Point de Paris* (2–4), width 6, length 4.5

Monogram and bold lines of satin stitching: red, width 2, length 0.4–0.6

Inside lattice: royal blue, large counted cross-stitch (2–18), preset

Ribbon: purple, two threads through same needle, straight stitch, length 2.5

"Viking" lettering: red, preset

Iron freezer paper to wrong side of square. Trace crest pattern in Fig. 11.23. Transfer pattern to square, using dressmaker's carbon and empty ballpoint pen.

Stitch everything in red first. Start with flowers. Stitch one petal, stop, then pivot fabric slightly to make the next. Continue until flower is complete.

Design your initials to fit in the center of the crest. It is a lot easier to stitch a block style, rather than a script type, monogram. Transfer initials to fabric with vanishing or water-erasable marker. Stitch initials, using the satin stitch setting above. Program the word "Viking" and stitch it in the center of the ribbon.

To center a word, mark a straight line with fabric marker and stitch a word sample first. Measure it and find the center. The word "Viking" is stitched on a curve, so cut the sample word out in a strip. *Without cutting the letters apart*, snip fabric strip from the top of letter to just above the line so you can spread letters on a curve. Measure from the center to the front of the curved word. Mark the center of the ribbon. Draw a curved line in the ribbon for word placement. Place sample word in ribbon, centering it on the curved line. Mark the beginning of the word using the stitch sample as a guide.

Note: To center a word that will be stitched on a straight line, draw a line on a scrap. Stitch the word and find the center of it. Draw a line on your project and center the word on the line using the stitch sample as a guide.

Next, stitch everything in forest green. Stitch large leaves first, the smaller leaves

Fig. 11.23 Pattern for Viking square in Fig. 11.22.

166

next. Once you have finished one motif, go on to the next without cutting thread. You have programmed the finishing button before and after each motif, so it's not necessary to tie each thread off. Go on to stitch the fronds, frond branches and bold satin stitching at the lower part of crest.

Satin stitch branches in spring green.

Rethread machine with purple thread top and bobbin. Stitch the horizontal boxes, using the *Point de Paris* hemstitch (2–

4) with setting described above. Rethread top with two purple threads through the same needle and stitch ribbon, using a straight stitch, length 2.5.

Finish crest with royal-blue thread. Stitch center latticework of crest with the large counted cross-stitch (2–18). Stitch the sides with a 2 width satin stitch. Stitch flower centers.

Remove freezer paper and finish square as described in Chapter 12.

Lesson 39. Machine accessories used with decorative stitches

Seven-hole foot

I am a nut for Viking accessories. One of my favorites is the 7-hole cording foot, which accommodates up to seven strands of yarn, pearl cotton cord or embroidery floss. It comes with a handy threader. The number and types of cord you use, the colors and stitches you select, can create eye-catching results.

Make your own trim and use it to define a yoke, cuff, front tab or belt. Thread foot with four or more strands of pearl cotton or floss. For more interest, thread the holes with contrasting colors, metallics, or fine variegated yarn; or, try a contrasting color through the middle hole. The more variety, the better. I thread each hole with a strand at least a yard long so I don't have to keep rethreading.

Select a thread color that contrasts with the cord and/or fabric. Topstitch over cord with the decorative stitch of your choice. My favorites are the closed heart (2–27), ball (2–28), square stitch (2–26), daisy (2–5) or open heart stitch (2–25). Better yet, use the Viking programming feature to combine decorative stitch patterns with letters and numbers. The thread covers part of the cord for a few stitches, giving a two- or three-toned effect. When you come to a corner, sew to the bottom edge, then cross over first row of stitching as shown in Fig. 11.24. Snip cording off close to the stitch or slightly beyond.

Texturize a solid fabric, using a short variation of the technique described above. Stitch cord to fabric with one or two closed motifs. The square (2–26), closed heart (2–27), or ball stitch (2–28) are good choices. Remember to use the finishing button after programming each stitch. Another idea is to sew a longer row, crossing rows as shown in Fig. 11.25A. A friend of mine used a variety of flat and metallic cords to stitch crosses on a beautiful ecclesiastical stole this way.

To finish, cut cord long or short. If you leave it long, knot it up to the stitch, then trim cord ½" (13mm) from knot, creating a tassel. You may prefer to leave cord long enough to thread beads onto it, then knot, or alternate knots and beads. If you leave cord short, cut it at an angle about ⅜" (10mm) from stitch (Fig. 11.25B).

I sometimes have trouble finding the right color soutache or middy braid for a project, so I make my own and sew it on in

Fig. 11.24 Cross over first row of stitching at corner with 7 hole foot, threaded with pearl cotton.

one step, using the 7-hole foot. Thread six holes with the same color pearl cotton or floss. Thread middle hole with contrasting floss. Use a matching thread, nylon monofilament, or metallic thread; couch over cord using a bridging stitch (2–6), or the three-step zigzag, stitch length 1–3, width 6, depending on stitch selected.

Another attractive effect is created by using the open heart (2–25) on its programmed setting. The foot tracks over cord to join it together, and you are able to stitch in almost any direction without struggling to keep cord under the stitch.

Project
Vest with
Corded Design

Decorate a jacket back, the front of a sweatshirt, or accent a pocket. I added the styling detail in Fig. 11.26 to the front of a favorite denim vest.

Stitch width: 4–6
Stitch length: 1.5–2
Needle position: center
Needle: #90/14 stretch
Feed dogs: up
Pressure: normal
Pressure foot: 7-hole foot
Utility stitches: three-step zigzag or bridging (2–6) stitch
Tension: *top*, normal; *bobbin*, normal
Fabric suggestion: restyle an old denim vest or use a stiff, firmly woven fabric
Thread: Zwicky cotton thread to match pearl cotton; size #5 or #8 pearl cotton
Accessories: dressmaker's carbon for dark fabric; tracing paper; empty ballpoint pen; water-erasable marker

Fig. 11.25 A. Stitch crosses on ecclesiastical stole, using 7 hole foot and metallic cord. B. Cut cord at an angle, about ⅜" (1cm) from stitch.

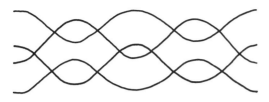

Fig. 11.26 Add this styling detail to vest or jacket front using 7 hole foot and pearl cotton.

Enlarge pattern in Fig. 11.26 until the small curve is at least 3″ long. Repeat motif until it is long enough for the garment you are restyling. Transfer design to the front of the garment.

Thread foot with five to seven strands of pearl cotton at least 1 yard (1 meter) long,

depending on what you intend to decorate. On a scrap, test which stitch you prefer (see suggestions above). On the right side of vest, stitch first curved row of 7-hole cording. Repeat for other four rows. Pull cord ends through to the back, threading them through a large-eye hand needle; tie them off.

Friendship Bracelets

Make friendship bracelets with colorful leftover cord and the bridging stitch (2–6) or three-step zigzag (Fig. 11.27). Use a 6 stitch width and 1.5–2 stitch length. Hold cord behind foot to get started. The feed dogs grab the cord and stitch it together without fabric underneath. Knot cord ends

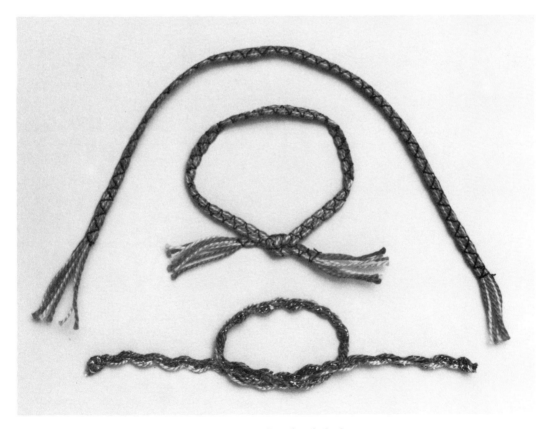

Fig. 11.27 Friendship bracelets or trim created with 7 hole foot.

to finish. Once cord is joined, you may want to twist or braid two or three bracelets together for a wider bracelet. (You can also use this technique to make cord for a pendant.) If you use a soft rayon or silk floss with the bridging stitch (2–6) on a 6 width, 2 length, you create a rickrack that can be used separately or joined together for a trim.

Hemstitching

Hemstitching is lovely on children's clothing, but kids outgrow things so quickly, you may prefer to spend your valuable time stitching something for yourself. I found some handkerchief linen that was perfect for hemstitching, so I chose to create my own heirloom blouse with a hemstitched collar (Fig. 11.28).

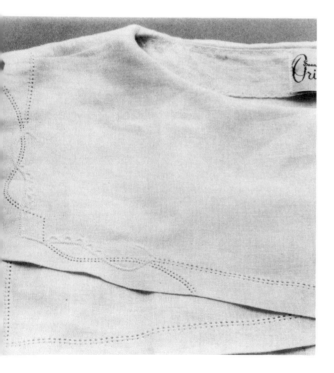

Fig. 11.28 Hemstitched linen collar in two layers.

Stitch width: varies
Stitch length: varies
Needle position: center
Needle: wing and 2.0mm double needle
Feed dogs: up
Pressure: normal
Presser foot: transparent appliqué foot
Tension: normal
Fabric suggestions: linen, batiste, or organdy
Thread: Zwicky darning (size #70 or #100 cotton) or fine machine-embroidery thread
Accessories: tissue paper; water-erasable marker; spray starch (optional)

The best fabrics to use are those that have a high natural fiber content and that are evenly woven. I used a square-collared blouse pattern which called for a 1½″ (3.8cm) hem. The hemstitched area was sewn on a double layer of fabric, so cut the collar with a 3″ (7.6cm) hem. Excess will be trimmed away later.

Create your design on a lightweight piece of tissue paper, using a water-erasable marker. Place tracing paper over fabric and trace the design so the ink from the marker penetrates tissue paper and bleeds through to the fabric. Remove the pattern and fill in the lines where necessary.

Another option is to darken the lines on the tissue pattern, then place the pattern under your fabric on a glass-top table. Shine a light up through your work and trace directly onto the fabric with a water-erasable fabric marker. Use the technique that works best for you.

Miter corners as described in pattern instructions and press up the hem. I used a number of stitches to create the collar detail. Test stitches on a double layer of scrap fabric first. If fabric puckers, starch with spray starch.

The hemstitches were done with a wing needle and darning thread to match fabric. Hems: *Point de Paris* (2–3), width 3, length 3. Hemstitched curves at the corner of top collar: stitch (2–4), width 3, length preset.

170

Right side of diamond in the corner of top collar: elastic straight stitch, width 0, length 3.

The following stitching was done with 2.0 double needles and regular sewing thread to match fabric. Left side of diamond; curves above and below diamond: straight stitch, width 0, length 2–2.5. Double needle scallops, arch stitch (2–8), width 2.5, length 0.6–0.8.

Stitch hem ¾″ (19.0mm) from edge so presser foot rests on a double layer of fabric. Trim excess fabric away up to the stitch and around hemstitching. This way, the hem is stitched in place as the hemstitch prevents fabric from raveling.

Project
Hemstitched, Fagoted and Embroidered Detachable Collar

I had some beautiful linen in my fabric stockpile, but none of the pieces were large enough to cut the collar I wanted. So I fagoted four pieces of linen together, using the hemstitch fork, to create the detachable collar in Fig. 11.29.

Stitch width: 0
Stitch length: 4–6
Needle position: center
Needle: #80/11 all-purpose
Feed dogs: up
Pressure: normal
Presser foot: standard A or rug foot
Utility stitch: straight stitch
Tension: loosened slightly to 4
Thread: Zwicky cotton thread to match fabric
Fabric suggestion: linen or cotton linette
Accessories: hemstitch fork

With right sides facing, pin fabric together; put pins ⅛″ (3.2mm) from, and parallel to, cut edge. Slip hemstitch fork between the fabric layers, snugging fork up to the pins. Place your work under the needle so the curved end of the fork is toward you. Turn flywheel by hand and put needle through the fabric, in between the prongs of the fork. Lower presser foot.

Begin stitching slowly. When you are almost to the end of the fork, leave the needle in the fabric and lift the presser foot. Pull the fork toward you, lower the presser foot again, and continue stitching as before. Because you move the fork as you go along, you can make a row of fagoting as long as you like.

Join the four fabric strips as described above, creating a piece of fabric large enough to cut collar front. Press fagoted seam allowances open. On either side of fagoting, anchor seam allowance with a closed embroidery stitch (Fig. 11.29). I used Satin Elements 2–34, 31, and 35 preset. This way, you don't have to finish the raw edges, and the decorative stitch keeps the seam allowance pressed flat no matter how many times the collar has been cleaned.

Stitch width: 0
Stitch length: 2–4.5
Needle position: center
Needle: #80/11 all-purpose; wing needle
Feed dogs: up
Pressure: normal
Presser foot: utility B, or transparent appliqué foot
Utility stitch: straight; elastic straight
Tension: normal
Thread: Zwicky cotton to match fabric; white darning thread size #70 or #100
Accessories: double roll of bias tape on 1″ (25mm) self-bias fabric; snap or Velcro dot

This collar pattern, too, came from a commercial blouse pattern. Cut collar from fagoted yardage made above. Staystitch around neckline. (If you don't

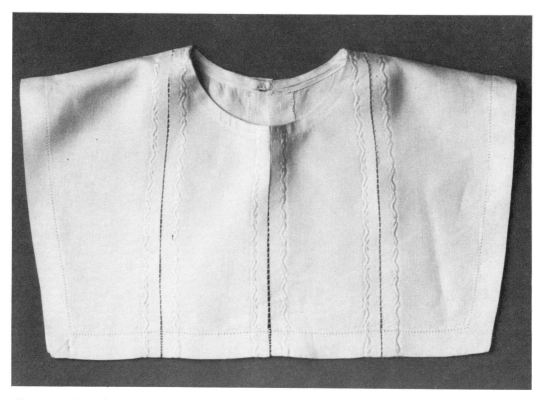

Fig. 11.29 Detachable linen collar, fagoted, embroidered, and hemstitched.

staystitch, you may accidentally pull out some fagoting stitches and have a mess on your hands.)

Miter corners and press up hem 1" (2.5cm). Finish hem by topstitching ¾" (19.0mm) from hem edge with the elastic straight stitch, length 3–4.5, using a wing needle and darning thread. Guide so presser foot is resting on a double layer of fabric. Trim excess fabric to stitching line.

Face neckline with a piece of self-bias or bias tape. On the left side of collar, extend the bias strip ¾" (19.0mm) past neck edge. Clip and turn bias strip right-side-out, as you would a facing. Press and topstitch ⅜" (9.5mm) from seamline using a size #80/11–12 all-purpose needle and normal sew-ing thread. Finish bias extension and sew a snap or Velcro dot on it for the closure.

This collar gives a new look to a blouse or dress. It even looks great under an existing, smaller collar. It's a welcome gift or fashion accessory for yourself.

AFTERWORD

My idea file is still bulging at the seams with things I want to create on my Viking. It's impossible to include everything in one chapter, but I hope the ideas here will help you think creatively and that you had fun learning about the decorative potential of your machine. If you didn't have fun, you aren't sewing on a Viking.

CHAPTER **12**

Making the Tote Bag

The year I became program chairman for an embroiderer's guild, I began to assess previous programs: Why was one a success, another a failure? I remembered the many needlework workshops I had taken, the many projects I had started in those classes and never finished because they were too big or demanded too much of my time. And I knew I wasn't the only one who felt this way, as other members also had boxes of half-finished needlework.

That's when I came up with the idea of the tote bag. I asked the teachers that year to gear their workshops toward making samples small enough to fit in a 6" (15.2cm) square frame. The fabric squares could then fit into the frames made by the handles on a tote bag I designed. Each new square could easily slip in and out. Not only were the class projects small enough to complete easily, but they were useful and decorative as well.

I'm using the same tote bag for this book (Fig. 12.1). After you've made the tote bag, it can be used to show off the sample squares found in the lessons.

First, I'll explain how to finish the squares you made throughout the lessons in this book. Then I'll explain the tote bag.

Finishing the squares

Specific instructions for each square are included in the lessons. A brief recap: Start with a piece of fabric large enough to fit in a 7" (17.8cm) hoop, if you will be working with one. I suggest starting with a 9" (22.9cm) square, as it is better to have extra fabric than not enough. The finished square will be 6¾" (17.1cm). The area that will show in the frame will be 6" (15.2cm)

Fig. 12.1 The tote bag, with one of the squares in position on the pocket.

square. Cut a piece of acetate or cardboard 6¾″ (17.1cm) square to use as a template.

After completing the embroidery, quilting, appliqué—whatever the lesson calls for–center the acetate pattern over the square. If you can't find acetate, cut a piece of tracing paper 6¾″ (17.1cm) square. You can see your work through the tracing paper. Center paper over work, then mark fabric by putting a dot at each corner. This way you don't ruin your embroidered square by cutting it off-center. Draw cutting lines at the edge of the acetate or cardboard all the way around with a water-erasable marker or white chalk pencil.

Back the square with stiff fabric, fleece, or fusible interfacing if it is not stiff enough for the pocket. Stitch along the line you've drawn and cut off the extra fabric to that line.

Slip typing paper or heavy tear-away stabilizer under the square. Finish by satin stitching at stitch width 4–6 around the edge. Dab the corners with Fray-Check to keep them from raveling.

Glue or stitch Velcro dots under the corner of each square to correspond to the ones in the pocket frame. (If the square is stiff enough, this will not be necessary.) An alternative to Velcro is an idea from Marilyn Tisol of Hinsdale, Illinois. She backs each square she makes by first cutting a piece of plastic canvas the size of the square; then she attaches the fabric square to it by whipping the edges together. The plastic is rigid enough to keep the square in the frame.

Tote bag construction

My tote bag is made of canvas, but it can be made of any heavy-duty fabric. I used canvas because I wanted a bag that would stand by itself. If the fabric you've chosen is not heavy enough, press a layer of fusible webbing between two layers of material. Whatever you choose, pre-wash and press all fabrics before you cut.

174

Supplies:

1½ yards (1.4m) of 36″ (0.9m) canvas (includes body of bag, handles, pockets, and bottom of bag)

3⅛ yards (2.9m) of 1″ (2.5cm) wide fusible webbing

Teflon pressing sheet

Four Velcro dots

Sewing thread to match canvas, or monofilament

Rotary cutter and board are timesavers

24″ × 6″ (61.0 × 15.2cm) plastic ruler

Water-erasable marker, pencil or sliver of soap

Blind hem D and standard A feet

#90/14 jeans needle

My tote (see cover) is made up of many colors and looks as if Dr. Seuss invented it. It includes royal blue for the bottom, yellow pockets, green handles, and red for the body of the bag.

I chose those colors because the striped lining fabric included them all. I backed the lining with Pellon fleece and quilted down each stripe to give my bag even more body. I added pockets to the lining, too.

Lining is optional, but if you choose to include one, you will need another piece of fabric at least 34″ × 20″ (86.4cm × 50.8cm). Add 20″ × 20″ (50.8cm × 50.8cm) to this if you wish to make pockets for your lining.

The layout of the bag is provided in Fig. 12.2; note that the layout is predicated on cutting all pieces from a single length of cloth, rather than several different colors.

Body of bag:
34″ × 20″ (0.85m × 50.8cm)

1. Cut out fabric. Fold in half and notch bottom on both sides, 17″ (43.2cm) from top. Draw a line between the notches on the inside (Fig. 12.3).

2. Place a 1″ (2.5cm) strip of fusible webbing along both 20″ (50.8cm) edges on the right side of the bag and fuse in place using the Teflon pressing sheet. Fold at the top

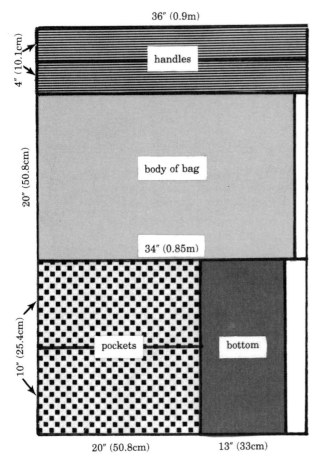

Fig. 12.2 Layout for the tote bag.

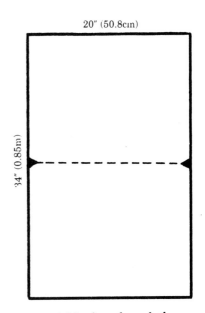

Fig. 12.3 Notch and mark the inside of the bag.

Fig. 12.4 Mark the outside of the bag.

of the webbing to the backside. Press the fold, using the Teflon pressing sheet on top to protect your iron. Then fold over 1″ (2.5cm) again, using the pressing sheet *between* the fusible webbing and the body of the bag.

3. Mark a line down the length of this piece 6¼″ (15.9cm) from each side, as shown in Fig. 12.4 to use later as guidelines for construction of the bag.

Pockets: 10″ × 20″ (25.4cm × 50.8cm); cut 2

1. Use the ruler and marking pen to indicate stitching lines from top to bottom–

6¼″ (15.9cm) from each side. Center area will be 7½″ (19.1cm).

2. Cut slits 1½″ (3.8cm) down from the top on these lines. Make a mark ¾″ (19.0mm) from the top and another ¾″ (19.0mm) down from the first. Draw lines through those marks across the top of the pockets (Fig. 12.5A). It is easier if you mark the middle section on the *back* of the fabric, so you'll be able to see the lines as you fold. Fold on the lines as follows: Each side should be folded twice toward the inside of the bag. The middle 7½″ (19.1cm) should be folded twice toward the front of the fabric. This middle flap creates the top of the frame.

3. Stitch across the top of all three pockets ⅛″ (3.2mm) from the top edge. Do this on both pocket pieces.

4. Then stitch across side pocket sections through all three layers of fabric at ⅛″ (3.2mm) from each bottom fold. Finish

both side pockets on both pocket pieces this way (Fig. 12.5B).

5. Open out the top of the middle sections on both pocket pieces to enable you to stitch across the folds without stitching them to the pockets. Stitch across the 7½″ (19.1cm) middle sections on both pocket pieces at ⅛″ (3.2mm) from each bottom fold. This flap will create the top of the frames in which you'll slip the 6″ (15.2mm) squares.

Handles: 4″ × 36″ (10.2cm × 0.9m); cut 2

1. Stitch down one long side 1″ (2.5cm) from edge. Fold. Do the same with the other side. (This stitching is used as a guide to make folding the handles easier and more accurate.) Bring folded edges together and fold again, creating the 1″ (2.5cm) wide handles. Place strips of 1″ (2.5cm) fusible webbing inside the length of the handles and press to fuse. The handle is four layers (plus fusible webbing) thick (Fig. 12.6).

2. Topstitch both sides ⅛″ (3.2mm) from edge. Use the blind hem D foot with needle position at far left. Then sew ¼″ (6.3mm) in from those lines of stitches on both sides.

Bottom: 12½″ × 20″ (31.8cm × 50.8cm)

1. Fold over 1″ (2.5cm) top and bottom along the 20″ (50.8cm) edges and topstitch across ⅛″ (3.2mm) from the fold. Draw a line ¾″ (19.0mm) from each fold.

2. Fold the bottom in half the long way and notch on the fold on both sides, 6¼″ (15.8cm) from top and bottom (Fig. 12.7).

Assembly

1. First sew pockets to the bag. The pockets will be 3″ (7.6cm) from the top. (Remember that the bag has been folded over 2″ (5.1cm) at the top. Measure from the top of the last fold. Line up the markings, 6¼″ (15.9cm) from each side on bag and pockets and pin in place. Stitch on the

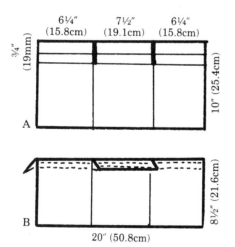

Fig. 12.5 Pocket construction. A. Mark lines to indicate the pockets. Then mark lines across the pockets, ¾″ (19.0mm) and 1½″ (3.8cm) from the top. Cut down 1½″ (3.8cm) between the pockets. B. Fold the tops of the side pockets to the back, the top of the middle pocket to the front.

176

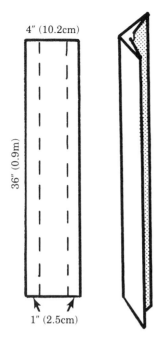

4" (10.2cm)

36" (0.9m)

1" (2.5cm)

Fig. 12.6 Stitch down the length of the handles 1" (2.5cm) from each side. Fold down 1" (2.5cm) at each side, the length of the handle. Then fold the handle in half. Place strip of fusible webbing inside and press in place. Stitch the handles together.

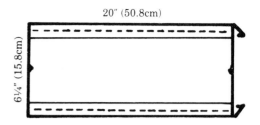

20" (50.8cm)

6¼" (15.8cm)

Fig. 12.7 Follow this diagram to fold, mark and stitch the bottom piece of the bag.

lines you've drawn to create pockets and, using a ¼" (6.4mm) seam allowance, stitch down each side and across the bottoms of the pocket pieces.

2. Sew handles next. Find the center of the bag by folding it double the long way. Measure 3" (7.6cm) from the center to each side of the bag and make a mark with the water-erasable marker; 6" (15.2cm) will be open in center. Using the 24" × 6" (61.0cm × 15.2cm) ruler, draw guidelines through these marks the length of the bag. Pin handles in place outside those lines. Stitch across the bottom of the handles and up, ⅛" (3.2mm) from the edge, on the existing outside stitching. Extend your stitching all the way to the top of the bag. Do this on the next outside lines as well (you will often stitch on top of other lines of stitching). The top edge of the bag will not be sewn down until later, but sew through the folds as you attach the handles.

3. To make the open frame, stitch only the top of the handles above the pockets on both sides. Leave ¾" (19.0mm) around the frame to insert workshop squares (Fig. 12.8).

4. Attach bottom next. Match notches with those of the bag and pin the bottom in place. Stitch over the ⅛" (3.2mm) stitching line to ¾" (19.0mm) from each side of the center pocket (see Fig. 12.8). *Do not* stitch across the center pocket. Then stitch all across the bottom piece on the ¾" (19.0mm) mark. This will create the bottom of the frame. Double check. Is the frame done correctly? Be sure you can slip a fabric square inside.

5. Finish the side edges of the bag with a zigzag stitch (Fig. 12.9). Then put it all together. Fold at center bottom notches with right sides together. Check to see that pockets and bottom meet at each side. Stitch in a ⅝" (15.9mm) seam line from top to bottom. Now refold the top edge of the bag and press in place to fuse. Topstitch in place at the top edge and bottom fold.

6. Bag corners should be finished this way: On the inside, pinch the bottom by matching the side seam with the line

177

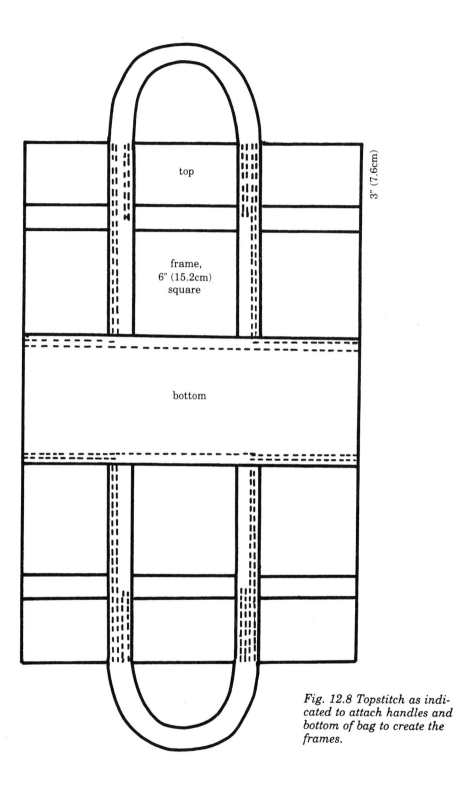

top

frame,
6" (15.2cm)
square

3" (7.6cm)

bottom

Fig. 12.8 Topstitch as indicated to attach handles and bottom of bag to create the frames.

Fig. 12.9 Finish the edges with zigzag stitches. With right sides together, stitch each side of the tote bag.

Fig. 12.10 Make the tote bag corners by stitching lines perpendicular to the side seams, 2″ (5.1cm) up from the points.

drawn across the inside of the bottom of the bag (Fig. 12.10). Measure, on the seam line, 2″ (5.1cm) from the point. Draw a line across. Be sure it is exact on each side so stitching is perpendicular to the side seams. Stitch on drawn line for corners. This forms the bottom of the bag. If you wish to cut a piece of ⅛″ (3.2mm) Masonite or linoleum tile to fit the bottom, do so now before you line your bag.

7. Press one side of four adhesive-backed Velcro dots into the four corners of the frame and stitch.

Lining

If you line your bag, create the lining as if making another bag. Do not include bottom, pockets or handles. However, if you wish to add pockets to the lining, then cut out two pieces of 10″ × 20″ (25.4cm × 50.8cm) fabric, the same size as the bag pockets. At the top of each pocket piece, turn over 1″ (2.5cm) two times and sew down at the top and at the fold. Press up 1″

(2.5cm) at the bottom. Place the pocket pieces 3″ (7.6cm) from the top of the lining and pin in place. Sew across the bottom of the pocket at the fold and ¾″ (19.0mm) from the first stitching line. (The double line of stitching will add strength to the pockets.) Then attach the pockets to the sides of the lining by stitching down on each side with a ¼″ (6.4mm) seam allowance. With a ruler and water-erasable marker, draw lines down the pocket pieces to indicate where you will divide the fabric for pockets. Stitch those in place.

Sew up the sides of the lining, using a ⅝″ (15.9mm) seam allowance and create the bottom corner. Fold over the top as you did for the bag. I use the double fold for stability.

Whip stitch invisibly by hand around the top to keep the lining and bag together. With heavy canvas, you may prefer to make the lining and then place wrong sides together (bag and lining) and machine stitch around the top.

A Brief History of Viking

When Viking Sewing Machine Company merged with White Sewing Machine Company in 1986, each company brought more than 100 years of experience, innovation and high quality in the home sewing industry to the partnership.

Viking's parent company, Husqvarna, was established in 1689. The company is now owned by A. B. Electrolux, one of Sweden's largest corporations and—with the acquisition of White Consolidated Industries—one of the largest appliance companies in the world.

In the beginning, Husqvarna was a royal arms factory. Since the area in Southwest Sweden was the scene of many battles between the Swedes and the Danes during the seventeenth century, it's not surprising that the manufacture of weapons such as crossbows, arrows, and, later, muskets began as a cottage industry and grew into one of the region's main concerns.

The Husqvarna factory was established directly below a waterfall in the town of Huskvarna. The word *huskvarna* means "watermill" and today that same waterfall provides power for the factory.

In the late 1800s, Husqvarna had to make a difficult decision: production either had to be adapted to the diminishing demands of firearms or had to be directed toward new products. Production switched to the manufacture of stoves, heaters, and hunters' guns. On February 5, 1872, the Board of Directors decided to manufacture sewing machines. The company's first machine was the Nordstjernan or "North Star." Although the machine never worked well, Husqvarna decided to contin-

ue making sewing machines. They manufactured an American machine under license and were able to turn things around, selling 3,212 machines.

In 1883, successful Freja was introduced and remained the top seller for 46 years. Another model, the Triumf, was introduced in 1885. Both machines gave Husqvarna its reputation for producing quality products at a profit.

The same year Wilber Wright succeeded in getting his plane off the ground, 1903, Husqvarna introduced the oscillating central bobbin (CB). This feature dominated the industry for more than 50 years.

The 30s were characterized by functionalism. Rather than the ornate wildflowers that decorated earlier models, the styling of the machine was more practical. The CBN Class 12 was also Husqvarna's first electric model (1934), a success with one million manufactured.

The Swedish company presented their first free-arm sewing machine in 1947, the Husqvarna Zig-Zag. Made of die-cast aluminum, it was easy to carry. A new die-cast zigzag machine was launched in 1953. It was called Class 20 and featured a rotating hook.

The 60s and 70s brought new innovations to the Viking. With the advent of knits in 1961, Husqvarna introduced the 2000. It had easy-to-operate color settings and Trimotion stitches for knit seams. In 1971, Husqvarna introduced the first lubrication-free domestic sewing machine. As early as 1977, Husqvarna stepped into the world of electronics with electronic speed control on model 5710 and the "needle-selectric stop right'' feature on the 6570.

Viking entered the computer age in the 80s with the introduction of the 6690, the world's first "writing" sewing machine. By 1983, Viking was not only the first writing, but the first "thinking," sewing machine with the introduction of the Sewing Advisor. Once the operator tells the Sewing Advisor what type of fabric to sew, the machine automatically selects the best stitch, length, width, and tension, and tells which presser foot is best for the job.

What will Viking dream up next? Who knows? But if it is possible to make an even better sewing machine or one that is easier to operate, it will be a Viking from Husqvarna.

Viking Presser Feet and Attachments

See Charts 1.1 and 1.2 for manufacturer's ordering numbers.

Standard Feet with Machine Purchase

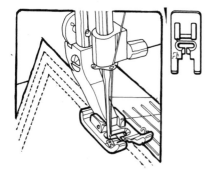

A. Standard (topstitch) foot

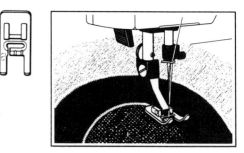

B. Utility foot

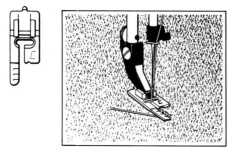

C. Buttonhole foot

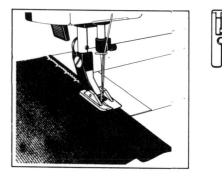

D. Blind hem foot

E. Zipper foot

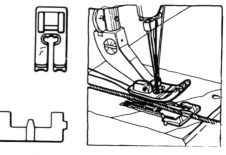

F. Raised seam foot & guide

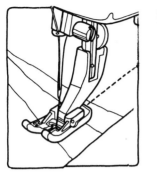

H. Teflon foot

J. Overcast
(edging) foot

Button reed/clearance plate

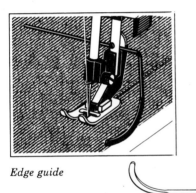

Edge guide

Transparent appliqué foot

Extra Feet and Attachments

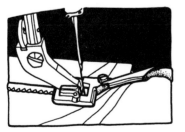

Bias binder

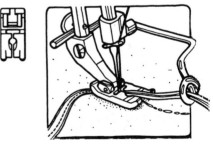

Braiding foot & guide

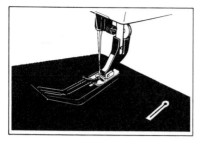

Buttonholer

Circular sewing attachment

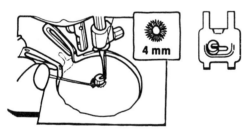

Darning foot

Dual feeder

Eyelet plate (4mm)

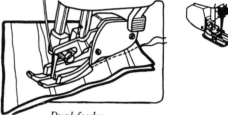
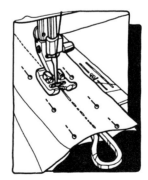

Gathering foot

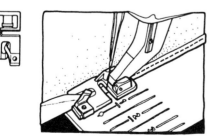

Hemmer (2mm)

Hemstitch fork

184

Narrow braiding foot

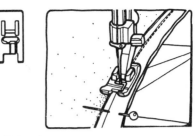

Piping foot

Roller presser

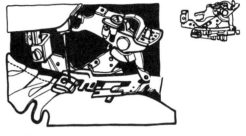

Ruffler

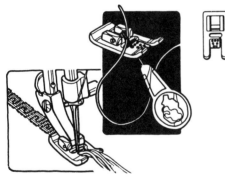

Seven-hole cording foot & threader

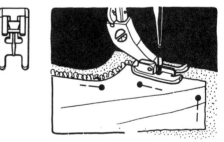

Special marking foot

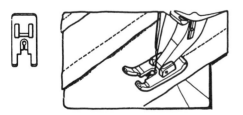

Straight stitch foot

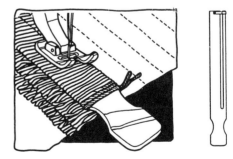

Weaver's reed

185

Sources of Supply

Viking Information

Husqvarna A.B.
S 561 81
Huskvarna, Sweden

Viking Sewing Machines
A division of VWS, Inc.
11750 Berea Rd.
Cleveland, OH 44111
or 2300 Louisiana Ave., North
Minneapolis, MN 55427

Viking White Sewing Machine Company publishes a wide range of educational materials too numerous to list here. Check with your local dealer. Of particular interest are:

Pictogram™ Idea Book (comes with the Viking 990)
Your Second Pictogram™ Idea Book
Your Third Pictogram™ Book
Viking Owner's Handbook, model 990 and fabric kit
Viking Owner's Handbook, model 980/ 960 and fabric kit
Viking Owner's Handbook, model 950 and fabric kit
Viking Owner's Handbook, model 940 and fabric kit
Viking Owner's Handbook, 6000 series and fabric kit
Viking Owner's Handbook, 100 series and fabric kit
Classica 100 Viking Owner's Handbook Supplement
Huskylock Owner's Handbook, 431/530 and fabric kit; 435/5350 and fabric kit

Video Tapes:
Viking Owner's Handbook, model 990 (VHS and Beta)
Viking Owner's Handbook, 100 series (VHS and Beta)

Sewing Techniques (VHS and Beta; five-part program includes introduction to one Viking sewing machine, how to's on machine embroidery, French sewing, ruffler tehniques and programming of the Viking 980. 50 minutes.)

(**Note**: The following listings were adapted with permission from *The Complete Book of Machine Embroidery* by Robbie and Tony Fanning [Chilton, 1986].)

Threads

Note: Ask your local retailer or send a pre-addressed stamped envelope to the companies below to find out where to buy their threads.

Extra-fine

Assorted threads
Robison-Anton Textile Co.
175 Bergen Blvd.
Fairview, NJ 07022

DMC 100% cotton, sizes 30 and 50
The DMC Corporation
107 Trumbull Street
Elizabeth, NJ 07206

Dual-Duty Plus Extra-fine, cotton-wrapped polyester
J&PCoats/Coats & Clark
PO Box 6044
Norwalk, CT 06852

Goldzack Elastic Thread
Viking White Sewing Machine Co.
11750 Berea Rd.
Cleveland, OH 44111

Iris 100% silk—*see* Zwicky

Madeira threads
Madeira Co.
56 Primrose Drive
O'Shea Industrial Park
Laconia, NH 03246

Mettler Metrosene Fine Machine Embroidery cotton, size 60/2
Swiss-Metrosene, Inc.
7780 Quincy Street
Willowbrook, IL 60521

Natesh 100% rayon, lightweight
Aardvark Adventures
PO Box 2449
Livermore, CA 94550

Paradise 100% rayon
D&E Distributing
199 N. El Camino Real #F-242
Encinitas, CA 92024

Pearl cotton #5
Viking White Sewing Machine Co.
11750 Berea Rd.
Cleveland, OH 44111

Sulky 100% rayon, size 30
Viking White Sewing Machine Co.
11750 Berea Rd.
Cleveland, OH 44111

Zwicky 100% cotton, sizes 30/2, 60/2, 70/2, silk and silk twist
Viking White Sewing Machine Co.
11750 Berea Rd.
Cleveland, OH 44111

Ordinary

Dual Duty Plus, cotton-wrapped polyester —
see Dual Duty Plus Extra-fine

Also Natesh heavyweight, Zwicky in cotton and polyester, Mettler Metrosene in 30/2, 40/3, 50/3, and 30/3, and Metrosene Plus

Metallic

YLI Corporation
45 West 300 North
Provo, UT 84601

Troy Thread & Textile Corp.
2300 W. Diversey Ave.
Chicago, IL 60647
Free catalog

Machine-Embroidery Supplies

(hoops, threads, patterns, books, etc.)

Aardvark Adventures
PO Box 2449
Livermore, CA 94550
Also publishes "Aardvark Territorial Enterprise"

Clotilde Inc.
1909 Southwest 1st Ave.
Ft. Lauderdale, FL 33315

Craft Gallery Ltd.
PO Box 8319
Salem, MA 01971

D&E Distributing
199 N. El Camino Real #F-242
Encinitas, CA 92024

Verna Holt's Machine Stitchery
PO Box 236
Hurricane, UT 84734

Nancy's Notions
PO Box 683
Beaver Dam, WI 53916
Catalog $.60 in stamps

Patty Lou Creations
Rt 2, Box 90-A
Elgin, OR 97827

Sew-Art International
PO Box 550
Bountiful, UT 84010
Catalog $2

Speed Stitch, Inc.
PO Box 3472
Port Charlotte, FL 33952
Catalog $2

SewCraft
Box 1869
Warsaw, IN 46580
Also publishes newsletter/catalog

Treadleart
Suite I
25834 Narbonne Ave.
Lomita, CA 90717

Sewing Machine Supplies

The Button Shop
PO Box 1065
Oak Park, IL 60304
Presser feet

Sewing Emporium
1087 Third Avenue
Chula Vista, CA 92010
  Presser feet, accessories

Miscellaneous

Applications
871 Fourth Ave.
Sacramento, CA 95818
  Release Paper for appliqué

Berman Leathercraft
145 South St.
Boston, MA 02111
  Leather

Boycan's Craft and Art Supplies
PO Box 897
Sharon, PA 16146
  Plastic needlepoint canvas

Cabin Fever Calicoes
PO Box 54
Center Sandwich, NH 03227

Clearbrook Woolen Shop
PO Box 8
Clearbrook, VA 22624
  Ultrasuede scraps

The Fabric Carr
170 State St.
Los Altos, CA 94022
  Sewing gadgets

Folkwear
Box 3798
San Rafael, CA 94912
  Timeless fashion patterns—$1 catalog

The Green Pepper Inc.
941 Olive Street
Eugene, OR 97401
  Outdoor fabrics, patterns—$1 catalog

Home-Sew
Bethlehem, PA 18018
  Lace—$.25 catalog

Libby's Creations
PO Box 16800 Ste. 180
Mesa, AZ 85202
  Horizontal spool holder

LJ Originals, Inc.
516 Sumac Pl.
DeSoto, TX 75115
  TransGraph

Lore Lingerie
3745 Overland Ave.
Los Angeles, CA 90034
  1 lb. of silk remnants, $9.45

Osage Country Quilt Factory
400 Walnut
Overbrook, KS 66524
  Washable fabric spray glue

The Pellon Company
119 West 40th St.
New York, NY 10018
  Machine appliqué supplies

The Perfect Notion
115 Maple St.
Toms River, NJ 08753
  Sewing supplies

Prym Sewing Notions
William Prym, Inc.
Main St.
Dayville, CT 06241
  Earring forms

Salem Industries, Inc.
PO Box 43027
Atlanta, GA 30336
  Olfa cutters, rulers

Solar-Kist Corp.
PO Box 273
LaGrange, IL 60525
  Teflon pressing sheet

Stacy Industries, Inc.
38 Passaic St.
Wood-Ridge, NJ 07075
  Teflon pressing sheet

Summa Design
Box 24404
Dayton, OH 45424
  Charted designs for knitting needle machine sewing

Susan of Newport
Box 3107
Newport Beach, CA 92663
  Ribbons and laces

Tandy Leather Co.
PO Box 791
Ft. Worth, TX 76101
  Leather

Theta's School of Sewing
2508 N.W. 39th Street
Oklahoma City, OK 73112
 Charted designs for knitting needle
 machine sewing, smocking directions
 and supplies for the machine

Magazines
(write for rates)

Aardvark Territorial Enterprise
PO Box 2449
Livermore, CA 94550
 Newspaper jammed with all kinds of
 information about all kinds of em-
 broidery, design, and things to order.
 I ordered the gold rings from them.

disPatch
1042 E. Baseline
Tempe, AZ 85283
 Newspaper about quilting and machine arts

Fiberarts
50 College St.
Asheville, NC 28801
 Gallery of the best fiber artists, including those who work in machine
 stitchery.

Needlecraft for Today
PO Box 2011
Harlan, IO 51537
 Creative uses of the sewing machine

SewCraft
Box 1869
Warsaw, IN 46580
 Newspaper and catalog combination
 containing machine embroidery arti-
 cles, designs and supplies.

Sew It Seams
PO Box 2698
Kirkland, WA 98083
 Bimonthly magazine on sewing

Sew News
PO Box 1790
Peoria, IL 61656
 Monthly tabloid, mostly about gar-
 ment sewing

Threads
Box 355
Newton, CT 06470
 Magazine on all fiber crafts

Treadleart
25834 Narbonne Ave., Ste. I
Lomita, CA 90717
 Bimonthly about machine embroidery

Bibliography

Alexander, Eugenie, *Fabric Pictures*, Mills and Boon Ltd., London, 1967.

Ashley, Clifford W., *The Ashley Book of Knots,* Doubleday & Co., 1944.

Bennet, dj, *Machine Embroidery with Style*, Madrona Publishers, 1980.

Butler, Anne, *Machine Stitches*, BT Batsford, Ltd., 1976.

Clucas, Joy, *Your Machine for Embroidery*, G. Bell & Sons, 1975.

Coleman, Anne, *The Creative Sewing Machine*, BT Batsford, 1979.

Coles, Myra, *The Complete Computer Sewing Book*, Wm. Heinemann, 1988.

Ericson, Lois, *Fabrics. . .Reconstructed* (Lois Ericson, Box 1680, Tahoe City, CA 95730), 1985.

———, *Belts. . .Waisted Sculpture,* 1984.

Fanning, Robbie and Tony, *The Complete Book of Machine Quilting*, Chilton Book Co., 1980.

———, *The Complete Book of Machine Embroidery*, Chilton Book Co., 1986.

Gray, Jennifer, *Machine Embroidery*, Van Nostrand Reinhold, 1973.

Hall, Carolyn, *The Sewing Machine Craft Book*, Van Nostrand Reinhold, 1980.

Harding, Valerie, *Textures in Embroidery*, Watson-Guptill, New York, 1977.

Hazen, Gale Grigg, *Sew Sane* (The Sewing Place, 100 W. Rincon Ave., Ste. 105, Campbell, CA 95008; $14.95 postpaid), 1985.

Hoover, Doris and Nancy Welch, *Tassels* (out-of-print), 1978.

James, Irene, *Sewing Specialties*, I. M. James Enterprises, 1982.

Ladbury, Ann, *Make the Most of Your Sewing Machine*, BT Batsford, 1988.

Lawrence and Clotilde, *Sew Smart,* IBC Publishing Co., 1984.

———, Supplement, IBC Publishing Co., 1984.

Macor, Alida, *And Sew On*, Alida Macor, 1985.

McNeill, Moyra, *Machine Embroidery — Lace and See-Through Techniques*, BT Batsford, 1985.

Nicholas, Annwen, *Embroidery in Fashion*, Watson-Guptill, 1975.

Ota, Kimi, *Sashiko Quilting* (Kimi Ota, 10300 61st Ave. So., Seattle, Washington 98178), 1981.

Pullen, Martha, *French Hand Sewing by Machine* (518 Madison St., Huntsville, AL 35801), 1985.

Saunders, Janice S., *Illustrated Speed Sewing: 103 Machine Shortcuts*, Speed Sewing, Ltd., 1985.

Shaeffer, Claire B., *The Complete Book of Sewing Short Cuts*, Sterling Publishing Co., Inc., 1984.

Short, Eirian, *Quilting*, BT Batsford, London, 1983.

Skjerseth, Douglas Neil, *Stitchology*, Seth Publications (PO Box 1606, Novato, CA 94947), 1979.

Tecla, *Greeting Cards by the Dozen* (120 E. Birch, Brea, CA 92621), 1986.

Thompson, Sue, *Decorative Dressmaking*, Rodale Press, 1985.

Warren, Virena, *Landscape in Embroidery*, BT Batsford, 1986.

Wiechec, Philomena, *Celtic Quilt Designs,* Celtic Design Co., 1980.

Zieman, Nancy, with Robbie Fanning, *The Busy Woman's Sewing Book*, Open Chain Publishing (PO Box 2634-V, Menlo Park, CA 94026; $11 postpaid), 1988.

Index

accessories, 6-8, 167-172
Alençon lace, 96-98
appliqué, 57-79
  application methods for,
    57-59
  in bird collage project, 47
  blindstitch for, 15, 63
  blurring on, 68
  bubbles in, 79
  cording for, 67
  edge-stitched, 63
  fabrics for, 57
  with feed dogs lowered, 67-72
  with feed dogs up, 60-61
  modified reverse, tote bag
    square with, 61-63
  reverse, 60-61
  satin stitch for, 60-61
  scribbling in, 70-71
  three-dimensional, 77-79
  tote bag square with, 63-65,
    65-67, 104-106
  with transparent fabric, 74
appliqué paper, 58-59
Applique Pressing Sheet, 11

ballpoint needles, 10
bangles, silver, 47
batiste, appliqués of, 72
Battenberg lace, 85-88
Battenberg rings, 6
batting, 11
baubles, attaching, 43-46
beads, attaching, 43-46
bed linens, 83
belt loops, 142
bias binder, 6, 183
bias strip, 42
bias tape, 133
bird collage project, 47-51
blind hem foot, 182
blind hemming, 129-130
blindstitch, 15. *See also* Hemstitch
blurring, applique with, 68
bobbin

elastic thread on, 53
loosening tension on, 35-36
thick thread on, 35-38
winding of, 2
bracelets, friendship, 169-170
braiding foot, 30-31, 34, 183
bridal veiling, 38
  for Alençon lace, 96
brides, 81
bridging stitch
  for seams, 125
  for smocking with elastic, 54
bubbles, fixing in appliqué, 79
butterfly-shaped lace project,
  85-88
button loops, 142
button project, 21-24
button reed plate, 183
button shank, 43
buttonhole foot, 3, 182
buttonholer, 184
buttonholes, 2
buttons
  attaching, 43
  Pictogram motif project with,
    158-159

cablestitching, with double needle, 149-151
cabling
  with free embroidery, 37
  tote bag square with, 38-39
canvas-type fabric, hems on,
  128-129
Carrickmacross, 72
  doily project with, 72-74
cassettes, 13
Christmas ornaments project,
  94-96
Christmas stocking project,
  154-157
circular sewing attachment, 6,
  184
cleaning, of machine, 12
closed stitches, 13, 149
collar project

hemstitched, fagoted and embroidered, 171-172
with tassels, 143-144
cord
  covering, 135
  gathering with, 55
  making, 140-142
cording
  for appliqué edges, 67
  for edges, 135-137
  Italian, 107-109
  using raised seam guide, 35
  vest project with, 168-169
cordonnet
  for Alençon lace, 96
  gathering with, 55
  smocking with, 53
  for texture, 29
corners
  with Italian cording, 109
  thick threads at, 34
cotton thread, 8
couching, 30-35
  blindstitch for, 15
  in Carrickmacross, 73-74
covered wire tassel project,
  144-145
crochet cotton
  on bobbin, 35
  for texture, 29
crocheted edges, 136-137
cutwork, 80-83
  needlecase project with,
    81-83

darning foot, 17, 184
  for couching yarn, 34
darning stitch, 18
decorative messages project,
  152-153
decorative stitches, 13-15,
  148-172
  hemming with, 128-129
  rows of, 149
  for seams, 125-126
denim needles, 10

191

denim rug project, fringed, 41-42
doily project, with Carrickmacross, 72-74
doll tassel project, 145
double needles, 10
  cablestitching with, 149-151
  on knits, for hems, 127-128
dual feed foot, 7, 184

earrings, Pictogram motif project with, 158-159
edge guide, 183
edge stitching, to attach appliqué, 63
edges. *See also* hems
  of applique, cording for, 67
  binding, 6
  cording, 135-137
  crocheted, 136-137
  piping, 139
  rolled and whipped, 112-114, 117
  shaped, covering wire for, 134-135
edging, lace, gathering of, 117
edging foot, 183
elastic
  applied with raised seam guide, 35
  gathering with, 55
  reshaping knits with, 137
  smocking with, 51, 53-54
  stitching seam over, 125
embroidery scissors, 2
encroaching zigzag, 29
English eyelets, 6
entredeaux, 111-112
  attaching to lace insertion, 117
  using, 115-117
eyelet plate, 6, 184
eyelets, 83
  in Carrickmacross, 73

fabric
  for appliqué, 57
  canvas-type, hems on, 128-129
  fringing, 40
  heavy, topstitching, 139
  for samples, 8
  transparent. *See* sheers
fagoting, 118
  for collar, 171-172
fake lapped seam, 123-124
feather stitch, 21
  for seams, 125
feed dogs, 4

fiberfill, 11
  for trapunto, 107
filler stitching, 27-29
Fine Fuse, 11
finishing button, 2, 15, 26
fishing line, for shaped edges, 135
flannel, 11
flat-felled seam, 7
flatlock, for seams, 125
fleece, 11
florist's wire, 135
flower motif, 38
flower project, with sheers and overlays, 68-70
flowers, creating, 26-27
foot pedal, 2
frame, and picture planning, 49
free-machining, 15-21
  for appliqué, 67-72
  button and pendant project with, 21-24
  cabling with, 37
  for needlelace, 83-85
  for quilting, 106
freezer paper, as stabilizer, 11
French handsewing by machine, 110-119
French seams, 112
friendship bracelets, 169-170
fringe fork, 40
fringed denim rug project, 41-42
fringing, 40
  thread, 137-138
fusibles, 11
  plastic sandwich bags as, 59
  webbing as, 58

gathering, 55
  for lace edging, 117
  of rolled and whipped edges, 114
  with smocking, 52-53
gathering foot, 55, 184
gimp, gathering with, 55
glacé-finish quilting thread, 9
glue stick, 43
Goldzack elastic thread, 53
greeting card project, 31-35
guide plates, 7

hand piecing on quilts, imitating, 125
handkerchief project, wedding, 119-122
heavy fabric, topstitching, 139
hemmers, 184
  narrow, 7-8, 123, 182
hems, 127. *See also* Edges

attaching scalloped lace to, 131
bias tape for, 133
blind, 129-130
narrow, 130-132
quilting, 129
roll and shell, 132
rolled, 7
on sheers, 128
shell edging for, 132
turning once, 127-129
with utility or decorative stitches, 128-129
zigzagging a narrow edge, 134
hemstitch fork, 184
hemstitching, 89, 170-171
  for appliqué, 59, 63
honeycomb stitch, for seams, 125
hoops, 8, 15-17
  for appliqué, 57
Husqvarna, 180

infant's bonnet project, 90-94
insertion, applying, 115
interfacings, vs. stabilizers, 11-12
Italian cording, 107-109

Japanese Sashiko, 36
jeans, seams in, 7
jeans needles, 10
jewels, attaching, 46
Jiffy Fuse, 11

knits
  double needles on, 127-128
  reshaping with elastic, 137
  yarn on, stitching of, 124-125

lace, 55. *See also* needlelace
  Alençon, 96-98
  appliquéd, 72
  attaching entredeaux to insertion, 117
  Battenberg, 85-88
  as edging, gathering of, 117
  as insertion, 115
  narrow hems and, 130-131
  scalloped, 115, 131
  sewing to lace, 118
  straight-edged, attaching to rolled and whipped edges, 117
lacy spiderwebs, 83
layering transparent fabrics, 74-77
leather, seams in, 7
leather needles, 10

lining, of tote bag, 174, 179

machine stitchery, 3
machine-embroidery, supply
   sources for, 187
machine-embroidery cotton, 8
machines
   maintenance for, 12
   settings for, 12, 14
magazines, 189
   ideas from, 1-2
Magic Polyweb, 11
markers, 8
marking foot, special, 118-119
Milliner's wire, 135
mirror images, 14-15
mohair, on bobbin, 35
monk's cord, 24, 140-141
monofilament, 9, 37
   for attaching beads, 44, 45
motifs, 157-167

nametags, 152
narrow braiding foot, 185
narrow hemmer, 7-8, 132
   for seams, 123
narrow hems, 130-132
needlecase cutwork project,
   81-83
needlelace, 45
   free machining for, 83-85
needles, 9-11
   applying thick thread
      through, 30
   double. See double needles
needleweaving, 99-102
notebook of samples, 1, 14, 80
nylon filament, for shaped
   edges, 134
nylon thread, 9

open space stitching, 80-98
   Alençon lace as, 96-98
   Battenberg lace as, 85-88
   cutwork as, 80-83
   hemstitching as, 89-94
   in rings, 94-96
   on sleeves, 99-102
open stitches, 13, 149
organdy, for attaching shisha
   mirrors, 47
organza, for shadow work, 75
overcast foot, 183
overlays, flower project with,
   68-70

paper
   sewing, pleating and folding,
      153-154

as stabilizer, 11
patch pocket, 15
pearl cotton, 35
   for Alençon lace, 96
   for texture, 29
pendant project, 21-24
Pictograms, 2, 8, 13, 23,
   157-167
   landscape tote bag square
      with, 161-164
pintucking, 91
pintucking foot, 151
piping edges, 139
piping foot, 185
plaids, creating, 151
plastic, water-soluble, 12, 80
plastic sandwich bags, as fusible, 11, 59
plates, eyelet, 6
pleating, 7
Point de Paris hemstitch, 89
presser feet, 3-6, 182-185. *See
   also* individual foot

quilting, 36, 103-109
   free-machining for, 103-106
   of hems, 129
   imitating hand piecing on,
      125
   tote bag square with,
      104-106
quilting thread, 9

raised seam foot, 151, 182
raised seam guide, attaching
   cord using, 35
rayon thread, 8
reverse appliqué, 60-61
   modified, tote bag square
      with, 61-63
ribbon
   on bobbin, 36
   rose from, 93
rickrack effect, 36
rickrack stitch, 99
rings, stitching in, 94-96
roll and shell hemming, 132
rolled edges, 7, 112-114
   attaching straight-edged lace
      to, 117
   gathering, 114
roller foot, 7
roller presser, 185
rose, from ribbon, 93
rosettes, 122
ruffle, estimating fabric for, 55
ruffler, 7, 185
rug project, with fringed denim,
   41-42

safety pins, for holding quilting
   work, 103
samples
   fabric for, 8
   for notebook, 1, 14, 80
Satin Elements, 2, 8, 13
   design lines for, 159-161
satin ribbon, on bobbin, 36-37
satin stitching, 22, 55
   for appliqué, 60-61
scallop stitch
   for hemming, 128
   joining veiling with, 125
scalloped lace, 115
   attaching to hem, 131
scribbling, in appliqué, 70-71
seams, 110-126
   fake lapped, 123-124
   with feed dogs lowered, 126
   flat-felled, 7
   French handsewing by ma-
      chine for, 110-119
   rolled and whipped edges for,
      112-114
   with side-cutter, 124
   utility and decorative stitches
      for, 125-126
seed beads, attaching, 44
serger, 124
seven-hole foot, 31, 167-168,
   185
shadow work, 74
   picture project with, 74-77
shank of button, 43
sheers
   flower project with, 68-70
   hems on, 128
   layering, 74
sheets, for quilt backing, 103
shell edging, for hems, 132
shell tuck, 8, 15, 149
shirred effect, 53
shisha mirror, attaching,
   46-47
side-cutter, seaming with, 124
silver bangles, 47
sleeves, openwork on, 99-102
smocking, 51-54
   with cordonnet, 53
   with elastic, 53-54
   gathered, 52-53
   with thick thread in bobbin,
      53
snap-on feet, 4
soutache, 34
special marking foot, 118-119,
   185
spool pins, extension for, 151
stabilizers, 11-12, 16, 80

stained-glass satin-stitch appliqué, 60
stair-step zigzag fill-in, 29
Stitch Witchery, 11
stitches
    closed, 13, 149
    feather, 21
    filler, 27-29
    length conversions for, 12
    open, 13, 149
    6mm width for, 2
    Trimotion, 89
    utility and decorative, 13-15, 125-129, 148-172
stones, attaching, 46
stop right control, 3
straight stitch foot, 185
straight stitches
    to fill in background, 27-28
    tote bag square appliquéd with, 65-67
stripes, creating, 151
supplies, 8-12

T square, 8
tassels, 142-147
    collar project with, 143-144
    covered wire project, 144-145
    doll project with, 145
    tops for, by machine, 145-147
Teflon foot, 7, 183
Teflon pressing sheet, 11, 58
tension, adjustment of, 2, 14
tension of bobbin, loosening, 35-36
texture, 25-56
thick threads, 29-31
    on bobbin, 35-38, 53
    greeting card project using, 31-35
threads, 8-9
    couching, 30-31
    drawn out of fabric, 99-102
    fringe of, 137-138
    pulling together, 55-56
    sources of, 186-187

Goldzack elastic, 53
three-dimensional appliqués, 77-79
three-step zigzag, for smocking with elastic, 54
topstitching, 139
topstitching needles, 10
    for thick thread, 30
tote bag, 173-179
    construction of, 174-179
tote bag squares
    with appliqué and quilting, 104-106
    with cabling, 38-39
    with edge-stitch appliqué, 63-65
    finishing, 173-174
    with Italian cording, 107-109
    landscape pictogram for, 161-164
    with modified reverse appliqué, 61-63
    with straight stitch appliqué, 65-67
    with Viking crest, 164-167
tracing paper, sewing on, 153-154
transparent appliqué foot, 3, 183
transparent fabric. See sheers
trapunto, 79, 107
Trimotion stitches, 89
triple needles, 10
twill tape, 16

Ultrasuede, 125
universal-point needles, 10
utility foot, 3, 182
utility stitches, 13-15
    hemming with, 128-129
    for seams, 125-126

veiling. See bridal veil
vest project, with corded design, 168-169
Viking button reed, 43

Viking crest, tote bag square with, 164-167
Viking Sewing Advisor, 2
Viking Sewing Machine Company, 180, 186
vinyl, seams in, 7

walking foot, 7, 184
water-soluble stabilizers, 12, 80
waxed quilting thread, 9
weaver's reed, 40, 185
wedding handkerchief project, 119-122
wedge needles, 10
weed-trimmer line, for shaped edges, 135
weft threads, 99
whipped edges, 19-20
    gathering, 114
    for seams, 112-114
    straight-edged lace attached to, 117
White Sewing Machine Company, 180
winding, of bobbins, 2
wing needles, 10
wire, covering for shaped edges, 134-135
Wonder-Under Transfer Fusing Web, 11, 58
woolly overlock, 9

yarn
    on bobbin, 35
    couching, 34
    fringing, 40
    on knits, stitching of, 124-125

zigzag stitches, 14, 35
    to fill in design, 27, 28-29
    for narrow hems, 134
    three-step, for smocking with elastic, 54
zipper foot, 182